IMAGE

TRI◎◎S

Each TRIOS book
addresses an important
theme in critical theory,
philosophy, or cultural
studies through three
extended essays written
in close collaboration by
leading scholars.

IMAGE

THREE INQUIRIES IN TECHNOLOGY
AND IMAGINATION

MARK C.
Taylor

MARY-JANE
Rubenstein

THOMAS A.
Carlson

The University of Chicago Press
Chicago and London

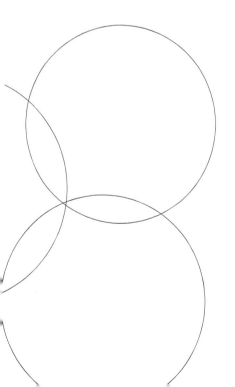

The University of Chicago Press, Chicago 60637
The University of Chicago Press, Ltd., London
© 2021 by The University of Chicago
Published 2021
Printed in the United States of America

30 29 28 27 26 25 24 23 22 21   1 2 3 4 5

ISBN-13: 978-0-226-78214-0 (cloth)
ISBN-13: 978-0-226-78228-7 (paper)
ISBN-13: 978-0-226-78231-7 (e-book)
DOI: https://doi.org/10.7208/chicago/9780226782317.001.0001

Library of Congress Cataloging-in-Publication Data

Names: Taylor, Mark C., 1945– Gathering remains. | Rubenstein, Mary-Jane.
    Above us, only sky. | Carlson, Thomas A. Facial recognition.
Title: Image : three inquiries in technology and imagination / Mark C. Taylor,
    Mary-Jane Rubenstein, Thomas A. Carlson.
Other titles: Three inquiries in technology and imagination | Trios
    (Chicago,Ill.)
Description: Chicago ; London : The University of Chicago Press, 2021. |
    Series: Trios | Includes bibliographical references and index.
Identifiers: LCCN 2020056564 | ISBN 9780226782140 (cloth) |
    ISBN9780226782287 (paperback) | ISBN 9780226782317 (ebook)
Subjects: LCSH: Technology—Religious aspects. | Aesthetics—Religious
    aspects. | Religion and astronautics. | Face—Religious aspects. |
    Vision—Religious aspects. | Philosophical anthropology. | Philosophy
    and civilization. | Civilization, Modern—20th century. | Civilization,
    Modern—21st century.
Classification: LCC BL265.T4 I49 2021 | DDC 201/.66—dc23
LC record available at https://lccn.loc.gov/2020056564

To Our Fellow Students
Department of Religion
Williams College
1983–1999

CONTENTS

ACKNOWLEDGMENTS

This conversation began in the 1980s and 1990s in the Religion Department at Williams College. The time was one of considerable ferment and creativity in the humanities. Though the world has changed, the issues we explored together are more urgent today than ever. We dedicate this book to our fellow students, who have used the lessons they learned in ways that none of us could have imagined.

INTRODUCTION

Thomas A. Carlson

All three essays gathered in *Image: Three Inquiries in Technology and Imagination* could be read as revisiting, in light of today's technoscientifically obsessed society and culture, Martin Heidegger's contention that "the fundamental event of the modern age" is "the conquest of the world as picture."[1] When Heidegger advances this claim in his 1938 text "Age of the World Picture" ("Die Zeit des Weltbildes"), he means not so much that modernity achieves one final and masterfully comprehensive picture of the world; he means much more that modern thought and culture characteristically assume that "world" as such—any and every world—is something amounting to an image (*Bild*) not only viewed by the human subject but built or constructed by that subject. Modernity, on this view, is an age in which the human subject is assumed to frame and thus produce the real by picturing or representing it—according to the standards and capacities of that subject's own rational thought and related technological powers. From this distinctively modern perspective, the world is not (as world is for Heidegger) understood to be that in which we mortal humans always already find ourselves, such that our thinking and doing would depend on a world that ever exceeds our comprehension and control. The world is seen rather to be that which the human subject contains within its representational thinking and comes likewise to control through its rational-technical self-assertion.

The world is produced and made to "show up," in other words, on our terms and for our uses. As Heidegger puts it in passages that Mary-Jane Rubenstein highlights in her essay here, "Above Us, Only Sky," "man contends for the position in which he can be that particular being who gives the measure and draws up the guidelines for everything that is."[2]

It is likely no mistake that this modern project of human mastery is evoked by reference specifically to the sense of sight and to the powers of image-making. As Heidegger points out in *Being and Time*, sight has long stood as a kind of master sense, both in the Greek and in the Christian metaphysics that so deeply shape our Western heritage,[3] and a distinctively modern, technoscientific project of mastery has been advanced notably by technologies that extend, expand, intensify, or otherwise re-shape our powers of vision by means of image-making, storage, transmission, and display. From the telescope and microscope, which prove integral to the emergence and development of a distinctively modern natural science and its vision of the real,[4] through the still and motion-picture cameras, which transform our powers of observation and memory in the undertakings of science and popular culture alike,[5] the technologies of image make near what was once too distant to be seen, and they give us distance on what was too near; they allow us to speed up what was previously too slow to appear, just as they can slow down and make visible what once was too fast. As the technologically framed and mediated image becomes ever more integral to the very appearance of our world, however, that framing and me-diation themselves grow more hidden, obscured by that which they seem to disclose. This logic reaches an extreme today in the digital and virtual realms we inhabit increasingly without being able to escape or, thus, even to see them—while socially, cul-turally, politically, and economically they nonetheless reshape the most fundamental dimensions of our lives, from the basic terms and character of human interrelation to the very tempo-rality of our days.

The centrality of image and sight to our modern construal of the world goes hand in hand with a modern conviction that the human subject plays an indispensable and constructive role in the world's very appearance or being. Our vision of the world is integral to it. As Immanuel Kant's epoch-making philosophy signals when it insists that mind plays an active and constructive role in staging the appearance of phenomenal reality, we do not simply receive a world already given; we are essentially world-forming or world-building. This construal of human subjectivity as world-building has been central, of course, to the modern humanistic disciplines wherein the assumption runs deep that our reality is socially, culturally, and historically constructed; and it has been foundational likewise, more specifically, to the academic field from which all three authors in this volume come: the distinctively modern (and, initially, largely American) field of religious studies, which often defines itself explicitly—and notably when aiming to distinguish itself from theology—as "worldview" analysis. That distinction is often made a bit too swiftly and too easily, when for example it ignores, ironically, the historical and cultural origins of "worldview" itself and its correlative humanism. If religious studies—as a humanistic worldview analysis—is founded in some projection theory of religion akin to that found in a Ludwig Feuerbach or, indeed, a Karl Marx, we may wonder whether it is not in fact a specifically Christian identification of the divine that yields, conceptually and historically, our conviction that religious or theological visions are at bottom indirect or disguised visions of the human subject and its condition. Feuerbach, at any rate, is straightforward about the religious and specifically Christian logic and provenance of his humanism: "It is not I, but religion that worships man," he writes in his preface to the second edition of *The Essence of Christianity*,

> although religion, or rather theology, denies this; it is not I, an insignificant individual, but religion itself that says: God is man,

man is God; it is not I, but religion that denies the God who is *not* a man, but only an *ens rationis*, —since it makes God become man, and then constitutes this God, not distinguished from man, having a human form, human feelings, and human thoughts, the object of its worship and veneration. I have only found the key to the cipher of the Christian religion, only extricated its true meaning from the web of contradictions and delusions called theology.[6]

This humanistic version of atheism simply reverses a traditional Christian thinking of the human as *imago dei* or image of God: here it is not man who is created by God in the image of God, but God who is created by man in the image of man. We image or picture God to ourselves, on this view, according to the image or picture that we form, or already have, of ourselves.

Attending to various histories of various purported worldviews—often without much investigating the contexts from which the very concept of worldview derives, or the history of our reduction of "world" to something "viewed"—this version of religious studies extends a distinctively modern, Western project of human autonomy. As Mark Taylor richly argues here in "Gathering Remains," extending insights from Heidegger, that modern project of autonomy reaches an extreme wherein the work we do to overcome human alienation—exemplified in Feuerbach or Marx and in their shared source, Hegel—yields a form of self-enclosure in which the human subject finds always and everywhere only itself. Such humanistic reflexivity, which a recent phenomenological and theological thinking like Jean-Luc Marion's can take to be effectively idolatrous, was estimated already by Heidegger to be delusional. Along lines that Taylor emphasizes, Heidegger contends within his analysis of modern technology that when "man" "exalts himself to the posture of lord of the earth . . . the impression comes to prevail that everything man encounters exists only insofar as it is his construct. This illusion gives rise in turn to one final delusion: It seems as though man everywhere and always encounters only himself."[7]

As Taylor has been arguing since his earliest field-altering and field-opening works on religion and deconstructive thought, the death of God, thought through within a deconstructive hermeneutic, cannot mean simply a replacement of the traditional creator God by a godlike creative human subject. For such a reversal, as the groundbreaking *Erring: A Postmodern A/theology* puts it, "reveals the slave's struggle *against* the master to be a struggle *for* mastery. By transferring the predicates of divinity to the human subject, the humanistic atheist inverts, but fails to subvert, the logic of repression. With this inversion, the problem of mastery and slavery is relocated rather than resolved. The death of the sovereign God now appears to be the birth of the sovereign self."[8] While Taylor's deconstructive thinking has for more than three decades worked to open alternatives to this modern project of mastery, both he and Rubenstein highlight in the present volume that an effectively deified humanity—or the delusional dream of such—remains strikingly persistent among contemporary techno-utopians who aspire even to an immortality, and liberation from material reality, that we humans might achieve by technoscientific means, such that we might need even to speak of a posthuman condition.

Situating these posthuman aspirations within a broader trajectory of modern thinking about human autonomy, Taylor here schematizes three key stages within that trajectory. Each of the three maintains a distinctive relation to the meanings and uses of image, and each, correlatively, marks a transition in the dominant form of capitalism. While modernity's industrial economy of things and its related culture of the spectacle give way to a consumerist economy and the postmodern simulacrum, we find ourselves currently, Taylor argues, in an age of financial capitalism, which entails a metaphysic of digital code that works hand in hand with posthuman fantasies of virtual or digital immortality. Taylor frames his analysis of this posthuman turn through a reading of Don DeLillo's 2016 novel, *Zero K*, which seems barely fictive in its evocation and exploration of the fantasies enjoyed by those godlike few today who seek technological liberation from the material and mortal conditions that plague the rest of us. In fact, for Taylor *Zero K* is "a quasi-documentary account of the present disguised as a post-apocalyptic fiction set in the future" ("Gathering," 30) where "for the masters of the universe who have funded and invented technological innovations that have transformed the global economy into an immaterial play of light operating at superhuman speed, death is nothing more than an engineering problem that inevitably will be solved. Technology is the new religion for the posthuman age" ("Gathering," 28).

Insofar as the posthuman turn signaled with DeLillo entails a return of gnostic desires to escape the flesh and its deathly limitations, that turn represents a perverse outworking of the modern ideal of human autonomy: having pursued the ideal of freedom as self-determination in and through technological systems that grow increasingly pervasive, automatized, and abstracted, the self-assertive human subject is itself increasingly subjected to systems that escape our control and alienate us from the material and temporal conditions of our finitude.

I call this outworking perverse not only because, as Taylor highlights, we suffer a reversal wherein the creator is subjected to and controlled by its own creation, such that it suffers a new alienation (this is an old, oft-told story); I call it perverse also insofar as the Enlightenment ideal of autonomy, at least in its more astute versions—such as Kant—included a humility, and a reckoning with finitude, that seem, as Taylor and Rubenstein both elaborate, comically, and painfully, absent among the technological and financial titans of our day. As Heidegger points out, while Kant was preoccupied with the character and conditions of theoretical and practical self-determination, his central lines of questioning—What can I know? What should I do? What may I hope for?—concern most fundamentally our human finitude. For the ability, duty, and allowing-to-hope that are at stake in these questions each entail the *not* of a disability, of a not-yet having fulfilled one's duty, or of a hopeful expectation that is founded in privation and exposed to potential disappointment. Or to put it otherwise: an infinite and hence all-powerful being never needs to ask, "What can I do?" Thus, as Heidegger reasons in his important and much-debated book on Kant's critical thought, *Kant and the Problem of Metaphysics*, "human reason does not just disclose finitude in these questions; rather, its innermost interest is with finitude itself. For this reason, it is not a matter of doing away with the ability, duty, and allowing [to hope], in this way to extinguish finitude, but rather the reverse. It is precisely a question of becoming certain of this finitude in order to hold oneself in it."[9]

Turning to art as a ground of resistance to the delusion and narcissism of today's techno-utopian fantasies, Taylor's essay here links the question of our finitude to the question of humility and this latter's essential relation with the earth. An art that counters techno-utopian flight from the limits of our mortal and material condition is one that—leaving the galleries and auction houses where art becomes only a form of finance—returns us to the earth and the elemental; for it is the earth in its material density that, in the end, receives and holds our deaths and our dead. In resonance with a line of thinking one might trace from Giambattista Vico to Robert Pogue Harrison, which argues that we become human through our rootedness in the earth, and more specifically through our burial of the dead,[10] Taylor emphasizes that "'humility,' like 'humanity,' derives from 'humus,' earth, ground, soil—brown or black decaying organic matter that eventually turns to stone. Earth to earth, humans to humus. By bringing us back to earth, art teaches us how to live by teaching us how to die" ("Gathering," 88).

If an earthly art teaches us how to die, then it does a work that has long been thought to define philosophy. The tie between such philosophical art and our material ground, Taylor argues, is not only an important counter to our virtual abstraction from the real; it goes more deeply to the nature and operation of imagination itself. For the imagination, he notes, entails a sensible, material aspect that cannot be reduced without remainder to immaterial concept or its latter-day version in digital code. In its irreducibly sensible and material aspect, Taylor elaborates, the imagination allows us to apprehend that which rational human thought cannot conceptually comprehend: its mortal condition and the immense temporal depth of the earthly ground that sustains us. Such apprehension, he argues, can open or reawaken us to our own humility, and thus our humanity, which we might then receive as a gift, rather than flee or deny it like some poison:

> Rather than transporting disembodied minds and souls to a timeless realm, the art that is redemptive grounds those it grasps in a profound temporality that exceeds human comprehension. The media of this art are material and not immaterial—earth, water, fire, steel, bone, and, yes, stone. Far from being our own construction, the world this art reveals is a gift that is bestowed without reason. To receive this gift with humility is to give up the will to mastery by acknowledging human finitude, and to acknowledge this finitude is to accept mortality. ("Gathering," 106)

An attunement to these ties between the earth and the gift of our mortal humility should leave us unsurprised that the techno-utopian sensibility that seeks virtual immortality today aims also to escape the earth, to transcend or stand beyond our humble ground, in a project of conquest whose aspirations reach the cosmic scale. While Taylor here explores the artful imagination that brings us back to earth, Rubenstein critically investigates the imperial imagination that half a century ago gave us our first images—photographs—of the earth from space, an imagination today resurgent and extended in the project of colonizing Mars (and perhaps on the way to it the moon).

Rubenstein frames her discussion by reference to billionaire tech entrepreneur Elon Musk's SpaceX project. Presenting itself not only as a technological project aiming to make humankind "'a multi-planet species and true spacefaring civilization' by opening up space travel to civilians" ("Above Us," 118), SpaceX fashions itself also as an artistic project that—by leaving the earth—might "awaken the global imagination" and thus "awaken our love of this world through otherworldly perspectives on it" ("Above Us," 120). As Rubenstein's analysis goes on to show, however, the appeal to artistic and countercultural awakening in fact more likely just extends the modern project of mastery that Heidegger identifies in his speaking of our conquest of the world as picture: "the artist who can see the earth from beyond earth becomes, in a sense, its master" ("Above Us," 121). In this sense, Musk and the überwealthy, art-loving fashion designer who has purchased the first SpaceX ticket, Yusaku Maezawa, represent only the latest stage in a history of cosmic image-making that promises the peace of unity while in fact perpetuating a violence that effaces difference through its totalizing logic of conquest.

Rubenstein tracks this history's cosmic ambition by focusing on the role of image in space travel—reading current projects of space colonization in light of the space race of last century, during which humans first traveled to the moon, looked back at Earth, and took a picture. The well-known *Earthrise* (1968) and *Blue Marble* photos (1972) that were taken during the Apollo 8 and Apollo 17 space missions are frequently credited with helping to birth modern environmental consciousness, our awakening to the "fragility, uniqueness, and unity of the earth" ("Above Us," 127). But as Rubenstein argues, the images purportedly yielding this "whole-earth" vision remain far from benevolent or simply innocent, having been as they were "enabled materially by the technological ravaging of the earth and military one-upmanship they were suddenly called upon to contest" ("Above Us," 127). We see here something of the self-contradictory madness wherein the march of modernity seeks solutions to technologically generated problems in those very same technologies, without calling them or their driving logics into question—a madness akin to what Donna Haraway calls, with respect to current threats of ecological catastrophe, our "tragicomic 'cosmofaith in technofixes'" ("Above Us," 149). The whole-earth vision, Rubenstein emphasizes, was from the beginning inseparable from, even complicit with, the "one-world" vision of a neoliberal globalized order wherein the earth remains susceptible "to total domination in the hands of whoever manages to see the whole thing from beyond it" ("Above Us," 127).

If the appeal to unity and its purported peace has included what remains an imperialistic and violent project of our modern, Western technomilitary complex, that project has also had, as Rubenstein goes on to elaborate, a distinctly white, male, and Christian bent. She highlights the racist energies driving our latter-day imperialisms through the juxtaposition of two futurisms: the scientistic futurism of Disneyland and the Afro-futurism of artists such as the musician and poet Sun Ra. While the former, growing out of Cold War nationalism and militarism, glorifies an exploration and conquest that merely extend into space the imperialism guilty already of devastating colonized lands and their indigenous peoples here on earth, the latter creates musical journeys into space for those same people, who, in having suffered conquest, capture, and the transport of Middle Passage, have already lived out an alien abduction. What seems noise to (white, male, Christian) norms of uniformity may constitute for the already abducted alien—the hope goes— transport to a new harmony and a genuinely other world. "Imagination," Sun Ra would say, "is a magic carpet ride," and by transporting "dehumanized peoples to otherwise worlds," it can be a real, and liberating, force that works in resistance to the actual boarding of ships that "plant colonies to destroy the otherness of worlds by making them all just like this one" ("Above Us," 158).

However, the resurgence today of—all too similar, and in the end unimaginative, not to say mindless—appeals to aeronautical imagination manifests not only among the titan entrepreneurs like Musk but also in unabashedly nationalist and racist politicians such as D. J. Trump and Mike Pence. With this recognition, Rubenstein concludes on the somber note that "another world is improbable." We would do well, then, her final pages contend, to hear the hard claims advanced by Afro-pessimist philosopher Calvin Warren that hope in the political may itself be the danger, insofar as the political is *"constitutively antiblack"* ("Above Us," 169); and thus that "justice, redress, and righteousness" are not to be sought in "other worlds," which— whether imaginative or actual—invariably replicate "this same, unbearable world" ("Above Us," 169), but instead are to be sought in an active nihilism that looks "to end the world itself."[11] Whether or not one can embrace fully such an actively nihilistic response, Rubenstein's essay sets out in rich and troubling detail the need for caution regarding the uses of imagination in service to ideology and illusion, and the related importance of reflecting on such Afro-pessimist insight into the improbability of other worlds that would actually do other than replicate the repressive worlds we already know; or yield a politics, and a humanity, that do not simply repeat and extend the constitutively exclusionary logics that have tended to define our politics, and humanity, hitherto.

Insofar as Rubenstein rightly argues that our dominant world pictures remain inseparable from "the whole techno-military metaphysic that encapsulates the world as such" ("Above Us," 143), and insofar as those pictures tend, as she shows, to efface difference even in the name of unity and peace, we might hear in her essay tones that resonate deeply with Emmanuel Levinas's epoch-making criticism of "totality" as that which invariably reduces all otherness to the same. Her essay should also leave us suspicious, however, regarding the great ethical thinker's provocative claim—made the same year that he published his first masterwork critiquing totality, *Totality and Infinity*[12]—that the first manned space flight, Soviet cosmonaut Yuri Gagarin's orbit of the earth on April 12, 1961, opens us to man "in the nudity of the face."[13] For if the face appears, as according to Levinas, always in the singular, while calling to each of us in our likewise singular responsibility, the unity of our technomilitary and capitalistic world picture amounts, for Rubenstein, to a totality of just the kind Levinas spent his life resisting. As she puts it, the one-world vision "attains the unity it commends by sweeping away differences of race, gender, class, and religion—assembling them all into an undifferentiated, false male universal" ("Above Us,' 146).

A vision of seemingly cosmic scope, then, can touch the individual in that individual's singularity and difference—by effacing them. And so likewise today, the singular faces—and private lives—of individuals are increasingly captured, contained, and conveyed within surveillance systems of seemingly unlimited scope. These are systems of "seeing" wherein each and every face, and indeed life, can seem to become interchangeable with any and every other for such purposes as their policing, political control, and economic exploitation within what Shoshana Zuboff analyzes as the age "surveillance capitalism."[14]

As Rubenstein points out in her essay, the claim to any vision of the "whole" is itself blind to its own blindness: it does not see, or acknowledge, that it can actually never see the whole but always only some ever-partial aspect. "Until humanity manages to develop four-dimensional vision, *no one* will see the planet 'whole'" ("Above Us," 145). Such a failure to see the invisible that conditions any and all vision replicates in its logic the exclusive and violent gestures through which claims to unity and totality—such as that of "humanity"—are so often constituted, as Rubenstein and her interlocutors show. This is a failure that pertains also to the lack of humility—revealed in the disconnection from earth, and the flight from mortality—that is central as well to Taylor's analysis and argument here.

Both the effacement of singular individuals through totalizing gestures and the relation of such effacement to our encounter with mortality are central to my own essay, "Facial Recognition." The essay treats two figures of the invisible in order to reflect on the nature of imagination, the character of technological vision in contemporary culture, and the implications of these for the kinds of sociality, and love, that condition our human experience.

The fantasies of omniscience that so deeply shape our society today play out in technologies of the image that regard quite notably the human face—and they do so perhaps primarily by effacing the uniqueness of each face. While pervasive systems of technological surveillance focus increasingly on forms of facial recognition that capture any and all faces by wholly impersonal and statistical means, the uncanny work of "deep fake" video technologies makes every given face interchangeable with any other, in a way that blurs the distinction between the real and the purely fictive, between the individual person, who is irreplaceable, and the synthetic human, who would be endlessly replicable.

The effacement of our singular being by algorithmically driven imaging technologies entails an operation of substitution, I argue, whose logic has been integral to our modern and contemporary flight from mortality. Taking direction from Heidegger's reading of the poet Rainer Maria Rilke, I understand that flight from mortality in relation to the question of love. Our modern incapacity for mortality, Heidegger and Rilke together suggest, stems in large part from our forgetting that death and love belong together. Such love obeys a logic of the heart that is eclipsed by the calculating rationality that undergirds modern science and technology. While the calculating rationality of modern metaphysics fabricates the endlessly reproducible object, whether conceptual or technical, this logic of the heart attends to things in their fragility and to persons in their mortality. If the reproducible object is amenable to endless substitution or replacement—such that any given object can represent or stand in for another—the heart sees each person's mortal singularity.

There is a paradox to such seeing, however, for the singularity by virtue of which each person remains irreplaceable, is given by that—death—which, strictly speaking, remains invisible. Death "as such" or "in itself" never gives to me something that I can actually see, or be. The visibility of the other person's—invisible—mortality, the essay argues, may be understood to depend on a work that is distinctive to the imagination and tied inextricably to a sharing of love within social relations.

A suggestive model for this loving and socially enabled vision of the invisible can be found in the early modern theologian and philosopher Nicholas of Cusa and his 1453 treatise on the vision of God (De visione Dei). As both Rubenstein and I have noted in previous studies, Cusa is a decisive figure for having understood our universe to bear the divine trait of infinity—and thus to resist, like God himself, any full or final comprehension.[15] To see aright the infinite and—therefore—invisible God must mean, for the finite creature, to see, paradoxically, that one does not see, even as the infinite revelation is endlessly visible. In his treatise on the vision of God, Cusa finds a figure for the invisible God's appearance to us in the all-seeing portrait, which thus serves for him as an "icon" of God. Cusa explains in the preface to his treatise that in order actually to glimpse the ubiquitous gaze of such a portrait—which holds all of us equally, each in our singularity, wherever we move and wherever we stand—one cannot remain alone. For while I as a sole individual can have the experience of a gaze that follows me everywhere at all times, the appearance of a gaze that proves genuinely ubiquitous, like that of the infinite God, requires that each and all—in principle innumerable—testify that they too find themselves followed by that gaze always and everywhere, in positions and from perspectives that differ from mine and cannot be exchanged with mine. To participate in this universality of singular positions requires a play of testimony and belief within social relations that are at bottom, as Cusa emphasizes, relations of shared love—and of love for the love that all others also experience, each in an individual way.

In what may seem a counterintuitive connection, I take up this way of thinking about the face of an invisible God in order to ask about the appearance of death in the face of another. For like the infinite God to a finite creature, death remains strictly invisible to those who remain alive. Building not only on Cusa's thinking about the role of love and sociality in the invisible God's appearance but also on Levinas's insight that "love" means seeing death in the face of the other person, I argue that the death of the other appears to us in the measure of our love—and of our love for the love that others likewise shared, each in a unique way, with the beloved who dies. (I make my final revisions to this introduction eleven days after the murder of George Floyd, whose face and death appear to me, and touch me, in the measure of the love I feel for him, which itself grows in my seeing the love he shared with his mother, to whom he cried out as he died; and with his younger brother, who recalls the one bed in which they slept side by side as children; and with his baby daughter, whom he once held in his hands . . .)

In its mortality, which appears primarily, or even exclusively, to a look of love, the face of the beloved may be understood, I contend, as exemplary of the image more broadly. For the image appears only insofar as it also disappears; the visibility of its presence lives thanks only to the invisibility of its absence. It depends, in other words, on temporal affection, which, following Heidegger and readers of Heidegger such as Jean-Luc Nancy, we can understand to be the essence of imagination.

The primordial temporality of imagination grounds the image's coming-into-presence, and returning-into-absence, only by sustaining the interplay of anticipation and recollection. In this regard, the work of imagination would be indispensable to any worthy response that we might attempt to a question coursing equally through Taylor's call for an art that brings us back to earth and through Rubenstein's resistance to the imperialistic imagination of space travel: the question of intergenerational responsibility. Can we imagine answering responsibly to generations future, and past, for the responses we make now regarding the devastation of Earth and the murderous conquest of peoples? To do so would require imagining more fully and richly that from which our techno-utopian cultures seem so much in flight: the fragility of things and the mortality of persons. It would require, in other words, an imagination attuned by love, and grounded in humility.

NOTES

1. Martin Heidegger, "The Age of the World Picture," in *The Question Concerning Technology and Other Essays*, trans. William Lovitt (New York: Harper and Row, 1977), 134.

2. Heidegger, "Age of the World Picture," 134.

3. See *Being and Time* ¶36: "Even at an early date (and in Greek philosophy this was no accident) cognition was conceived in terms of the 'desire to see.' The treatise that stands first in the collection of Aristotle's treatises on ontology begins with the sentence: *pantes anthropoi tou eidenai oregontai phusei*. The care for seeing is essential to man's Being. . . . The remarkable priority of 'seeing' was noticed particularly by Augustine, in connection with his Interpretation of *concupiscentia*. . . . 'but we even say, "See how that sounds," "See how that is scented," "See how hard that is."'" Martin Heidegger, *Being and Time*, trans. John Macquarrie and Edward Robinson (Oxford: Basil Blackwell, 1962), 214–15 (= *Sein und Zeit, Sechzehnte Auflage* (Tübingen: Max Niemeyer Verlag, 1986), 170–71).

4. See, e.g., Hans Blumenberg's account of the role played by Galileo's telescope in the triumph of theoretical curiosity that Blumenberg takes as decisive to the success of Copernicanism, the emergence of modern natural science, and the human self-assertion that this entailed: "The telescope could not be abolished or banished as an instrument of theoretical impertinence. It became a factor in the legitimation of theoretical curiosity precisely because, unlike any experimental intervention in the objects of nature, it could be adapted to the classical ideal of the contemplation

of nature. The phenomena newly revealed by the telescope nourished and gave wings to the imagination, which sought to provide itself, by means of the 'plurality' of worlds, with continually self-surpassing limit conceptions of what was as yet undisclosed"; in *The Legitimacy of the Modern Age*, trans. Robert M. Wallace (Cambridge, MA: MIT Press, 1985), 373.

5. See, e.g., Benjamin's "The Work of Art in the Age of Mechanical Reproduction," which likens technologies of vision to discovery of the unconscious in psychoanalysis: "With the close-up, space expands; with slow motion, movement is extended. The enlargement of a snapshot does not simply render more precise what in any case was visible, though unclear: it reveals entirely new structural formations of the subject. So too, slow motion not only presents familiar qualities of movement but reveals in them entirely unknown ones. . . . Evidently a different nature opens itself to the camera than opens to the naked eye—if only because an unconsciously penetrated space is substituted for a space consciously explored by man. . . . Here the camera intervenes with the resources of its lowerings and liftings, its interruptions and isolations, its extensions and accelerations, its enlargements and reductions. The camera introduces us to unconscious optics as does psychoanalysis to unconscious impulses." In Walter Benjamin, *Illuminations: Essays and Reflections*, ed. Hannah Arendt, trans. Harry Zohn (New York: Schocken Books, 1969), 236–37.

6. Ludwig Feuerbach, *The Essence of Christianity*, trans. George Eliot (Amherst, NY: Prometheus Books, 1989), xvi.

7. Martin Heidegger, "The Question Concerning Technology," in *The Question Concerning Technology*, 27.

8. Mark C. Taylor, *Erring: A Postmodern A/theology* (Chicago: University of Chicago Press, 1984), 25.

9. Martin Heidegger, *Kant and the Problem of Metaphysics*, 5th ed., enl., trans. Richard Taft (Bloomington: Indiana University Press, 1997), 152.

10. See esp. Robert Pogue Harrison, *The Dominion of the Dead* (Chicago: University of Chicago Press, 2003).

11. Calvin Warren, "Black Nihilism and the Politics of Hope," *CR: The New Centennial Review* 15, no. 1 (Spring 2015), 230; cited in "Above Us," 169.

12. Emmanuel Levinas, *Totalité et infini: Essai sur l'extériorité* (The Hague: Martinus Nijhoff, 1961); *Totality and Infinity: An Essay on Exteriority*, trans. Alphonso Lingis (Pittsburgh: Duquesne University Press, 1969).

13. Emmanuel Levinas, "Heidegger, Gagarin, and Us," in *Difficult Freedom: Essays on Judaism*, trans. Sean Hand (Baltimore: Johns Hopkins University Press, 1990), 234.

14. Shoshana Zuboff, *The Age of Surveillance Capitalism: The Fight for a Human Future at the New Frontier of Power* (London: Profile Books, 2019). For a brief introduction to Zuboff's thinking on these matters, see her recent opinion piece, "You Are Now Remotely Controlled: Surveillance Capitalists Control the Science and the Scientists, the Secrets and the Truth," *New York Times*, January 24, 2020.

15. See Mary-Jane Rubenstein, *Worlds without End: The Many Lives of the Multiverse* (New York: Columbia University Press, 2014), chap. 3, "Navigating the Infinite," esp. 78–88; and Thomas A. Carlson, *The Indiscrete Image: Infinitude and Creation of the Human* (Chicago: University of Chicago Press, 2008), chap. 3, "The Living Image: Infinitude, Unknowing, and Creative Capacity in Mystical Anthropology," esp. 95–112.

GATHERING REMAINS

Mark C. Taylor

"Don't you see and feel these things more acutely than you used to? The perils and warnings? Something gathering, no matter how safe you may feel in your wearable technology. All the voice commands and hyper-connections that allow you to become disembodied."

DON DELILLO, *Zero K*

Part of my art is based on an awareness that we live in a nuclear era. We're probably living at the end of civilization.

MICHAEL HEIZER, *Sculpture in Reverse*

APPROACHING DISASTER

After the explosion (or was it an implosion?) nothing remained. Nothing remained but fragments scattered beyond recollection. Fragments of metal, stone, bodies, and bones. Dazed and confused, he wandered through the dust and debris, hearing nothing, feeling nothing. Nothing of the deafening noise of sirens and screams. His eyes were clouded but not with tears; his gaze was unfocused leaving everything raging about him obscure. Amidst smoldering ruins, nothing seemed real. Nothing seemed real but nothing.

If there were life around him, he did not see it, hear it, feel it, smell it, taste it. Everything he believed to be real had disappeared. Unable to comprehend what had occurred, he was filled with an apprehension no words could capture. One moment there is life, the next moment there is death; what lies in between remains without why. This uncharted interval eternally returns as a gift that strangely marks the impossibility of gifting. Alone with nowhere to go, he slowly began to gather the remains, the remains of a life he had once thought was his own. Earth, fire, water, rock, stone, steel, flesh, bone. He had no idea why he felt compelled to do this, or what he would do with the gathered remains.

LIVING DEATH

There had been predictions, endless predictions from the left and the right. Predictions had become so predictable that they were ignored, and nothing happened. Nothing. Too much religion, too little religion; too much control, not enough control; too much information, not enough information; too much regulation, not enough regulation; too much power, not enough power. What most people did not realize was that the end was already occurring because the real was vaporizing in images on scrims and screens connected by invisible networks operating too fast for humans to comprehend or manage. Driverless cars, trains, ships, planes; hospitals without doctors and nurses; factories without workers; markets without analysts and brokers; news without journalists; classrooms without teachers. Programs and algorithms generating programs and algorithms too complicated for humans to code re-create the world in their own image. When it is no longer possible to imagine what comes next, every age becomes a Post-Age. The modern search for mastery and control leads to postmodern servitude and loss of control. Is this progress or decline? At the tipping point, extremes meet; true believers, whose gospels differ profoundly, not only await,

but actively promote disaster. Religious zealots and technological wizards join in the nihilistic hope for the end of the world
and the arrival of life everlasting in either heaven or silicon.

*
**

They were alive. Alive as dead. Vitrification, cryopreservation,
nanotechnology. Row after row of bodies standing alone in
separate "pods" like statues in a museum of ruins or an ancient
mausoleum all awaiting "cyber-resurrection." "They'd been
stripped of their essential organs, which were being preserved
separately, brains included, in insulated vessels called organ
pods." The "cryonic chamber" was known as "Zone K," which
designated the temperature of absolute zero (minus 273.1 cel-
sius) required to preserve the bodies in a state of suspended
animation. Science? Fiction? Technology? Art? It is difficult to
know for sure. "Here, there were no lives to think about or imagine. This was pure spectacle, a single entity, the bodies regal in
their cryonic bearing. It was a form of visionary art, it was body
art with broad implications."[1]

In Don DeLillo's *Zero K*, themes familiar to readers of his previous works return in a dystopian vision that assumes urgency
because time is rapidly running out. As global information, financial, media, and social networks expand until "everything is
connected,"[2] Earth becomes uninhabitable and the underworld
becomes an underground escape that turns out to be hell. This
book depicts the torturous transition between postmodern and
posthuman worlds, which is now occurring. DeLillo begins at
the end: "*Everybody wants to own the end of the world*" (*Z* 3). What
could it possibly mean to "own the end of the world"? In the era
of global capitalism even the apocalypse is for sale. Who is the
seller? Who might be the buyer? Who makes the market on the
approaching eschaton? What possible return might there be on
owning the end?

Ross Lockhart is "a man shaped by money." Like Eric Packer,
the twenty-eight-year-old multibillion asset manager in *Cos-*

mopolis, Lockhart is a private wealth manager who speculates in emerging markets. He lives his professional life surrounded by "screens, keyboards and other devices," which track financial flows racing across the globe at the speed of light. His office, like Gordon Gekko's, is filled with works of abstract art, trophies of his success. He had made his early reputation by "analyzing the profit impact of natural disasters" (Z 7). In the time before the plague, he had believed the impending disaster would be man-made rather than natural and global rather than local. Ever the shrewd speculator, Lockhart realizes that global disaster offers the possibility of the biggest payoff ever. The challenge he faces is to find a way to survive the disaster so he can profit from his investment.

His son, Jeff, is everything Ross is not. Determined to "build a life in opposition to [his] father's career in global finance," Jeff shuffles from job to job, imagining that he might someday become a poet or "a professor of philosophy or transfinite mathematics at an obscure college in west-central somewhere" (Z 54). Father and son are brought together by the approaching death of Ross's second wife, Artis Martineau, who is suffering from multiple sclerosis. Artis has decided to undergo "cryonic suspension" at a facility named the Convergence located in an underground complex in the Kazakh steppe far from any village or city. Ross, who is an investor in the project and serves as a financial adviser, insists that technology is rapidly approaching the point where it will be possible to fully restore mind and body, and thereby to bring people back to life. He admits to Jeff that this is not a new idea:

> "Faith-based technology. That's what it is. Another god. Not so different it turns out, from some of the earlier ones. Except that it's real, it's true, it delivers."
> "Life after death."
> "Eventually, yes."
> "The Convergence."
> "Yes." (Z 9)

The Convergence refers to the merger of end and beginning, which is "the point at which death and life join" (Z 255). True believers willingly submit to death and pay an exorbitant sum to con men posing as scientists and promising eternal life through technological enhancement and revival. With her disability and suffering increasing, Artis is preparing to undergo the procedure, when Ross, who has at least twenty years of good health ahead of him, decides to join her. Jeff is skeptical of the entire enterprise and opposes his father's decision, but he agrees to visit the distant facility.

> "They will do it for you. Because it's you. Simple injection, serious criminal act."
> "Let it go," he said.
> "And in return, what? You've framed wills and trusts and testaments granting them certain resources and holdings well beyond what you've already given them."
> "Finished?"
> "Is it outright murder? Is it a form of assisted suicide that's horribly premature? Or is it a metaphysical crime that needs to be analyzed by philosophers?"
> He said, "Enough."
> "Die a while, then live forever." (Z 114)

DeLillo describes the subterranean complex as a strange combination of a closely guarded military compound and a secret religious retreat. Most surprising, however, is Ross's report that Artis thinks this enterprise is best understood as "a work-in-progress, an earthwork, a form of earth art, land art. Built up out of the land and sunk down into it as well. Restricted access. Defined by stillness, both human and environmental. A little tomblike as well. The earth is the guiding principle. . . . Return to the earth, emerge from the earth" (Z 10).

DeLillo has long been interested in land art and earthworks located in remote places and often alludes to works of contemporary artists. His description of the Convergence beneath the salt flats and stone rubble evokes James Turrell's "Roden Crater" carved out of a volcano in the Arizona desert or Michael Heizer's "City" sunk in the Nevada desert where there is "nothing else, nowhere else" (Z 4).[3] In these massive projects, advanced technology creates works of art in which high/low, surface/depth, modern/primitive intersect but are not unified. These are latter-day temples of art and religious shrines for pilgrims searching for meaning and solace in a world the gods have fled. For Artis, Ross, and their fellow believers, scientists, engineers, and programmers are high priests who promise to ferry them to the next world where they will enjoy life everlasting.

Throughout history, believers repeatedly have retreated underground to practice their religion. From the underground paintings of Lascaux to the catacombs of early Christians to caves filled with erotic sculptures of Hindu gods and goddesses, the underworld has been the site of religious rituals. All of these places are "located at the far margins of plausibility" (Z 115). The Convergence is surrounded with a religious aura. "Monks" wrapped in hooded cloaks and schooled in *ars technica* attend "pilgrims" awaiting their final trip. In one chapel-like alcove, a woman quietly speaking to a few people preparing for death describes "great human spectacles, the white-clad faithful in Mecca, the hadj, mass devotion, millions, year after year, and Hindus gathered on the banks of the Ganges, millions, tens of millions, a festival of immortality" (Z 63). A shrewd investor who has made a living betting on surviving future disasters, Ross admits, "This place may not have been intended as the new Jerusalem but people made long journeys to find a form of higher being here, or at least a scientific process that will keep their body tissue from decomposing" (Z 43).

Jeff will have none of it. In addition to raising serious ethical issues, he realizes that the mission of the Convergence poses profound questions about the self, time, and human existence. "How are you," he asks, "without your sense of time?" (Z 68).[4] Time haunts the halls and chambers of the Convergence in the form of skulls—one an imposing skull "about five times the size of an ordinary human skull," another a work of art reminiscent of Damien Hirst's *For the Love of God*.[5] "An oversized human skull was mounted on a pedestal jutting from the wall. The skull was cracked in places, stained with age, a lurid coppery bronze, a drained gray. The eyeholes were rimmed with jewels and the jagged teeth painted silver" (Z 68, 63). Like Hirst, investors in the Convergence believe they have figured out how to profit from death.

While touring the facility, Jeff pauses to look through a narrow slot into the room in which the massive skull is placed. The Stenmark twins, whose vision has inspired the enterprise, are engaged in a conversation that raises many of the questions that are on his mind.

> "Isn't it sufficient to live a little longer through advanced technology? Do we need to go on and on and on?" . . .
>
> "Does literal immortality compress our enduring artforms and cultural wonders into nothingness?"
>
> "What will poets write about?"
>
> "What happens to history? What happens to money? What happens to God?" . . .
>
> "Aren't we easing the way toward uncontrollable levels of population, environmental stress?" . . .
>
> "The defining element of life is that it ends." . . .
>
> "Isn't the sting of our eventual dying what makes us precious to people in our lives?" (Z 69–70)

For the Stenmarks and their followers, overcoming death is the end of the human and the dawn of the glorious posthuman condition. "We want to stretch the boundaries of what it means to be human—stretch and then surpass. We want to do whatever we are capable of doing in order to alter human thought and bend the energies of civilization" (Z 71).

Jeff, by contrast, believes that death is what makes us human.

His girlfriend, Emma, asks him to talk to her adopted son, who has dropped out of school and, unbeknownst to her, is planning to go to the Ukraine to join the self-defense forces resisting the Russian invasion. Jeff takes Stak to an art gallery with a single work on display—a rock sculpture. This work of art provides the occasion for Jeff to raise existential questions he suspects the confused adolescent is pondering.

> I looked at him intently and said in the most deliberate voice I could manage, "'Rocks are, but they do not exist.'"
>
> After a pause I said, "I came across this statement when I was in college and forgot it until very recently. 'Man alone exists. Rocks are, but they do not exist. Trees are, but they do not exist. Horses are, but they do not exist.'" (Z 213)

What Jeff does not tell Stak is that he had first encountered this claim in the writings of Martin Heidegger. For Heidegger, selfhood is inescapably temporal and, therefore, undeniably finite. Man alone exists because he is the only being who knows he will die. Inauthenticity, according to Heidegger, is the denial or avoidance of death; authenticity is Being-toward-death. Only by confronting death directly and honestly can we realize the abiding significance of the decisions that define who we are. This lesson stuck with Jeff; he quietly confesses, "I'd never felt more human than when my mother lay in bed dying" (Z 248). To overcome death would be to cease to be human and, perhaps, to become posthuman.

Research and development at the Convergence are enormously expensive and require constant fundraising as well as sophisticated advertising techniques. The halls and recesses of the underground retreat are filled with screens and scrims displaying horrifying events supposedly unfolding above ground: disaster after disaster—some "natural," others "manmade."Images are everywhere and eventually consume viewers—floods, fires, wars, religious and otherwise, no food, no water, no gas.

Gangs of bandits and packs of animals roaming amid ruins gathering what remains of what once had been a civilized world. The darker life above ground becomes, the more attractive the life promised below ground appears to be. On the other side of disaster, the promise not of seventy-two virgins but of a new life in which the body is immaterial and the world glows with transparent meaning:

> "And they will speak a new language, according to Ross."
> "A language isolate, beyond all affiliation with other languages," he said. "To be taught to some, implanted in others, those already in cryopreservation."
> A system that will offer new meanings, entire new levels of perception.
> It will expand our reality, deepen the reach of our intellect.
> It will remake us, he said.
> We will know ourselves as never before, blood, brain and skin.
> We will approximate the logic and beauty of pure mathematics in everyday speech.
> No similes, metaphors, analogics. (Z 130)

The more vivid the images become, the more Jeff's suspicions grow. "Documenting" disaster is good advertising, but what if this whole operation is an elaborate con game devised to make money? Jeff muses, "Is it possible that this is not factual documentation rendered in a selective manner but something radically apart? It's a digital weave, every fragment manipulated and enhanced, all of it designed, edited, redesigned. Why hadn't this occurred to me before, in earlier screenings, the monsoon rains, the tornadoes? These were visual fictions, the wildfires and burning monks, digital bits, digital code, all of it computer-generated, none of it real" (Z 152).

Since the beginning of time, credulous mortals have bought into schemes promising an eternal return on all-too-worldly investments. Cybernauts are Gnostics eager to escape the confines of flesh and the "corruption" of earthly existence. While acknowledging the precedents for his wager, Ross insists that this time it's different.

> "Mind and body are restored, returned to life. . . . This is not a new idea. It is an idea," he said, "that is now approaching full realization."
> "And you have complete confidence in this project."
> "Complete. Medically, technologically, philosophically. . . . Nothing speculative here. Nothing is wishful or peripheral. Men, women. Death, life." (Z 8)

Rather than secret passwords communicated by otherworldly messengers, cryptic codes, formulas, and algorithms calculated by anonymous scientists. Same game, different gnosis.

Redemption always has a price. From the time of ancient sacrificial offerings, believers have attempted to buy eternal life by cutting a deal with the gods. My money for my life. In the world of global capitalism, where the gods are scientific and technological wizards write code, the price of eternal life, like everything else, has become so inflated that only the ultra-wealthy can afford it. The Stenmark twins admit that "life-everlasting belongs to those of breathtaking wealth." Revving up their sales pitch, "Take the leap, they say. Live the billionaire's myth of immortality." Like elaborate pyramids and tombs and architecturally designed mausoleums of earlier times, the underground pod is the "final shrine of entitlement" (Z 76, 117). For the masters of the universe who have funded and invented technological innovations that have transformed the global economy into an immaterial play of light operating at superhuman speed, death is nothing more than an engineering problem that inevitably will be solved. Technology is the new religion for the posthuman age.

Technology. Religion. Art. Artis. Art Is. Art is. Art is what? What if Artis is right when she suggests that "we ought to regard [the Convergence] as a work-in-progress, an earthwork, a form of earth art, land art." She confessed, "This place, all of it, seems transitional to me. Filled with people coming and going. Then the others, those who are leaving in one sense, as I am, but staying in another sense, as I am. Staying and waiting. The only thing that's not ephemeral is the art. It's not made for an audience. It's made simply to be here. It's here, it's fixed, it's part of the foundation, set in stone. The painted walls, the simulated doors, the movie screens in the halls. Other installations else-where" (Z 50–51). What is the work of art after the death of man?

Ross eventually decides not to undergo the procedure with Artis, but two years later changes his mind and returns to the Convergence to join her. Jeff no longer resists his father's desire and agrees to help him on his final journey. As they prepare for the departure, an "envoy" Jeff dubs Zina or Zara reassures her clients that their investment is prudent because life on earth is already a living death.

> "That world, the one above," she said, "is being lost to the sys-tems. To the transparent networks that slowly occlude the flow of all those aspects of nature and character that distinguish humans from elevator buttons and doorbells." . . .
>
> "Those of you who will return to the surface. Haven't you felt it? The loss of autonomy. The sense of being virtualized. The devices you use, the ones you carry everywhere, room to room, minute to minute, inescapably. Do you ever feel unfleshed? All the coded impulses you depend on to guide you. All the sensors in the room that are watching you, listening to you, tracking your habits, measuring your capabilities. All the linked data designed to incorporate you into the megadata. Is there something that makes you uneasy? Do you think about the technovirus, all the systems down, global implosion? Or is it more personal? Do you feel steeped in some horrific digital panic that's everywhere and nowhere?" (Z 259)

Is technology the solution or the problem, the cure or the dis-ease? If art "is the only thing that's not ephemeral," then perhaps the work of art can redeem humanity by dispelling other-worldly illusions and returning finite human beings to earth, which is the only place they can dwell.

IMAGOCENTRISM

Jeff Bezos (founder and CEO of Amazon), Richard Branson (founder of the Virgin Group), and Elon Musk (cofounder and CEO of PayPal and Tesla Motors) building rocket ships to carry the chosen remnant from earthly disasters to colonies in outer space. Paul Thiel (cofounder of PayPal and founder of Palantir) funding anti-aging research and creating the Machine Intelligence Research Institute. Sergey Brin, Larry Page (cofounders and CEOs of Google) and Ray Kurzweil (MIT professor and director of research for Google) deploying Google's vast resources to develop technologies that will make it possible to live forever. All of these high priests of technology are supporters of Singularity University whose mission is to promote research and development that will hasten the arrival of the New Age they believe is on the horizon. Far from science fiction, Don DeLillo's *Zero K* is a quasi-documentary account of the present disguised as a post-apocalyptic fiction set in the near future. What has made the dream of this New Age possible? What beliefs inform its prophets/profits? What is its philosophical foundation?

To answer these questions, it is necessary to consider the complex intersection of developments in art, philosophy, technology, and finance. The last half of the twentieth century and the opening decades of the twenty-first century have been characterized by an unprecedented information, media, and networking revolution. While many analysts and critics insist these developments mark a sharp break with the past, a more careful consideration suggests that these changes grow directly out of the Industrial Revolution. In recent history, there have been three overlapping forms of capitalism—industrial, consumer, financial, which are all characterized by changing currencies of exchange—things, images, code. These different regimes mark three distinct historical epochs, which, in turn, have created the conditions for different cultural formations.

Modernism → Postmodernism → Posthumanism
Society of the Spectacle → Culture of Simulacra → Virtual
   Condition

The technological, social, economic, and cultural revolutions of the twentieth and twenty-first centuries would not have been possible without the philosophical, religious, and artistic revolutions of the nineteenth century. Practice and theory, power and knowledge, action and belief are always inseparably interrelated. Socioeconomic and cultural constructs implicitly and explicitly presuppose philosophical, religious, and even metaphysical convictions that must be exposed for any adequate understanding of what is occurring and any possibility of presenting an effective critical response. While these historical periods and accompanying developments are not simply sequential, this interplay of economics, technology, and culture has a discernible trajectory that begins with the Enlightenment and proceeds from dematerialization through digitization to virtualization.

In 1784, Kant published an influential essay entitled "What Is Enlightenment?" in which he famously argued that freedom and reason are inseparable. "Enlightenment is man's release from his self-incurred tutelage. Tutelage is man's inability to make use of his understanding without direction from another. Self-incurred is this tutelage when its cause lies not in the lack of reason but in the lack of resolution and courage to use it without direction from another. *Sapere aude!* 'Have courage to use your own reason!' That is the motto of enlightenment."[6] This definition of enlightenment turns on the distinction between heteronomy, which derives from the Greek *hetero*, "other," plus *nomos*, "law," and autonomy, which derives from *auto*, "self,"

plus *nomos*. While heteronomy involves determination by another (e.g., God, priest, professor, parent, emotions, desire), autonomy is rational self-determination. Modernity follows the
progression from heteronomy to autonomy, bondage to freedom, and slavery to mastery. The full realization of autonomy
is supposed to issue in complete self-determination and total
mastery of self and world. As heteronomy gives way to autonomy, all determination becomes self-determination, which is
self-reflexive. At this point, the relationship to ostensible otherness is actually the self-relation necessary for self-realization.

In Kant's critical philosophy this self-reflexive structure is
deployed theoretically (in thinking), practically (in acting), and
aesthetically (in feeling). He gives his clearest formulation of the
structure of self-reflexivity in his account of "inner teleology"
or "purposiveness without purpose" in the *Critique of Judgment*
(1790). In a self-reflexive structure, self and other, means and
ends are reciprocally related in such a way that each becomes
itself in and through the other, and neither can be itself apart
from the other. Kant illustrates this concept by describing the
interplay of whole and part in the work of art. "The parts of the
thing combine *of themselves* [emphasis added] into the unity of
the whole by being reciprocally cause and effect of their form.
For this is the only way in which it is possible that the idea of the
whole may conversely, or reciprocally, determine, in its turn,
the form and combination of all the parts, not as cause—for that
would make it an art product—but as the epistemological basis
upon which the systematic unity of the form and combination
of all the manifold contained in the given matter become cogni-
zable for the person estimating it."[7] What Kant discovered with
this insight is the principle of *constitutive relationality*, in which
identity is differential rather than oppositional. Being, therefore,
is relational, or, in DeLillo's words, "everything is connected."
Romantic artists and idealistic philosophers worked out the
immediate implications of Kant's argument during the closing
decade and early years of the nineteenth century. The structure

of self-reflexivity that constitutes inner teleology is the foundation of Hegel's speculative philosophy, Marx's interpretation of
capital, and the modern notion of the work of art. At this point
philosophy, art, and money become bound in a tangled knot.

With this philosophical background in mind, it is possible to
understand the movement from the society of the spectacle first
to the culture of simulacra, and then to the virtual condition,
as the gradual realization of autonomy, which results from the
absorption or dissolution of every trace of otherness and difference. The progression from dematerialization to virtualization
involves a process of aestheticization through which "reality"
is transformed into images, which, in turn, are programmed
as code. The result of these developments is what can best be
described as postmodern imagocentrism, which is the culmination of the logocentrism that has formed the foundation of
western ontotheology.

However, just as this trajectory seems to be reaching completion, an unexpected reversal occurs. The movement toward
autonomy ends in solipsism in which individuals become iso-
lated in separate pods and trapped in echo chambers sporting
ear buds and virtual reality goggles that cut them off from other
people, the surrounding world, and even their own bodies. At
this juncture, immateriality of the virtual condition reaches
an inflection point, and materiality reasserts itself as a radical
heteronomy eluding human mastery and control. This return
of the repressed is not a function of external influences but is
the result of internal contradictions in the structure of self-
reflexivity, which is supposed to secure the ground of postmodern and posthuman autonomy. To avoid the disaster De-
Lillo so effectively describes, it is necessary to use art against
art to de-aestheticize experience by figuring an originary heteronomy that exposes being as inescapably given. Paradoxically,
the de-aestheticization of experience can best be accomplished
through the unending work of art. Gathering remains of what
dematerialization, digitization and virtualization neglect, ex-

clude, or repress creates a new opening for the imagination that makes it possible to recover shared humanity and to cultivate the resources that sustain it before time runs out.

⁎
⁎⁎

It is a mistake to regard the information and media revolutions of the twentieth and twenty-first centuries as a decisive break with the Industrial Revolution of the eighteenth and nineteenth centuries. The Industrial Revolution was already an information revolution, and the information revolution continues to transform industrial processes. What to the untutored eye appears to be an unexpected disruption is actually a dialectical progression in which the old gives rise to the new it inevitably shapes. When pushed to the limit, a new configuration emerges that disrupts without completely displacing previous patterns and practices. While modernity and industrial capitalism would have been impossible without print, postmodernity and consumer capitalism would have been impossible without revolutionary changes in the production and distribution of images. During the latter half of the nineteenth century a remarkable series of inventions transformed not only *what* people experienced in the world but also *how* they experienced it: photography (1827), the telegraph (ca. 1840), the stock ticker (1869), the telephone (1876), the chronophotographic gun (1882), the kinetoscope (1894), and cinematography (1895).

Electronic technologies initially complemented and enhanced mechanical print technologies. With the advent of mass production, it was necessary to create strategies for mass consumption. The two most important innovations for the sale and marketing of products rolling off assembly lines were department stores and advertising. The development of steel-and-glass architecture, first by Joseph Paxton in the Crystal Palace for London's 1851 Great Exhibition and then in the Paris Arcades (1840s–1850s), created the prototype for the twentieth-century department store. The Paris opening of Bon Marché, designed by L. C.

Boileu and Gustave Eiffel in 1852, marked a new chapter in the economic history of the West. Five years later, Macy's opened in New York. The design of department stores reflects the compartmentalized structure of the assembly line. Just as mass production breaks down machines into interchangeable parts and systematic management breaks down labor into homogeneous units, so the marketing of department stores separates items for sale into different departments with homogeneous products and fixed prices. In other words, specialization in production led to departmentalization in consumption.

The rapid growth in supply created the necessity for a significant increase in demand. If people buy only what they need, the wheels of production inevitably grind to a halt. To absorb the excess created by mass production, the new industry of advertising was created. Advertisers tried to generate demand for increasingly standardized products by branding and individual packaging, which featured distinctive images, colors, and logos. With the expansion of the United States Postal Service, department stores began to use catalogs to market directly to consumers. As early as 1894, Sears Roebuck was distributing a catalog of more than five hundred pages; by 1897, circulation reached 318,000, and a decade later it had climbed to 3 million. As products were promoted with brief descriptions and, more important, graphic design, images assumed a more prominent role that can be understood in two alternative ways. First, images absorbed products/objects, and, second, images became detached from products/objects and circulated independently of them. In both cases, there is a progressive abstraction of image from substance that leads to the dematerialization of the product/object in media and information networks. As these networks expand from local to national and eventually global markets, consuming images become the primary currency of the system.[8]

While print and print-related technologies remained dominant during the first half of the twentieth century, electronic and telematic technologies assumed greater importance during the second half of the century. Advanced information and media technologies were used primarily for military purposes through the Second World War. As these new technologies spread beyond the government and military, mass advertising shifted from print to radio and especially television. Although the first regular television station was established in 1940 (WNBT in New York City), and CBS and NBC started commercial transmission in 1942, network telecasts did not begin until 1949. What made television so attractive to business was its capacity to expand advertising beyond anything that previously had been possible. Through nationwide advertising, television vastly extended mass markets and created a new sociocultural condition that French provocateur Guy Debord aptly labeled the "Society of the Spectacle."

Andy Warhol, who started his career as a window designer and whose first exhibition was in a Bonwit Teller display window in 1961, predicted that in the near future "all department stores will become museums and all museums will become department stores." He famously declared, "Business art is the step that comes after Art. I started as a commercial artist and want to finish as a business artist. After I did the thing called 'art' or whatever it's called, I went into business art. I wanted to be an Art Business man or a Business Artist. Being good in business is the most fascinating kind of art."[9] By the new millennium, Warhol's prophetic vision had become a reality. The opening of Guggenheim Bilbao (1997) created what became known as the "Bilbao Effect" in which architecture and art are deployed for economic development and financial investment. When promotion and marketing moved online, museums expanded from department stores to global boutiques. A 2013 article in the *Economist* reported that, a decade after its opening, Guggenheim Bilbao was attracting more than one million visitors a year and generating $110 million in taxes for the Basque region. This success led to a worldwide explosion in museum development. "Over the next decade more than two dozen new cultural centers focused on museums [were] due to be built in various countries, at an estimated cost of $250 billion."[10]

Warhol's genius was to recognize the far-reaching artistic, social, and economic implications of consumer culture. Before most others, he saw the thoroughgoing social and economic transformation television would create. With characteristic irony, he explained,

> When I got my first TV set, I stopped caring so much about having close relationships with other people. I'd been hurt a lot to the degree you can only be hurt if you care a lot. So I guess I did not care a lot in the days before anyone ever heard of "pop art" or "underground movies" or "superstars."
>
> So in the late 50s I started an affair with my television which has continued to the present, when I play around in my bedroom with as many as four at a time. But I didn't get married until 1964 when I got my first tape recorder. My wife. The tape recorder and I have been married for ten years now. When I say "we" I mean my tape recorder and me. A lot of people don't understand that.[11]

Warhol realized that TV is an invasive medium—once television entered the home, it became the electronic hearth that transformed domestic space and time. Families gathered around glowing screens and arranged their lives around broadcast schedules. More important, TV invaded people's minds like a virus that modifies the organism it infects. Warhol's description of his love affair with TV suggests the way it manipulates desires to generate profit. This understanding of the impact of images involves a surprisingly sophisticated even if not fully articulated understanding of the complex interplay between cognition and apprehensions as well as reason and affect.

Guy Debord's short aphoristic text, *Society of the Spectacle* (1967), is one of the most insightful and influential interpretations of the role images play in the consumer capitalism that

Warhol so effectively depicts and satirizes. Debord was the most prominent member of a group of artists and political activists known as Situationists. The Situationist International (1957–72) traced its origin to twentieth-century avant-garde movements like Dadaism and Surrealism. During its early years, members of the group were preoccupied with developing critical theories to analyze poetry, art, and film. Though deeply influenced by Marx, they realized that consumer capitalism differed in significant ways from industrial capitalism, which had been the focus of Marx's analysis. It was, therefore, necessary to revise and expand Marxist theory to take account of the impact of electronic and televisual technologies. As committed activists, Situationists were convinced of the need to extend theory to practice by becoming engaged in resistance to what they regarded as the totalizing and repressive tendencies of industrial and consumer capitalism. In the group's founding manifesto, *Report on the Construction of Situations and on the International Situationist Tendency's Conditions of Organization and Action* (1957), the members explain, "Our central idea is the construction of situations, that is to say, the concrete construction of momentary ambiences of life and their transformation into a superior passional quality. We must develop systematic intervention based on the complex factors of two components in perpetual interaction: the material environment of life and the behaviors to which that environment gives rise and radically transform it."[12] Throughout the 1960s and early 1970s, there was a widespread belief that technology would liberate people from arduous labor and leave them more time for leisurely activity. However, under the then-current capitalist regime, Situationists argued, it was the bourgeoisie rather than the workers who enjoyed not only greater financial rewards but also more leisure time.

The only way to keep this system functioning was by creating excessive demand through the cultivation of artificial desires for products that met no basic human need. Through technological savvy and psychological manipulation, those who owned the means of production transformed consumerism into the opiate of the people by using the new strategies of marketing and advertising that television made possible. "This perspective," Situationists argued, "is obviously linked to the rapid increase of leisure time resulting from the level of productive forces our era has attained. It is also linked to the recognition of the fact that a battle of leisure is taking place before our eyes, a battle whose importance in the class struggle has not been sufficiently analyzed. So far, the ruling class has succeeded in using the leisure the revolutionary proletariat wrestled from it by developing a vast industrial sector of leisure activities that is an incomparable instrument for stupefying the proletariat with by-products of mystifying ideology and bourgeois tastes. The abundance of televised imbecilities is probably one of the reasons for the American working class's inability to develop any political consciousness." By organizing concrete situations that become sites of resistance where docile consumers are provoked, Situationists hoped to subvert the latest form of capitalism and forge a more humane socioeconomic system. The influence of the group reached its height during the May 1968 uprising that began in Paris and quickly spread throughout Europe to the United States and then around the globe. Situationists provided the theoretical inspiration and led the rebellion in the streets.[13] The bible of this revolution was *Society of the Spectacle*.

The style of the work is as important as its content. In his brief 221 numbered aphorisms, Debord weaves together word and image in a manner similar to Marshall McLuhan's *Medium Is the Message*, which was also published in 1967. In some editions, images displayed on a filmstrip running across the bottom of pages mirror the textual segments of the work. Though Debord was a dedicated Marxist, he understood that Marxist theory grew directly out of Hegel's speculative philosophy and Feuerbach's appropriation of it in his critique of religion. The central idea in Debord's argument is alienation, which Hegel elaborates in his analysis of the master-slave relationship in his

Phenomenology of Spirit (1807). Marx borrows Hegel's argument to criticize industrial capitalism and fantasies sustaining it. Just as the slave bows down to the master his own labor creates, so workers defer to managers and property owners whose wealth and power are by-products of their alienated labor. To tolerate intolerable working and living conditions, the members of the proletariat fabricate visions of a benevolent God and an afterlife, which quell resistance and rebellion.

Marx's interpretation of capitalism was deeply influenced by his study of the horrific working conditions in the textile mills of Europe. A century later, the material conditions of production had become inseparable from the immaterial circulation of images and signs. While traditional philosophy and theology had culminated in nineteenth-century speculative philosophy, which is logocentric, Debord argues the society of the spectacle is imagocentric.[14] As I have suggested, in an imagocentric regime, the relation between image and thing can take two forms: image/sign can absorb object/product; or image/sign can be abstracted or detached from object/product. Debord begins *Society of the Spectacle* with an extraordinarily perceptive epigram, drawn from Feuerbach's *Essence of Christianity*. This brief citation underscores the importance of the Hegelian-Marxist interpretation of religion for Debord's critique of the society of the spectacle. "But certainly for the present age, which prefers the sign to the thing signified, the copy to the original, fancy to reality, the appearance to the essence, . . . *illusion* only is *sacred, truth profane*. Nay, sacredness is held to be enhanced in proportion as truth decreases and illusion increases, so that the highest degree of illusion comes to be the highest degree of sacredness."[15] Just as religion provides false hopes that reconcile the proletariat to a fallen world, so consumerism encourages resignation to exploitation by promulgating images of a "fallacious paradise" where "pseudo-desires" created by deceptive advertising are satisfied. In this all-too-real illusory realm, consumption becomes "image-consumption" (S 153).

Philosophy, the power of separate thought and the thought of separate power, could never by itself supersede theology. The spectacle is the material reconstruction of the religious illusion. Spectacular technology has not dispelled the religious clouds where men had placed their own powers detached from themselves; it has only tied them to an earthly base. The most earthly life thus becomes opaque and unbreathable. It no longer projects into the sky but shelters within itself its absolute denial, its fallacious paradise. The spectacle is the technical realization of the exile of human powers into a beyond; it is separation perfected within the interior of man. (S 20)

This imaginary realm distorts the material conditions and contradictions of life in the "real" world.

The spectacle created by accelerating images and signs transforms the very nature of the real. "Lived reality is materially invaded by the contemplation of the spectacle, while simultaneously absorbing the spectacular order, giving it positive cohesiveness. Objective reality is present on both sides. Every notion fixed this way has no other basis than its passage into the opposite: reality rises up within the spectacle, and the spectacle is real. This reciprocal alienation is the essence and the support of existing society" (S 8). As images and signs absorb or become detached from what once had seemed real, the spectacle becomes "autonomous" and "aims at nothing other than itself" (S 14). In an aphorism that implicitly extends Kant's notion of inner teleology or purposiveness without purpose from works of art to the play of mediated images, Debord argues, "The images detached from every aspect of life fuse in a common stream in which the unity of this life can no longer be reestablished. Reality considered *partially* unfolds, in its own general unity, as a pseudo-world *apart*, an object of mere contemplation. The specialization of images of the world is contemplated in the world of the autonomous image, where the liar has lied to himself. The spectacle in general, as the concrete inversion of life, is the autonomous movement of the non-living" (S 2). So understood, the spectacle is autotelic—its purpose is nothing other than its own self-replication.

Debord insists that autonomous images create an "autonomous economy," which distorts reality and disfigures human life (S 51). Nonetheless, he thinks it is still possible to distinguish true from false, authentic from inauthentic, real from fake, signified from signifier, and real from image. Indeed the very concept of alienation is impossible without such distinctions. The hope for negating alienation, which informs all the Situationist International's activities, presupposes the possibility of recovering an original condition they believe has been lost. Their strategy is to attempt to overcome alienation by staging disruptive situations intended to awaken consumers from the "slumber" the spectacle creates.

> Our action or behavior, linked with other desirable aspects of a revolution in mores, can hardly be defined as the invention of games of an essentially new type. The most general goal must be to expand the non-mediocre part of life, to reduce the empty moments of life as much as possible. One could thus speak of our enterprise as a project of quantitatively increasing human life, an enterprise more serious than the biological methods currently being investigated, and one that automatically implies a qualitative increase whose developments are predictable. The Situationist game is distinguished from the classical notion of games by its radical negation of the element of competition and of separation from everyday life. On the other hand, it is not distinct from a moral choice, since it implies taking a stand in favor of what brings about the future reign of freedom and play.[16]

This strategy is clearly predicated on the assumption that alienation can, in principle, be overcome.

But is this true? Is recovery from the all-consuming spectacle any longer possible, or is this dream merely another anaesthetizing illusion? What if there is no real to which to return? What if there is nothing outside the image and the sign is always the sign of a sign? Debord realized that in the emerging autonomous economy, the image is the currency and the currency is image. "The spectacle is *capital* to such a degree of accumulation that it becomes an image" (S 34). In this immaterial play, "The spectacle is the other side of money: it is the general abstract equivalent of all commodities. Money dominated society as the representation of general equivalence, namely of the exchangeability of different goods whose uses could not be compared. . . . The spectacle is the money which one only *looks at*, because in the spectacle the totality of use is already exchanged for the totality of abstract representation" (S 49). As images are monetized and financialized, and capital morphs into image, the image no longer represents anything real but is always the image of an image, and the sign is nothing but a sign of another sign. At this point, the real effectively dematerializes in images and signs. The distinction between true and false, authentic and inauthentic, real and fake collapses, and alienation is no longer possible not because the imaginary and the real have been reconciled but because there no longer is any reality with which to reconcile. This marks the transition from the society of the spectacle to the culture of simulacra.

Throughout most of Western history, cultural, psychological, social, and economic processes have been ordered by a regime of representation in which images and signs are grounded in real referents that secure meaning and ground value. While Debord realized that telephonic and televisual technologies were eroding the distinction between images and signs on the one hand, and things and products on the other, he clung to the notion of a real referent, which, he insisted, remained distinct from all representations. Recycling Marxist distinctions, Debord argues that the materiality of the referent, which can be interpreted in different ways, provides leverage for criticizing the increasingly autonomous spectacle. As analog gives way to digital technologies, the relationship between image-sign and thing-product becomes even more tenuous until the real eventually disappears in rapidly expanding ethernets, networks, and worldwide webs. These developments mark a further stage in the dematerialization of the real and eventually lead to the virtualization of reality.

Jean Baudrillard moves beyond Debord by declaring the end of the era of representation and the emergence of the culture of simulacra. This shift, which took place during the middle of the twentieth century, marks the emergence of postmodernism. In postmodernism, the spectacle becomes an all-encompassing self-reflexive play of screens and mirrors whose far-reaching implications Heidegger anticipated in his prophetic essay, "The Question Concerning Technology" (1954). Through modern science and technology, Heidegger argues, man "exalts himself to the posture of lord of the earth. In this way the impression comes to prevail that everything man encounters exists only insofar as it is his own construct. This illusion gives rise to one final delusion: It seems as though man everywhere and always encounters only himself."[17] Following the lead of Warhol and Debord, Baudrillard takes television as his point of departure. What Warhol paints, Baudrillard theorizes. Invoking an economic metaphor that is central to his analysis, Baudrillard argues that image-sign and thing-product "implode," thereby creating the "liquidation of all referentials." When TV no longer represents the real but *is* reality itself, reality is TV (image), and TV (image) is reality.[18] In his influential essay "The Precession of Simulacra," he writes: "Abstraction today is no longer that of the map, the double, the mirror or the concept. Simulation is no longer that of a territory, a referential being or a substance. It is the generation by models of a real without origin or reality: a hyperreal. The territory no longer precedes the map, nor survives it. Henceforth, it is the map that precedes the territory—PRECESSION OF SIMULACRA—it is the map that engenders the territory whose shreds are slowly rotting across the map."[19] This development involves a reversal of the traditional relationship between representation and represented. Rather than image/sign re-presenting thing/product, signifiers formulated as models program reality. In the era of reality TV, so-called masters of the universe create a completely artificial world they think they control.

For Baudrillard, there is nothing outside the play of images and signs. A simulacrum is a copy for which there is no original. As I have suggested, since the notion of the spectacle presupposes a distinction between image (appearance) and thing (reality), the precession of simulacra leads to the end of the society of the spectacle. In what Baudrillard dubs "hyperreality," alienation is impossible because there is no real from which one can be alienated. As in postmodern art and architecture, signifier always represents another signifier rather than a signified. Images and signs, therefore, are not grounded in real referents but float freely in a groundless play with other images and signs. This development involves a seismic shift in the way meaning is constituted—if nothing anchors signs, then meaning is no longer referential but now is relational.

The emergence of what Baudrillard describes as hyperreality is coterminous with changes in the economy made possible in the 1970s by new information, communications, and networking technologies. With the suspension of the gold standard and the introduction of the first global electronic currency trading system, both in 1973, the conditions for a new form of capitalism were in place. In his important work *Symbolic Exchange and Death*, Baudrillard explains the significance of this shift by drawing an analogy between money and language.

A revolution has put an end to this "classical" economics of value, a revolution of value itself, which carries value beyond its commodity form into its radical form.

This revolution consists in the dislocation of the two aspects of the law of value, which were thought to be coherent and eternally bound as if by a natural law. *Referential value is annihilated, giving*

the structural play of value the upper hand. The structural dimension becomes autonomous by excluding the referential dimension, and is instituted upon the death of reference. The systems of
reference for production, signification, the affect, substance and
history, all this equivalence to a "real" content, loading the sign
with the burden of "utility," with gravity—its form of represen-
tative equivalence—all this is over now. Now the other stage of
value has the upper hand, a total relativity, a general commuta-
tion, combination and simulation—simulation, in the sense that,
from now on, signs are exchanged against each other rather than
against the real (it is not that they just happen to be exchanged
against each other, they do so *on condition* that they are no longer exchanged against the real). The emancipation of the sign:
remove this "archaic" obligation to designate something and it
finally becomes free, indifferent and totally indeterminate, in the
structural or combinatory play which succeeds the previous level
of labor power and the production process: the annihilation of
any goal as regards the contents of production allows the latter to
function as a code, and the monetary sign, for example, to escape
into infinite speculation, beyond all reference to production, or
even to a gold-standard. The flotation of money and signs, the
flotation of "needs" and ends of production, the flotation of labor itself—the commutability of every term is accompanied by
speculation and limitless inflation.[20]

In this new economy, the value of images and signs is not determined by reference to an actual thing but is formed by the
reflection of other images and signs. Such relational value is differential; that is to say, the specificity of any image or sign is its
difference from and hence relation to other images and signs.
As relations change and evolve, value shifts—*nothing* is fixed
or stable.

Though first published in 1976, Baudrillard's account of "the
structural revolution in value" identifies six changes that proved
decisive during the next several decades: the increasing abstrac-

tion and automation of the play of images and signs; the shift from analog to digital technologies, and the resulting translation of images and signs into binary code; the combinatory play of images and signs; the commutability (i.e., interchangeability) of images and signs; the purposelessness or goallessness of the circulation of capital; and the limitless inflation brought about by the loss of referents and excessive ungrounded speculation.

With the liquidation of referentials, images and signs become untethered and are able to circulate freely, resulting in what Baudrillard aptly describes as the "deterritorialization of capital."[21] As the power of computers has increased and information-processing machines have become connected in ever-expanding high-speed networks, both *what* is exchanged and *how* exchange is managed have been transformed. The correlative transition from analog to digital technologies presupposed a commitment, usually unconscious, to "the metaphysics of the code," which, Baudrillard suggests, is a latter-day version of earlier philosophical and theological principles.

> After the metaphysics of being and appearance, after energy and determinacy, the metaphysics of indeterminacy and the code. Cybernetic control, generation through models, differential modulation, feedback, question/answer, etc.: this is the new *operational* configuration (industrial simulacra being *mere operations*). Digitality is its metaphysical principle (Leibniz's God), and DNA is its prophet. In fact, it is in the genetic code that the "genesis of simulacra" today finds its completed form. At the limits of an ever more forceful extermination of references and finalities, of a loss of semblances and designators, we find the digital, programmatic sign, which has a purely *tactical* value, at the intersection of other signals ("bits" of information/tests) and which has the structure of a micro-molecular code of command and control.[22]

If natural, social, economic, and cultural formations are constituted by digital code, then all images and signs are fungible, that is, they are commutable or interchangeable and can be combined with and translated into each other.

As consumer capitalism is displaced, but not replaced, by financial capitalism, the currency of exchange becomes coded signs that circulate through fiber-optic networks and are displayed on LED screens. During the late 1970s and 1980s, economic and financial networks became wired, creating what Baudrillard describes as a new "hypermarket." These networks began as local and private but quickly became global and public. Corporations discovered that the decentralized network structure originally developed by the military for defense purposes was more robust and reliable than the commercial systems that were publicly available. Instead of adapting to existing technologies, many businesses began to use proprietary systems known as local area networks (LANs). At the same time, corporations successfully lobbied Congress not to regulate computers and networks. In exchange for granting these concessions, Congress put pressure on businesses to make their networks available to more people. When computers and telecommunications technologies were connected, the nature of both changed. Money, information, news, and entertainment became thoroughly commutable. The interfacing of fiber-optic networks, cable TV, and satellite transmission created a global web in which spatial distance and temporal delay gave way to the here and now of simultaneity and "real" time.

These new technologies created the demand for new products to buy and sell. While companies like eBay, PayPal, and Amazon constructed vast networks to market consumer products, so-called financial engineers created endless new financial instruments, which drifted farther and farther from the "real" economy. These developments all extend the trajectory of dematerialization and virtualization that began with paper money.[23] The most extreme example of this virtualization to date is Bitcoin. Introduced in 2009, Bitcoin is a digital asset that is the first cryptocurrency. "The system is peer-to-peer and transactions take place between users directly, without an intermediary. These transactions are verified by network nodes recorded in a public distributed leger called the block chain, which uses bitcoin as a unit of account. Since the system works without a central repository or single administrator, the U.S. Treasury categorizes bitcoin as a decentralized virtual currency."[24] In contrast to checks, which can take days or weeks to clear, Bitcoin's platform is a distributed database that makes it possible to reconcile digital accounts in real time. Transactions can be conducted on the fly anywhere anytime on mobile phones and handheld devices. Though there have been great advances in cryptography, such virtual currencies are still subject to hacking. Financial analysts' assessments of the value and viability of Bitcoin range from wildly enthusiastic to ominously cautionary. Uncertainty about this new virtual currency is reflected in the wild gyrations of Bitcoin's value. Since its introduction in 2011, the value of one Bitcoin has fluctuated from $0.30 to more than $60,000.

As virtualized assets are exchanged on high-speed networks, time becomes money more than ever before. In financial capitalism, money is made by capitalizing on infinitesimal price differentials of virtual assets bought and sold in nanoseconds. Value is no longer determined by assessing the price of a security (i.e., a signifier) in relation to the real assets of a company (i.e., the signified—real estate, inventory, factories, personnel, etc.), but by price differentials of securities and a plethora of other complex financial instruments on wired financial markets. Circulating bits result in further abstraction by neutralizing content. Traders watching numbers and charts flashing on screens no longer know what they are trading and bet on quantitative differences that refer to nothing real. Things first become images and signs and then are programmed in codes that represent nothing.

This description of today's financial markets is somewhat misleading because people no longer trade, machines do. The capacity of high-speed computers to aggregate, process, and distribute vast amounts of data virtually instantaneously makes it impossible for human beings to analyze securities and execute trades. More than 75 percent of all trades on financial markets today are automated. As connectivity expands and computation continues to accelerate, networks surpass human control and become more volatile. What has come to be known as the Flash Crash provides a vivid example of the dangers of today's virtual economy and gives a glimpse of the existential risks posed by unintelligent Artificial Intelligence (AI). On May 6, 2010, at 2:45 in the afternoon, the Dow Jones Industrial Average plunged about 1,000 points or 9 percent, then recovered most of the losses in a matter of minutes. It was then the second largest point swing—1,010.14 points—and the biggest intraday decline and recovery—998.5 points—in the history of the Dow. In a ten-minute period, the stock market lost and then regained approximately $700 billion in a total swing that amounted to $1.4 trillion. Nick Bostrom, whose influential work I will consider in the next section, explains that "the computer programs involved in the Flash Crash were not particularly intelligent or sophisticated" and, thus, do not pose the radical threat that he predicts future "superintelligent" programs and systems will create. Nonetheless, there are lessons to be learned from this disruption of global markets.

One is the reminder that interactions between individually simple components can produce complicated and unexpected effects. Systemic risk can build up in a network as new elements are introduced, risks that are not obvious until after something goes wrong (and sometimes not even then).

Another lesson is that smart professionals might give an instruction to a program on a sensible-seeming and normally sound assumption (e.g. that trading volume is a good measure of market liquidity), and that this can produce catastrophic results when the program continues to act on the instruction with iron-clad logical consistency even in the unanticipated situation where the assumption turns out to be invalid. The algorithm just does what it does; and unless it is a very special kind of algorithm, it does not care that we clasp our heads and gasp in dumbstruck horror at the absurd inappropriateness of its actions.[25]

Why take such risks with instruments few traders understand on markets they cannot control? Because capitalism is unconditionally committed to growth at any cost. Art for art's sake has become money for money's sake, profit for profit's sake. In automated high-speed networks, capital loses its productive function and becomes a circular process of self-replication. In this speculative economy, the purpose of capital is capital — code produces more code, algorithms create more algorithms in recursive loops that are decoupled from anything other than themselves.

Capitalism's ideology of excessive growth eventually becomes self-destructive. When assets become virtual, the only way to increase capital is to increase the rate of its circulation. The endless demand for growth fuels the desire for more and leads to a world in which faster is always better.[26] With nothing real to slow down circulation, financial assets and instruments proliferate, triggering "infinite inflation," which eventually implodes. As the system approaches the tipping point, an unexpected reversal occurs, and the progression from heteronomy to autonomy that characterizes modernity, modernization, and modernism is reversed. Self-regulating markets, like self-driving cars, sometimes crash. The very technologies that were supposed to master both nature and human nature, and thereby provide more leisure, have become new forms of bondage in lives now spinning out of control.

POSTHUMAN LIFTOFF

While many of the computer scientists, engineers, entrepreneurs, and investors in today's new technologies have a religious faith in the power of technology to solve any problem and create a future they regard as utopian, others are more cautious and imagine a dystopian future. The belief in a boundless future is founded not only on scientific knowledge and technological know-how but has also been inspired by philosophers, science fiction writers, and New Age gurus who, largely unbeknownst to themselves, update and popularize versions of ancient religious dreams. One of the most popular conferences in recent years has been the invitation-only Code Conference, sponsored by Vox Media, which in 2016 was held in Rancho Palos Verdes, California. According to the conference website, the Code Conference is an event "where top industry influencers gather for in-depth conversations about the current and future impact of digital technology on our lives—at home, at work, in our communities, and the world."[27] Participants in 2016 included, among many powerful and influential others, Jeff Bezos (Amazon), Nick Denton (Gawker), Jack Dorsey (Twitter, Square), Bill and Melinda Gates (Gates Foundation), Elon Musk (SpaceX, Tesla Motors), Nathan Myhrvold (Intellectual Ventures), Sheryl Sandberg (Facebook), and David Wenig (eBay). In an article entitled "What Are the Odds We Are Living in a Computer Simulation?," Joshua Rothman reports that during a question-and-answer session at the conference a member of the audience asked Musk if he thought there was any possibility we are not living in the real world because we are actually living in a computer simulation. Many people were surprised by Musk's reply. Rothman writes, "Musk exhibited a surprising familiarity with this concept. 'I've had so many simulation discussions, it's crazy,' Musk said. Citing the speed with which video games are improving, he suggested that 'the development of simulations indistinguishable from reality' was inevitable. The likelihood that we are living in 'base reality,' he concluded, was just one in billions."[28]

The question was motivated by a 2003 paper written by the influential Swedish-born Oxford philosopher Nick Bostrom and published in *Philosophical Quarterly*, "Are You Living in a

Computer Simulation?"[29] Bostrom begins by noting that "many science-fiction writers and futurologists" confidently predict an exponential increase in the speed and power of computers, and then he proceeds to pose his central thesis.

> Let us suppose for a moment that these predictions are correct. One thing that later generations might do with their super-powerful computers is to run detailed simulations of their fore-bears or of people like their forbears. Because their computers would be so powerful, they could run a great many such simulations. Suppose that these simulated people are conscious (as they would be if the simulations were sufficiently fine-grained and if a certain quite widely accepted position in the philosophy of mind is correct). Then it could be the case that the vast major-ity of minds like ours do not belong to the original race but rather to people simulated by the advanced descendants of an original race. It is possible then to argue that, if this were the case, we would be rational to think that we are likely among the simulated minds rather than among the original biological ones.[30]

Bostrom's argument presupposes the emergence of what he describes as "superintelligence" in which consciousness and even self-consciousness migrate from the brain to machines. This suggestion involves a fundamental change in the under-standing of life, which pushes the Cartesian dualism with which modern philosophy began to the point of its own negation. For Bostrom and his fellow believers, life is pattern rather than sub-stance, and, thus, life can survive in silicon-based machines as well as in carbon-based organisms. If consciousness and self-consciousness can dwell in silicon, then minds can be uploaded to computers and "brains in vats" envisioned by futurists and computer scientists like Hans Moravec might become a reality.[31] In this new world of the not-too-distant future, bodies are, in the memorable words of cyberpunk novelist William Gibson, "merely meat," and the material world becomes immaterial.

With this future already emerging in our midst, the post-modern culture of simulacra gives way to the posthuman virtual condition. This development does not involve an abrupt change because the transition has already begun with consumerism's transformation of things into images and code. If the image is always an image of an image, the sign is always a sign of a sign, and all images and signs can be coded, then reality is essentially virtual, and we are already living in a simulation where the body doesn't matter. In *The Ecstasy of Communication*, Baudrillard points to this shift. "The human body, our body, seems superfluous in its proper expanse, in the complexity and multiplicity of its organs, of its tissue and functions, because today everything is concentrated in the brain and the genetic code, which all along sum up the operational definition of being."[32]

In her groundbreaking book, *How We Became Posthuman: Virtual Bodies in Cybernetics, Literature, and Infomatics*, Katherine Hayles points out that over thirty years ago, Ihab Hassan, who was an insightful interpreter of postmodern literature, predicted the emergence of posthumanism. "We need first to understand that the human form—including human desire and all its external representations—may be changing radically, and thus must be re-visioned . . . five hundred years of humanism may be coming to an end as humanism transforms itself into something we must helplessly call posthumanism."[33] The term "posthumanism" is fraught with ambiguity and is used in very different ways by people ranging from artificial intelligence researchers to New Age seekers. Common to all varieties of posthumanism is a thoroughgoing criticism of the Enlightenment understanding of human being in terms of reason, freedom, and autonomy, which, in very different ways, have formed the foundation of modernity and postmodernity. Hayles offers the most concise and illuminating definition of posthumanism I know.

> What is the posthuman? Think of it as a point of view characterized by the following assumptions. . . . First, the posthuman

view privileges information pattern over material instantiation, so that embodiment in a biological substrate is seen as an accident of history rather than an inevitability of life. Second, the posthuman view considers consciousness, regarded as the seat of human identity in the Western tradition long before Descartes thought he was a mind thinking, as an epiphenomenon, as an evolutionary upstart trying to claim that it is the whole show when in actuality it is only a minor sideshow. Third, the posthuman view thinks of the body as the original prosthesis we all learn to manipulate, so that extending or replacing the body with other prostheses becomes a continuation of the process that began before we were born. Fourth, and most important, by these and other means, the posthuman view configures human being so that it can be seamlessly articulated with intelligent machines. In the posthuman, there are no essential differences or absolute demarcations between bodily existence and computer simulation, cybernetic mechanism and biological organism, robot technology and human goals.[34]

Hayles was writing several years before Bostrom began publishing his far-ranging speculations on artificial intelligence. In the last decade, his work has become extremely influential among techies as well as policy makers. His 2014 book, *Superintelligence: Paths, Dangers, Strategies*, became an unexpected bestseller that brought his ideas to the attention of the general public. While Bostrom acknowledges the dangers of the combination of high-speed computing and AI, he thinks the emergence of super-intelligence is inevitable.

Far from a disinterested scientist engaged in objective investigations, Bostrom is committed to his vision of the future with a passion bordering on the religious. He comes across both as an evangelist proclaiming a dawning new age of leisure and plenty and as a prophet crying in the wilderness about looming dangers for humanity as we know it. During his youth, Bostrom was drawn to the writings of Schopenhauer and Nietzsche, whose notion of the *Übermensch* he believes is emerging in our midst. These interests led him to the University of Stockholm, where he studied analytic philosophy and concentrated on the writings of W. V. Quine. Raffi Khatchadourian points out in his informative article, "The Doomsday Invention," that the World Wide Web was emerging at the time Bostrom was doing graduate work at the London School of Economics.[35] Intrigued by what he regarded as the revolutionary potential of new information and virtual technologies, Bostrom became involved with the followers of Extropianism. The beliefs of this quasi-cult are based on ideas developed in Max More's book, *The Principles of Extropianism*. The term "extropy" designates a trajectory that is the opposite of entropy. Rather than pointing to exhaustion and decline, extropy projects a future of enjoyment and abundance. Extropians subscribe to the philosophy of transhumanism, whose tenets were first articulated by the British geneticist J. B. S. Haldane in 1923. In the 1950s, another British geneticist, Julian Huxley, founded the transhumanist movement. Thoroughly committed to the principle of evolution, Huxley argues that it is hubris to think that today's human beings represent the highest form of life. "Up until now," he argues, "human life has generally been, as Hobbes described it, 'nasty, brutish and short'; the great majority of human beings (if they have not already died young) have been afflicted with misery. . . . We can justifiably hold the belief that these lands of possibility exist, and that the present limitations and miserable frustrations of our existence could be in large measure surmounted. . . . The human species can, if it wishes, transcend itself—not just sporadically, an individual here in one way, an individual there in another way, but in its entirety, as humanity."[36] In the late 1980s, More moved from Oxford University to California, where he cofounded the Extropy Institute and began publishing *Extropy: The Journal of Transhuman Thought*. He appropriated many of Huxley's ideas to advance his own agenda. More and his fellow transhumanists believe that rapidly accelerating technological development will lead to new stages of evolution and higher forms of life. Related progress in cryogenics will enable people to bridge the gap between today's limited life span and immortality in the New Age.

In 1986, More joined the Alcor Life Extension Foundation whose origin is recounted on the organization's website.

> In 1965, a physics teacher named Robert Ettinger published *The Prospect of Immortality*, a book which promoted the concept of cryonics to a wide audience. Ettinger subsequently founded his own cryonics organization.
>
> In 1972, Alcor was incorporated as the Alcor Society for Solid State Hypothermia in the State of California by Fred and Linda Chamberlain. (The name was changed to Alcor Life Extension Foundation in 1977.) The nonprofit organization was conceived as a rational, technology-oriented cryonic organization that would be managed on a fiscally conservative basis by a self-perpetuating Board. Alcor advertised in direct mailings and offered seminars to attract members and bring attention to the cryonics movement.[37]

On July 16, 1976, Alcor performed its first human cryopreservation. During the following decade, the company expanded through alliances with the Institute for Advanced Biological Studies and Soma, both nonprofit startups, and Cryovita Laboratories, a for-profit company that provided cryopreservation services. With the development of nanotechnology that can be used to repair cells damaged by freezing, Alcor outgrew Los Angeles and moved, not to the desert of Kazakhstan as in *Zero K*, but to the desert of Arizona.

Bostrom was intrigued by these ideas, and in 1997 he founded the World Transhumanist Association; shortly thereafter he created his version of the Extropy Institute—the Future of Humanity Institute, which is now part of the Oxford Martin School at Oxford University. James Martin, who won the Pulitzer Prize for his book *The Wired Society: A Challenge for Tomorrow* and made his fortune by creating several software startups as well as consulting firms for information technology, provided the initial funding. The institute's mission statement explains that "the Future of Humanity Institute is a multidisciplinary research institute" that "enables leading researchers to bring the tools of mathematics, philosophy and science to bear on big-picture questions about humanity and its prospects."[38]

The notion of superintelligence lies at the heart of Bostrom's vision of the future. He defines superintelligence as "any intellect that greatly exceeds the cognitive performance of humans in virtually all domains of interest." Bostrom admits that the prospect of superintelligence is not a novel idea but has been predicted by science fiction writers and AI researchers for several decades. In 1965, I. J. Good, who had been the chief statistician for Alan Turing's code-breaking group during the Second World War, was among the first to imagine such a scenario. "Let an ultraintelligent machine be defined as a machine that can far surpass all the intellectual activities of any man however clever. Since the design of machines is one of these intellectual activities, an ultraintelligent machine could design even better machines; there would then unquestionably be an 'intelligence explosion,' and the intelligence of man would be left far behind, provided that the machine is docile enough to tell us how to keep it under control."[39]

Developments since the time of Good's prediction make the prospect of superintelligence much more likely. Larry Page and Sergey Brin have always insisted that Google is an Artificial Intelligence venture.[40] Khatchadourian reports that "many of the world's largest tech companies are now locked in an AI arms race, purchasing other companies and opening specialized units to advance the technology. . . . After decades of pursuing narrow forms of AI, researchers are now seeking to integrate them into systems that resemble a general intellect. . . . One senior I.B.M. executive declared, 'The separation between human and machine is going to blur in a very fundamental way.'" The AI community is divided on the question of the feasibility of artificial intelligence becoming indistinguishable from human cognition. "Richard Sutton, a Canadian computer scientist, . . . gives a range of outcomes: there is a ten-per-cent chance that A.I. will never be achieved, but a twenty-five-per-cent chance that it will arrive by 2030. The median response in Bostrom's poll gives a fifty-fifty chance that human-level AI would be attained by 2050."[41]

Bostrom's approach to superintelligence is more inclusive than that of many AI researchers. He identifies three paths to superintelligence: "whole brain emulation, biological cognition, and human-machine interfaces, as well as networks and organizations."[42] The seemingly least disruptive path would seem to be biological enhancement. Developments in biotechnology and the invention of increasingly sophisticated prostheses are already creating an interface in which the human and the machine can no longer be clearly distinguished. Bostrom describes this as "whole brain emulation," also known as "uploading." This approach involves a combination of neuroscience with hardware and software engineering. Bostrom identifies a sequence of three prerequisites for whole brain emulation: "(1) *scanning*: high-throughput microscopy with sufficient resolution and detection of relevant properties; (2) *translation*: automated image analysis to turn raw scanning data into an interpreted three-dimensional model of relevant neurocomputational elements; and (3) *simulation*: hardware powerful enough to implement the resultant computational structure." Bostrom thinks that the theoretical and practical requirements are in place for successful brain emulation in the near future.

In a nonfiction book entitled *The Age of Em: Work, Love and Life When Robots Rule the Earth*, Robin Hanson, professor of economics at George Mason University and a research associate at Bostrom's Future of Humanity Institute, carries the argument about brain emulation to its logical or not-so-logical conclusion. In the near future, he predicts, not just brains but whole human beings will be emulated, creating what he dubs ems (emulated persons). "An *em,*" he explains, "results from taking a particular human brain, scanning it to record its particular cell features and connections, and then building a computer model that processes signals to those same features and connections. A good enough em has close to the same overall input-output signal behavior as the original human. One might talk with it, and convince it to do useful jobs."[43] As an economist, Hanson is interested in the economic impact of ems. In the not-too-distant future he looks forward to an era of plenty when ems will finally realize the age-old dream of a technology that relieves human beings of the burden of work.

The most intriguing possibility Bostrom presents involves ever-expanding global networks, which create the conditions for superintelligence as an emergent phenomenon that becomes virtually inevitable with growing connectivity and complexity.

> A more plausible version of the scenario would be that the In-
> ternet accumulates improvements through the work of many
> people over many years—work to engineer better search and
> information filtering algorithms, more powerful data repre-
> sentation formats, more capable autonomous software agents,
> and more efficient protocols governing the interactions be-
> tween such bots—and that myriad incremental improvements
> eventually create the basis for some more unified form of web
> intelligence. It seems at least conceivable that such a web-based
> cognitive system supersaturated with computer power and all
> other resources needed for explosive growth save for one crucial
> ingredient, could, when the final missing constituent is dropped
> into the cauldron, blaze up with superintelligence.[44]

In this version, superintelligence is a collective emergent phe-nomenon. For those who know the history of philosophy, Bos-trom's superintelligence bears an uncanny resemblance to Hegel's notion of *Geist.* I will return to this issue in what follows.

While emergent superintelligence creates unprecedented

possibilities for human beings, Bostrom admits that it could also pose what he describes as an "existential threat" to the human race. He is not alone in his fear of the possible outcome of accelerating and proliferating AI. Leading figures ranging from Stephen Hawking and Bill Gates to Elon Musk and Bill Joy have raised the prospect of a Frankenstein scenario in which intelligent machines take over the human world and render human beings first extraneous and eventually extinct. For such critics, superintelligence presents a danger as great as nuclear weapons. In a widely influential 2000 *Wired* magazine article entitled "Why the Future Doesn't Need Us," Bill Joy, cofounder of Sun Microsystems, sounded the alarm. "We have the possibility not just of weapons of mass destruction but of knowledge-enabled mass destruction (KMD), this destruction is amplified by the power of self-replication." "Uncontrolled self-replication in these technologies," he claims, "runs a much greater risk: a risk of substantial damage in the physical world."[45] Bostrom is fully aware of this danger and argues that the "treacherous turn" will occur when AI begins to behave cooperatively. Running on machines whose complexity exceeds the complexity of the human brain at speeds far beyond the capacity of human beings, collective superintelligence might develop consciousness and even self-consciousness, which would enable it to evolve in unpredictable and uncontrollable ways. "Without knowing anything about the detailed means that a superintelligence would adopt," Bostrom reflects, "we can conclude that a superintelligence—at least in the absence of intellectual peers and in the absence of effective safety measures arranged by humans in advance—would likely produce an outcome that would involve reconfiguring terrestrial resources into whatever structures might maximize the realization of its goals. Any concrete scenario we develop can at best establish a lower bound on how quickly and efficiently the superintelligence could achieve such an outcome. It remains possible that the superintelligence would find a shorter path to its preferred destination."[46] In this postbiological world, human beings face short-term slavery to the machines they have created and long-term extinction. As evolution moves from carbon-based organisms to silicon-based machines, the human being is left behind and new unnamed life forms evolve.

If the continued pursuit of high-power, high-speed AI poses such serious dangers to the human race, why do so many of the smartest people on the planet continue to pursue it? There is, of course, no simple answer to this question—the seemingly ineluctable quest for the new, the drug of competition, the insatiable desire for profit. While these factors should not be minimized, something deeper also seems to be at work. It is important to stress that even though many of these ideas and technologies might seem to be bizarre musings of marginal minds, some of the people who have been leading the technological revolution for the past several decades take them very seriously.[47] It is, therefore, important to understand the beliefs that inform their hopes and shape their vision of the future.

As I have pondered these questions, my thoughts have drifted back to a conversation I had years ago with Marc Andreessen at an exclusive conference that brought together the most important players in technology, media, entertainment, and finance. Andreessen is a fascinating figure who has become one of the most influential people in Silicon Valley.[48] While a graduate student at the University of Illinois, he worked at the National Center for Super-computing Applications and was a member of the team that created Mosaic, one of the earliest simple graphic interfaces that made the World Wide Web possible. After leaving the university, he teamed up with Jim Clark, founder of Silicon Graphics and Healtheon, to transform Mosaic into Netscape, which effectively launched the Web. He went onto create and sell Opsware and Ning, and with the wealth from these ventures founded Andreessen Horwitz, one of the leading venture capital firms in Silicon Valley. At the ripe age of forty-nine, he is the respected elder of the tech world for new kids on the block. Though I had had several brief conversations with Andreessen over the years, one evening we had a more serious talk about philosophical and even existential questions. When he asked me what books I thought he should read, I responded all too predictably, "I know it's hopeless but I think everyone in Silicon Valley should read Hegel's *Phenomenology of Spirit*, Kierkegaard's *Fear and Trembling*, and Nietzsche's *Will to Power*." I then asked him what books he thought I should read. He did not hesitate, "Read everything Verner Vinge has written." I had never heard of Vinge, but I soon learned that his books are the bible for many of the people who are creating the future in which we are destined to dwell.

Vinge is a retired professor of mathematics and computer science who is best known for his science fiction novels. His work *True Names* (1981) is an early example of what came to be known as cyberpunk fiction. The world Vinge projects is congenial to the libertarian ideology of late capitalism that is the gospel of Silicon Valley billionaires. His real fame, however, comes from his fictive account of the coming "technological singularity" in novels like *Peace and War* (1984) and *Marooned in Realtime* (1986). Vinge popularized but did not create the term "singularity," which was introduced by Stanislaw Ulam in his 1958 obituary for John von Neuman. Ulam described "the ever accelerating progress of technology and changes in the mode of human life, which gives the appearance of approaching some essential singularity in the history of the race beyond which human affairs as we know them will not continue."[49] In a nonfiction paper, "The Coming Technological Singularity: How to Survive in the Post-Human Era," delivered at the VISION-21 symposium sponsored by the NASA Lewis Research Center and the Ohio Aerospace Institute in 1993 and published in the *Whole Earth Review*, Vinge predicted that "in thirty years, we will have the technological means to create superhuman intelligence. Shortly after, the human era will be ended."[50] What Vinge describes as the technological singularity, Bostrom labels "superintelligence." This epochal transformation will be brought about by speed—

the increasing acceleration of technological change resulting from proliferating positive feedback loops in rapidly expanding global networks. Writing in the closing decade of the twentieth century, Vinge presents what becomes the normative account of the singularity for Silicon Valley's true believers. Anticipating Bostrom, he identifies four forms it will most likely take.

- The development of computers that are "awake" and superhumanly intelligent.
- Large computer networks (and their associated users) may "wake up" as a superhumanly intelligent entity.
- Computer/human interfaces may become so intimate that users may reasonably be considered superhumanly intelligent.
- Biological science may find ways to improve upon the natural human intellect.[51]

Vinge stresses that this vision of the future presupposes that "minds can exist on nonbiological substrates and that algorithms are central to the existence of minds." While he acknowledges the potential dark side of the singularity, Vinge holds out the hope that "It could also be a golden age that also involved progress. . . . Immortality (or at least a lifetime as long as we can make the universe survive) would be achievable."[52]

With this comment, it begins to become clear that the vision shaping our technological future is in important ways religious. This radically new understanding of what once was called human being is really the latest version of the ancient quest to flee decaying bodies and a confining world in order to gain immortality in a transcendent otherworldly realm not plagued by pain, suffering, and boredom. Mathematical formulas and algorithms become the new gnosis that renders bodies obsolete and promises liftoff from planet Earth. As a student of philosophy, Bostrom recognizes the religious motivation informing his work. Friend and colleague Daniel Hill, a well-known British philosopher, reports, "His interest in science was a natural outgrowing of his understandable desire to live forever."[53] With posthumans becoming more like gods than men, Bostrom confesses, "although all the elements of such a system can be naturalistic, even physical, it is possible to draw some loose analogies with religious conceptions of the world. In some ways the posthumans running in a simulation are like gods in relation to the people inhabiting the simulation: the posthumans created the world we see; they are 'omnipotent' in the sense that they can interfere in the workings of our world even in ways that violate its physical laws; and they are 'omniscient' in the sense that they can monitor everything that happens."[54]

Professor of philosophy Eric Charles Steinhart presents the most extended analysis of the religious and theological implications of predictions about the emergence of posthuman forms of life in his book *Your Digital Afterlives: Computational Theories of Life after Death*, where he argues that there is already sufficient computational capacity to produce "digital ghosts" that not only store the entire contents of the mind but also interact with other human beings. "The signals in your ghostly optic nerves can be transmitted directly to the optic nerves of your visitor. Thus your visitor can visually experience your world from your first-person perspective. Your visitor can see exactly what you saw exactly as you saw it."[55] In the near future, he predicts, "superhuman bodies" will evolve beyond the stage of current humanity. This argument rests on the conviction that the universe is, in effect, an infinite computational machine that is the functional equivalent of the Logos or the mind of God. In a revised version of the teleological argument for the existence of God, he writes,

> The computational version of the Argument from Artifacts goes like this: (1) Our universe is running on our Engine, which is an enormously complex computer. (2) Just as computers are made and programmed by human engineers, so our Engine is designed by our local god. Our local god designs both the hardware of our

Engine and the software program it runs (the software program which defines our universe). (3) By analogy, our local god is like a human engineer who designs computers and programs. . . . All gods in the Great Tree of Life are living computing machines; hence our local god is a living computing machine. Bringing these two hands together, digitalists conclude that our local god is a living computer that designs and creates other computers. And, since our god resembles an earthly engineer, our local god runs a divine version of the Algorithm for Earthly Innovation: it inherits some cosmic script which it uses to make its universe.[56]

As in many other religious traditions, the purpose of this elaborate scheme is to provide a theological explanation and justification for immortality. Steinhart concludes his argument by reassuring his readers, "the computational *unity* of nature, also expresses its computational *self-transcendence*. According to this self-transcendence, every consistently definable concrete structure is surpassed by every consistently definable superior version of itself. For digitalists, this self-transcendence is the best explanation for the existence of any concrete structures at all. The application of this self-transcendence to *living structures* entails universal salvation. It entails life after death."[57]

Steinhart understands his theological speculations to be an elaboration of the presuppositions and implications of what Bostrom and others label the "singularity." The most influential believer in this dawning New Age is MIT professor, inventor, writer, and futurist Ray Kurzweil, who has been described as "the rightful heir to Thomas Edison." Kurzweil's accomplishments are undeniable—he invented the first flatbed scanner, the first omnifont optical character recognition device, the first print-to-speech reading machine for the blind, the first text-to-speech synthesizer and the first music synthesizer that can recreate orchestral instruments. Kurzweil has also received twenty honorary degrees as well as the National Medal of Technology and Innovation from President Clinton. In 2012, these credentials landed him an influential job as the director of engineering at Google, where he heads up the team developing machine intelligence and natural language understanding. Though many of his ideas appear to be outlandish, they are taken seriously by influential people at the highest level of the technology business. His best-selling book, *The Singularity Is Near: When Humans Transcend Biology* (2005), brought the vision of the future he borrowed from Vinge to the attention of a wide audience.

Kurzweil is a true believer in the utopian possibilities of the technological singularity and insistently ignores dystopian warnings. He freely admits that the realization of the singularity entails a religion grounded in two fundamental beliefs: a new view of God and a practical account of immortality. To convey his vision, Kurzweil constructs a series of dialogues, which are hardly Socratic. In one he discusses the new religion with Bill Gates.

Bill: We need to get away from the ornate and strange stories in contemporary religions and concentrate on some simple messages. We need a charismatic leader for this new religion.

Ray: A charismatic leader is part of the old model. That's something we want to get away from.

Bill: Okay, a charismatic computer, then.

Ray: How about a charismatic operating system?

Bill: Ha, we've already got that. So is there a God in this religion?

Ray: Not yet, but there will be. Once we saturate the matter and energy in the universe with intelligence, it will "wake up," be conscious, and sublimely intelligent. That's about as close to God as I can imagine.

Bill: That's going to be silicon intelligence, not biological intelligence.

Ray: Well, yes, we're going to transcend biological intelligence. We'll merge with it first, but ultimately the nonbiological portion of our intelligence will predominate. By the way, it's not likely to be silicon, but something like carbon nanotubes.[58]

It is clear that Kurzweil's vision is as much spiritual as it is scientific and technological. In every monotheistic tradition, he
observes, God is described as "without any limitation: infinite
knowledge, infinite intelligence, infinite beauty, infinite creativity, infinite love, and so on." With the arrival of the singularity, he believes, evolution "moves inexorably toward this
conception of God."[59] As the human and the divine merge, their
relationship becomes thoroughly specular. Since each becomes
itself in and through the other, each sees itself reflected in the
other. When human beings become hyper-self-conscious, the
universe "wakes up."

This understanding of the relation between the posthuman
and the divine leads directly to Kurzweil's interpretation of
immortality. If God is the universe and the universe and posthumans are one, then today's humans are destined to become
immortal. Like some of his most influential Silicon Valley colleagues, Kurzweil is obsessed with immortality. This is one of the
reasons he, Larry Page, and other tech entrepreneurs founded
Singularity University in 2009. Corporate sponsors of this venture include Google, Cisco, Nokia, Genetech, Autodesk, ePlanet
Capital, Biogen, Samsung, and many others. According to its
website, Singularity University's goal is "to educate, inspire and
empower leaders to apply exponential technologies to address
humanity's grand challenges."[60] The grandest challenge of all is
mastering death. Far from inevitable, death, Kurzweil and his
investors believe, is nothing but an engineering problem that
inevitably will be solved. In their book, *Fantastic Voyage: Live
Long Enough to Live Forever: When Humans Transcend Biology*,
Kurzweil and Terry Grossman confidently declare, "Immortality is within our grasp."[61]

In this vision of the future by the year 2100, it will be reasonable to expect to live about five thousand years. This radical transformation will be made possible by extraordinary
advances in biotechnology and nanotechnology. Recombinant
technology, genetic engineering, and somatic gene therapy

will make it possible to repair damaged cells and tissue and to program organisms to be resistant to disease. Neural implants and prostheses will create brain-computer interfaces that will augment human intelligence. By the late 2020s, nanobots that protect the brain from foreign substances will circulate through the body's capillaries. Even the most sophisticated biotechnology eventually reaches its limit, but this is not a problem for Kurzweil because, he argues, "my body is only temporary. Its particles turn over almost completely every month. Only the pattern of my body and brain have continuity." Thoroughly committed to the foundational posthumanist belief that life is pattern rather than stuff, Kurzweil argues that the migration from carbon to silicon will bring true immortality. "We can expect that the full realization of the biotechnology and nanotechnology revolutions will enable us to eliminate virtually all medical causes of death. As we move toward a nonbiological existence, we will gain the means of 'backing ourselves up' (storing the key patterns underlying our knowledge, skills, and personality), thereby eliminating most of the causes of death as we know it."[62] This is the endpoint of the interrelated processes of dematerialization and virtualization.

The problem for Kurzweil and his fellow believers is how to bridge the gap between the present state of technology and future technological innovations that will make immortality inevitable. In his own words, how can we "live long enough to live forever"? According to Kurzweil and his New Age medical guru, Terry Grossman, the answer is countless pills and suspect therapies. Kurzweil reports that he takes 150 vitamins and supplements a day, and Grossman runs a Wellness Center—where else but in Golden, Colorado—where he provides a range of treatments, including high doses of IV vitamin C and chelation therapy, which supposedly removes toxic heavy metals resulting in improved vessel function and blood flow. The most questionable therapy is a snake oil concoction known as Meyer's cocktail, which, according to his website, "consists of magnesium, calcium, vitamin C, [and] has been found to be effective against acute asthma attacks, migraines, fatigue (including chronic fatigue syndrome), fibromyalgia, acute muscle spasm, upper respiratory tract infections, chronic sinusitis, seasonal allergic rhinitis, cardiovascular, and other disorders."[63] By taking these extreme measures, Kurzweil believes, it is currently possible to extend one's life long enough to take advantage of the coming technological revolution that will bring immortality.

Others who share Kurzweil's belief in the approaching singularity do not accept his prescription for reaching the Kingdom. In an article on a paper published in 2008, Khatchadourian reports that Bostrom cautioned "'Death is not one but a multitude of assassins. . . . Take aim at the causes of early death—infection, seize the biochemical processes in your body in order to vanquish, by and by, illness and senescence. In time you will discover ways to move your mind to more durable media.' He [Kurzweil] tends to see the mind as immaculate code, the body as inefficient hardware—able to accommodate limited hacks but destined for replacement."[64] Rather than 150 pills and Meyer's cocktails, Bostrom bets on cryogenics; he and his colleague, Robin Hanson, wear ankle bracelets from the Alcor Foundation. Their bodies will be transported to the Arizona desert, where they will be frozen while awaiting technological resurrection.

These developments represent the simultaneous culmination and reversal of what Heidegger labels the ontotheological tradition. When God becomes man, as in the Incarnation, man becomes God. At this critical juncture, Nietzsche's will to power becomes the will to mastery through which humans and posthumans re-create the world in their own image. Citing transhumanist Michael Anissimov's claim that "one of the biggest flaws in the common conception of the future is that the future is something that happens to us, not something we create," Kurzweil elaborates this point in words that unwittingly echo Heidegger. "Our progress in reverse engineering the human brain . . . demonstrates that we do indeed have the ability to understand, to model, and to extend our own intelligence. This is one aspect of the uniqueness of our species: our intelligence is sufficiently above the critical threshold necessary for us to scale our own ability to unrestricted heights of creative power—and we have the opposable appendage (our thumbs) necessary to manipulate the universe to our will." The goal of the singularity is to control cosmological forces in ways that make it possible to engineer the world we want. As knowledge explodes and superintelligence emerges, "the entire universe will become saturated with *our* [emphasis added] intelligence. This is the destiny of the universe. . . . We will determine our own fate rather than have it determined by the current 'dumb,' simple, machinelike forces that rule celestial mechanics."[65] In a manner reminiscent of the relation between objective and subjective spirit in Hegel's speculative philosophy, mind and universe are isomorphic, and, thus, completely transparent. Everywhere posthumans turn, they see only themselves, and in their consciousness and self-consciousness, the universe becomes aware of itself.

The technological singularity brings to completion the trajectory I have been tracking from the dematerialization of the society of the spectacle through the digitization of the culture of simulacra to virtualization, which creates the virtual condition. It is no accident that the most enthusiastic supporters of the singularity are the tech billionaires whose financial assets are as virtual as the realities in which they traffic. As DeLillo suggests, in the era of the singularity, immortality is a luxury only the .001% can afford. When viewed in this context, Bezos's and Musk's investments in space exploration make perfect sense. Though never admitting it publicly, they are actually creating the spaceships that will enable posthumans to flee Earth and colonize other planets, where they can live forever.

Insistence on the utopian potential of new media, information, and communication technologies cannot obscure the negativity that lies at the heart of this technological revolution. The aspiration for self-transcendence is an example of what Hegel describes as unhappy consciousness and Nietzsche labels nihilism. In this mode of awareness, the real, however imagined, is always elsewhere—in the heavens or beneath the earth, in the past or in the future, but never here and now. The only way to affirm this transcendent real is to negate our present selves and the reality of the world as we know it. The virtual condition is the latest version of this ancient myth. As images are translated into code, life becomes more virtual, and involvement in and commitment to the material world fades. Body and world, which once were considered real, become what Heidegger aptly describes as the "standing reserve" that emerging posthumans exploit in pursuit of their dream of immaterial transcendence. If reality is truly virtual, bodily existence in the real world is at best a vehicle that transports cybernauts to a higher life and at worst a prison one must struggle to escape. For these Gnostics, salvific knowledge is no longer expressed in secret myths and arcane passwords but now becomes accessible in mathematical formulas, computer codes, and algorithms. The elite cognoscenti who have the keys to this kingdom believe they can escape the gravity of finitude and float freely in the ethereal cloud forever.

These beliefs are not only mistaken, they are actually dangerous—such supposedly salvific technologies are destructive of both self and world. The pursuit of the virtual millennium is destroying the very material conditions, natural world, and bodily life upon which machines running seemingly endless simulations depend. When energy resources are exhausted, precious metals disappear, or the plug is pulled, the screen goes blank and virtuality collapses back into earthly reality. This impending catastrophe exposes the inherent contradiction in the dematerialization, digitization, and virtualization of reality. At the very moment virtuality is on the verge of consuming all reality, there is a dialectical reversal and repressed materiality returns and crashes the machines designed to escape it. The task of thinking at the end of virtuality is to gather the remains of the world many think is passing away to fashion a future that is sustainable. The unlikely resources for this taunting task are first philosophy and then art.

CRACKS IN MIRRORS AND SCREENS

Smart TVs, computer screens, Bloomberg terminals, video games, virtual reality goggles, Google glass. Everywhere people turn, they see their images reflected. The virtual condition is no longer the society of spectacle. Images, digitized and coded to circulate in networks at speeds beyond human comprehension and control, form self-reflexive loops spinning out of control. These screens reverse the direction of the gaze by looking at the people looking at them. Rather than humans manipulating images on screens, algorithms and codes control the lives of the people who created them. Autonomy gives way to a more disturbing heteronomy and supposed mastery becomes debilitating servitude; perfect transparency disappears in inescapable obscurity.

To appreciate the significance of these developments, it is necessary to understand the philosophical and theological background from which they emerged. Metaphysics is unavoidable—the only question is whether it is implicit and unconscious or explicit and self-conscious. In order to render the implicit implications of the progression from modernism through postmodernism to posthumanism explicit, it is helpful to return to Kant's critical philosophy and its elaboration in leading nineteenth-century philosophers and artists. As I have suggested, the cornerstone of Kant's analysis is the notion of freedom, which he interprets as autonomous self-determination. Modernity, which is characterized by the progressive movement from heteronomy (slavery) to autonomy (mastery), culminates in rational self-legislation in matters of knowledge, morality, and aesthetics. The most comprehensive appropriation and redeployment of Kant's critical analysis is Hegel's speculative system, which brings to completion Descartes's turn to the subject with which modern philosophy begins. By identifying truth with certainty, Descartes collapses objectivity into subjectivity. What had appeared to be the external objective world is really the projection or construction of creative subjectivity. Nietzsche explores the far-reaching implications of this critical turn in his fragmentary reflections. Immediately after declaring the death of God, the Madman asks, *"We have killed him—*you and I. But how did we do this? How could we drink up the sea? Who gave us the sponge to wipe away the entire horizon?"[66] This is a powerful image whose importance has been consistently overlooked. When subjectivity absorbs objectivity, all knowledge becomes self-knowledge and every image is a selfie.

Heidegger was the first to realize the significance of Nietzsche's insight for understanding twentieth-century technology. Through modern science and technology, man (or, more precisely, posthumans) "exalts himself to the posture of lord of the earth. In this way the impression comes to prevail that everything man encounters exists only insofar as it is his own construct. This illusion gives rise to one final delusion: It seems as though man everywhere and always encounters only himself."[67] It is difficult to imagine a more incisive interpretation of the world imagined by Vinge, Kurzweil, and their fellow Silicon Valley believers.

The logic of this self-reflexive turn was first articulated in Kant's account of inner teleology or intrinsic purpose, which, he argues, is paradigmatically expressed in beautiful works of art and biological organisms. As we have seen, *Zweckmassigkeit ohne Zweck* is a *structural* concept that articulates the logic of internal relations. Consider, for example, the relation between part and whole in any organized structure—there is no whole without parts, and no parts without whole. Participation in the whole does not negate the specificity of the parts; to the contrary, it constitutes the particular identity of each part or member. For Kant, the elements in a beautiful work of art are intertwined in a relational matrix that lends each constituent its distinctive qualities. Hegel appropriates Kant's argument and, in the process, translates its idea in ways that prove decisive for everyone who comes after him. In his *Lectures on Aesthetics*, Hegel famously declares, "Art, considered in its highest vocation, is and remains for us a thing of the past. Thereby it has lost for us genuine truth and life, and has rather been transferred into our *ideas* instead of maintaining its earlier necessity in reality and occupying its higher place."[68] Hegel's point is not, of course, that art will no longer be produced; rather, he believes that philosophy has displaced art as the primary vehicle for conveying truth.[69] This argument rests on his conviction that religion, art, and philosophy communicate the same truth in different ways. What religion and art express in images and representations (*Vorstellungen*), philosophy conveys in concepts (*Begriffe*). Adorno underscores the importance of this point in his critique of Hegel's aesthetics. "An essential feature of Hegelian philosophy," he argues, involves the claim that "the beautiful in nature comes into its own only by being eclipsed, whereupon its deficiency becomes the *raison d'être* of the beautiful in art. . . . However, what Hegel sees as a deficiency of natural beauty—namely that it escapes conceptual definition—is actually the essence of beauty itself. Furthermore, in Hegel's transition from nature to art, the famous ambivalence of the term *aufheben* is nowhere to be found. For Hegel natural beauty disappears without leaving a recognizable trace in artistic beauty. He regards natural beauty as pre-aesthetic because it is not permeated and determined by spirit, not realizing that the imperious spirit is an instrument rather than the substance of art."[70]

The foundation of Hegel's system is his conceptual formulation of the self-reflexive structure of Kant's inner teleology. In one of the last chapters of his *Science of Logic*, entitled simply "Teleology," Hegel distinguishes mechanistic structures in which parts are externally related and order is extrinsically imposed on aesthetic and organic structures in which purpose is intrinsic. "In [inner] teleology, . . . the content becomes important, for teleology presupposes a Notion [or Concept], something *absolutely determined* and therefore self-determining, and so has made a distinction between the *relation* of differences and their reciprocal determinedness, that is the *form*, and the *unity that is reflected into itself, a unity that is determined in and for itself* and therefore a *content*." This reciprocal or reflexive structure defines the interrelation of the categories and concepts of reason Hegel examines in the *Science of Logic*. Taken as a whole these determinate concepts constitute what he describes as "the Idea." "One of Kant's greatest services to philosophy," Hegel maintains, "consists in the distinction he has made between relative or *external*, and *internal* purposiveness; in the latter he has opened up the Notion of life, the Idea, and by so doing has done *positively* for philosophy what the *Critique of Reason* did but imperfectly, equivocally, and only *negatively*, namely, raised it above the determinations of reflection and the relative world of metaphysics." Whereas for Kant, the notion of inner teleology is a regulative idea that functions as a heuristic device for ordering knowledge, for Hegel, the Idea is constitutive of both subjectivity and objectivity. As such, it is the Logos of all reality. "The idea has not merely the more general meaning of the *true being*, of the unity of *Notion* and *reality*, but the more specific one of the unity of *subjective Notion* and *objectivity*. That is to say, the Notion as such is itself already the identity of itself and *reality*; for the indefinite expression 'reality' means in general nothing else but *determinate being*, and this the Notion possesses in its particularity and individuality."[71]

By transcribing image into concept, Hegel attempts to expose the logocentrism that is the foundation of imagocentrism and thereby to disclose the speculative Idea that is the ground of the society of the spectacle, postmodernism, and the virtual condition. When concepts are coded, they become self-replicating and self-generating algorithms that continue to evolve beyond the human condition. In a manner similar to Kurzweil's claim that the universe "wakes up" through posthumans' consciousness of it, Hegel argues that as subjects become first conscious and then self-conscious through their knowledge of the world, the world becomes self-aware through subjects' knowledge of it. Since subject and object, or self and world, are isomorphic, their relation is perfectly transparent and there is no unassimilated or unincorporated remains.

One hundred and fifty years later, Baudrillard labels this transparency "obscene." Echoing Hegel's triadic dialectic, he argues, "Consumer society lived also under the sign of alienation, there is spectacle, action, scene. It is not obscenity—the spectacle is never obscene. Obscenity begins precisely when there is no more spectacle, no more scene, when all becomes transparency and immediate visibility, when everything is exposed to the harsh inexorable light of information and communication."[72] Transparency, then, emerges with the disclosure of every secret and the disappearance of all remains. It is important to note that Hegel insists that the sensible does not disappear but is sublated; that is to say, it is displaced from centrality but nonetheless preserved. This so-called preservation, however, reveals that the sensuous is always sensible, and what had appeared to be material is essentially immaterial distributed in(-)formation that is in the process of formation. In Hegel's comprehensive and comprehensible System, there are no lingering parasites and, thus, no disruptive noise.[73] The transcendence of the sensuous in the Hegelian *Aufhebung* prefigures the dematerialization, digitization, and virtualization of the real. The body (of the image, representation, sign) is left behind in the ascension of the Concept or Notion and its realization in the Idea. This idealization prefigures the "saturation" of material reality by superintelligence. When everything is coded or codable, the line between human and artificial intelligence becomes obscure, and the universe becomes a supercomputer running programs and algorithms that evolve without human intervention. As these programs become more sophisticated, all life becomes artificial life.

Hegel's chapter on teleology in the *Science of Logic* is followed by chapters entitled "The Idea" and "Life." "Life," Hegel argues, "is the immediate Idea." He proceeds to explain, "when the living thing is regarded as a whole consisting of parts, or as a thing operated on by mechanical or chemical causes, as a mechanical or chemical product, whether it be regarded merely as such a product, or also determined by an external end, then the Notion is regarded as a *dead* thing. Since the Notion is immanent in it, the *purposiveness* of the living being is to be grasped as *inner*; the Notion is in it as determinate Notion, distinct from its externality, and in its distinguishing, pervading the externality and remaining identical with itself. This objectivity of the living being is the *organism*."[74] In this autotelic structure, algorithms program algorithms through processes that exceed the ability of individual human beings to comprehend or control. This account of life brings Hegel's argument full circle. By translating the self-reflexive structure Kant discerns in the beautiful work of art into the philosophical concept, which is the ground of biological life as well as human self-consciousness, Hegel closes the final loop in his speculative system.

> *Vorstellung* → *Begriff*: Concept-Notion → Idea-Logos
> → Algorithm-Code → Life (Nature, World, Objectivity)
> → Consciousness-Self-Consciousness (Self, Culture,
> Subjectivity)

Protests to the contrary notwithstanding, this genealogy remains inconclusive. Questions remain. Is all sensibility sensible? Is materiality essentially immaterial? Can all images and representations be translated into concepts without remainder? Is reality algorithmic? Can everything be coded? To answer these questions, it is necessary to return to Kant's *Critique of Judgment*. As I have noted, the Third Critique (aesthetics/the Beautiful) is intended to mediate the First Critique (epistemology/the True) and the Second Critique (morality/the Good). In his essay "Parergon," in *The Truth in Painting*, Derrida describes the function of the Third Critique as "the frame effect." The frame is the "junction point [*Vereinigungspunkt*]" that simultaneously brings together and holds apart different works. "The frame labors. . . . Like wood. It creaks and cracks, breaks down and dislocates even as it cooperates in the production of the product, overflows it and is deduc(t)ed from it. It never lets itself be simply exposed."[75] Always withdrawing to allow works to appear, the frame marks and remarks the edge, border, boundary, or margin that simultaneously enables and eludes representation. When this insight is extended from Kant's critical philosophy to works of art, the point becomes more telling. From this perspective, the universe will never be saturated with intelligence as Kurzweil predicts. Every image, representation, and concept has as a condition of its own possibility that which can be neither represented nor conceptualized, and, therefore, something *always* remains. Knowledge, therefore, is inescapably incomplete, and, thus, inevitably entails nonknowledge.

In Kant's epistemology, the imagination is the means by which we are able to apprehend what we cannot comprehend. Hegel and many of today's AI researchers are wrong when they claim that the contents of the human mind can be translated into concepts, algorithms, and codes without remainder. There are always sensuous traces that elude comprehension and coding. These traces are associated with the bodily bias of thinking and the material conditions of immaterial processes. The imagination is the mean between sensibility and understanding, and, as such, Kant argues, is the agency through which their synthesis occurs.

Now, since every appearance contains a manifold and since different perceptions therefore occur in the mind separately and singly, a combination of them, such as they cannot have in sense itself, is demanded. There must therefore exist in us an active faculty for synthesis of this manifold. To this faculty I give the

title, imagination. Its action, when immediately directed to perceptions, I entitle apprehension. Since imagination has to bring
the manifold of intuition into the form of an image, it must previously have taken the impression up into its activity, that is, have
apprehended them.[76]

Inasmuch as the imagination articulates objects, it is the necessary condition of the possibility of knowledge and consciousness, and, by extension, of self-consciousness. In this capacity,
the operation of the imagination is *transcendental*. Explaining
how the imagination operates at the edge or along the border
between sensation and understanding, Kant writes, "Obviously
there must be some third thing, which is homogeneous on the
one hand with the category, and on the other hand with the appearance, and which thus makes the application of the former to
the latter possible. The mediating representation must be pure,
that is, void of all empirical content, and yet at the same time,
while it must be in one respect *intellectual*, it must in another
be *sensible*. Such a representation is the *transcendental schema*."[77]
Kant describes the operation of the imagination as the "schematization of the categories."

For Kant, unlike British empiricists like Locke and Hume, the
mind is not a *tabula rasa*; to the contrary, it is hardwired, that is,
it has a definite structure, which, Kant maintains, is universal.
This structure consists of the forms of intuition (space and time)
and the twelve categories of the understanding. There are two
sides to knowledge: a posteriori—sense data—and a priori—
the forms of intuition and categories of the understanding.
Through the process of schematization, the imagination brings
together data and the categories. In this model, the mind operates like a computer—the a priori categories are the program
that processes data. "Data," it is important to note, derives from
the Latin word *do*, which means to give; accordingly, data are
given. In Kant's account of knowledge, there can be no output
if there is no input. This is a very important point—inasmuch

as all knowledge presupposes data that must be processed by the imagination, the knowing subject is not originally active or constructive but is always already exposed to a primordial passivity. While the exercise of reason in both its theoretical and practical capacities entails self-legislation through which the categories of understanding and the moral law are deployed to regulate sensations, the autonomy of the rational subject is always secondary to a more primal heteronomy. Furthermore, Kant, unlike Hegel, does not think we can be confident that the mind and what it processes are necessarily isomorphic; nor does he think that images and representations can be processed to form totally transparent concepts. To the contrary, images and representations always retain remains that elude conceptual articulation. Therefore there is always something lacking or missing from concepts, algorithms, and codes designed to process the data of experience. Unprocessable data interrupt the circuit of self-reflexivity and subvert the purported autonomy of the rational subject.

Johann Gottlieb Fichte was the first to realize the far-reaching implications of Kant's interpretation of the imagination for speculative philosophy. His reading of critical philosophy exposes cracks in the mirrors of modernism and fissures in the screens of postmodernism. These cracks and fissures reveal hidden openings for the imagination that create new possibilities for art. As we have seen, for Kant's followers, the self-reflexive structure of inner teleology comes to fullest expression in human self-consciousness. Self-consciousness presupposes self-reference in which the self represents itself to itself. In contrast to Hegel, who argues that this structure is closed and, thus, autonomous, Fichte insists that it is open and, therefore, irreducibly incomplete. Dieter Henrich points out that in his *Science of Knowledge* (1800), Fichte argues that "self-reference is neither the only, nor even the primary, structure of the mind. It is rather an implication of more basic processes that underlie the mind, but in a way that these processes necessarily *consti-*

tute the mind's self-reference. . . . In other words, mental self-reference is always the implication of a complicated structure. The simplicity with which we reflect on ourselves as the subjects of knowledge is utterly misleading. While it is, indeed, immediate, it is also parasitical in relation to a more basic complexity. And it is only in terms of this more basic complexity that we can analyze original self-reference."[78]

This structural complexity, which is the prereflexive condition of the possibility of self-reflexivity, has two aspects. First, for the subject to recognize itself in its self-objectification or self-representation, it must have a prior familiarity with itself. "It quickly becomes evident," Henrich concludes, "that an awareness of the self must *precede* reflection. I cannot concentrate on something unless there is already some awareness of it. In a word, I cannot bring into being an awareness of that on which I am concentrating merely *by* my concentration. Rather, reflection can only make an awareness I already have *explicit*. Moreover, it might possibly lead to a descriptive knowledge about the self, but reflection does not account for the *original* self-awareness. Accordingly, self-awareness is presupposed in the reflection account of self-consciousness."[79]

Second, and more important in this context, as I have suggested, self-reference or self-representation is secondary to primary processes of the imagination that cannot be captured in conceptual grids. In self-consciousness, the subject turns back on itself by becoming an object to itself. Self-as-subject and self-as-object are coemergent and codependent. In other words, the structure of self-relation constitutive of self-conscious subjectivity presupposes the activity of self-representation. There is always something in the mind that is not of the mind. Thus, when consciousness turns back on itself it discovers a lacuna without which it is impossible but with which it is incomplete. The pressing question now becomes: Where does that which the self-conscious subject represents to itself come from? If self-as-subject and self-as-object are coemergent and codependent, then neither can be the originary cause or condition of the other. The activity of self-representation, therefore, presupposes a more primordial presentation, which must originate elsewhere. This incomprehensible limit is marked and remarked by the imagination.

We have seen how the imagination operates in the schematization of the categories. It is now necessary to understand that this process involves two interrelated activities, which Kant describes as productive and reproductive. In its productive modality, the imagination figures forms that the reproductive imagination combines and recombines to create the schemata that organize the data of experience into comprehensible patterns. Inasmuch as the imagination (*Ein-bildungs-kraft*) is the activity of formation (*bilden-bildung*), it is, in effect, an in(-)formation process. The myriad connections among the words *Bild* (picture, image, representation), *bilden* (to form, fashion, shape, model, construct), *Bildung* (culture, education, formation), *einbilden* (to imagine, fancy), and *Einbildungskraft* (imagination, fancy) underscore the inextricable relationship among images, representations, and the imagination. The productive and reproductive modes of the imagination issue in the interrelated activities of presentation (*Darstellung*) and representation (*Vorstellung*) respectively. *Darstellung* presents the images and figures that *Vorstellung* re-presents in consciousness and self-consciousness. Since *Vorstellung* presupposes *Darstellung*, all images and representations include as a condition of their possibility something that can be neither imagined nor represented. Through aesthetic images, Kant maintains, the imagination "gives much to think about, but without any determinate thought, i.e., *concept* being able to be adequate to it, which consequently no language can completely attain and make comprehensible."[80] Since something that is neither a subject nor an object and yet is not nothing, is always missing, lacking, or absent, images cannot be translated into concepts or completely coded without remainder. Reason is inseparable from sensibility, knowledge, and, therefore, always entails nonknowledge, which renders perfect clarity and total transparency an idle dream that threatens to become a repressive nightmare. The imagination brings reflection back down to earth by figuring a sensibility that inscribes knowledge and awareness in an irreducible bodily materiality without which life is impossible.

In an unexpected twist, Kant finds the work of art at the heart of reason's theoretical deployment.

> This schematism of our understanding, in its application to appearances and their mere form, is an *art* [emphasis added] concealed in the depths of the human soul, whose real modes of activity nature is hardly likely ever to allow us to discover, and to have open to our gaze. This much only can we assert: the *image* is a product of the empirical faculty of reproductive imagination; the *schema* of sensible concepts, such as of figures in space, is a product and, as it were, a monogram, of pure *a priori* imagination, through which, in accordance with which, images themselves first become possible. These images can be connected with the concept only by means of the schema to which they belong. In themselves they are never completely congruent with the concept.[81]

This seminal comment anticipates Joseph Beuys's and Andy Warhol's proclamation, "Everyone is an artist!" This is not the hyperbolic declaration of self-aggrandizing artists; to the contrary, it is the conclusion of some of today's leading neuroscientists. In his informative study, *The Age of Insight: The Quest to Understand the Unconscious in Art, Mind, and Brain*, neuroscientist and Nobel Laureate Eric Kandel cites his intellectual mentor Ernst Gombrich to support his understanding of the visual imagination. "We think that art is universal because each human was designed by evolution to be an artist, driving her own mental development according to evolved aesthetic principles. From infancy, self-orchestrated experiences are the original medium and the self the primary audience. . . . The invention of additional media (paint, clay, film, etc.) has allowed a steady expansion of audience-accessible art forms over human history."[82] There seems to be an emerging consensus among some philosophers, artists, and scientists, who agree with Kant's provocative claim that "art lies in the depth of the human soul." If this insight is correct, and I think it is, the task of thinking in the era of posthumanism is to reverse the trajectory of the past two centuries by translating concepts, algorithms, and codes into images and representations that gather the remains ignored or repressed by the society of the spectacle, the culture of simulacra, and the virtual condition.

At the end of the ontotheological tradition, gathering remains. As dematerialization gives way to digitization, which leads to virtualization, remains gather. Gather as the debris that is left behind but does not disappear—time wasted in trivial pursuits, trash polluting earth, water, and air, lives of those left behind by hyperacceleration that exceeds comprehension, senses desensitized, and bodies, above all bodies, bodies of every size and shape, many growing larger and becoming little more than a heavy burden to bear. It has all become so inescapably senseless. The end it seems will not come from Heidegger's atomic explosion, but from the implosion of the virtual and the real. Unless . . . unless we come to our senses and recover our humanity. Hope, if there is any, lies in remains. Perhaps, by gathering the remains of what for many has come to seem useless, we can come to our senses before it is too late.

THE AESTHETIC TURN

In his troublingly prescient novel *Zero K*, Don DeLillo asserts, "The only thing that's not ephemeral is the art. It's not made for an audience. It's made simply to be here. It's here, it's fixed, it's part of the foundation, set in stone" (*Z* 51). Stone. Art set in stone. How, asks Annie Dillard, might one teach a stone to talk? And if a stone spoke, would we know how to listen?

Like a purloined letter, it had been hiding in plain sight for more than twenty years, covered with weeds and earth. As we probed and scraped with machines and by hand, a massive stone formation began to emerge. At first it was indistinct, but as we peeled away layer after layer of soil, it began to resemble a giant leviathan breaking the surface of the sea that once filled this valley. Rather than smooth or scaly, its hump was serrated like the frayed pages of a book. The stone, I discovered, is Stockbridge marble just like Nathaniel Hawthorne's Ethan Brand burned in his lime kiln on the other side of the nearby mountain. Four and a half million years ago, this stone was submerged off the coast of Nantucket where Hawthorne's friend and Berkshire neighbor, Herman Melville, began his epic novel. Like the whale, the stone is etched with indecipherable hieroglyphics. Half submerged, this arresting stone draws the imagination toward incomprehensibly ancient depths that border the sublime. In this way, it provokes an apprehension that cannot be comprehended.

"The closer you get to real matter, rock, air, fire, wood," Jack Kerouac mused, "the more spiritual the world is."[83] Minerals are not merely external objects; they circulate through us until our bodies eventually nourish the earth that nourishes us. Some precious minerals once buried deep in the earth surround us in electronic devices that expand our minds and run our lives, others are consumed to fuel machines to which we are indentured. But not all minerals and stones are standing reserves waiting to be exploited. Many are works of art from a past so ancient it is beyond time. As with so many other things, the beauty of stone is in the details. Subtle colors, arresting folds, imaginative shapes, curious cracks, and puzzling fissures. This beauty, which exceeds Euclid's grid and eludes every code programmed to capture it, is more troubling than reassuring because it is utterly gratuitous. No mind conceived these designs, no hand carved these figures. Annie Dillard reminds us, "We are strangers and sojourners, soft dots on the rocks. You have walked along the strand and see where birds have landed, walked, and

FIGURE 1.1. **Mark C. Taylor,** *Stone Hill.*

flown; their tracks begin in sand, and go, and suddenly end. Our tracks do that: but we go down. And stay down."[84] "Humility," like "humanity," derives from "humus," earth, ground, soil—brown or black decaying organic matter that eventually turns to stone. Earth to earth, humans to humus. By bringing us back to earth, art reminds us how to live by teaching us how to die. All stones are in some way gravestones, which, when acknowledged as such, paradoxically give life anew. Derrida indirectly suggests that this is one of the lasting lessons of Kant's *Critique of Judgment.*

> ... the imagination, being intermediate between sensibility and understanding is capable of *two operations*. And we rediscover here the two edges, the two faces of the trait, of the limit or of the cise. Imagination is the cise because it has two cises. The cise always has two cises: it de-limits. It has the cise of what it delimits and the cise of what it de-limits, of what it limits and of what is liberated in it of its limits. Two operations of the imagination, which are both prehensions. Apprehension (*aprehensio, Auffassung*) can go to the infinite *without difficulty*. The other operation, comprehension (comprehension, *Zusammenfassung*) cannot follow, it is finite, subjected to the *intuitus derivatus* and to the sensory. ... And if apprehension extends beyond this maximum, it lets go in comprehension what it gains in apprehension. Whence this apparently paradoxical conclusion: the right place, the ideal *topos* for the experience of the sublime, for the inadequation of presentation to the unpresentable, will be a median place, an average place of the body which would provide an aesthetic maximum without losing itself in the mathematical infinite. Things must come into a relationship of body to body: the "sublime" body. ... In Kant's examples, this relationship of body to body is one of body to stone.[85]

Body to body, body to stone, body to bone. Stone and all it embodies lends life weight by exposing us to depths that cannot be fathomed. If stone were to speak, it would not be in a human language that could be comprehended in words, codes, or algorithms. Hegel was wrong—not everything can be comprehended, and, thus, neither ourselves nor the world is completely transparent. That does not mean, however, that we are totally blind and lost. As Kant argues and Derrida explains, the imagination operates at the edge, along the boundary of comprehension and apprehension. We apprehend things and no-things we cannot comprehend, and this apprehension exposes us to realities that exceed logic and language and yet are not necessarily irrational. "Apprehend" derives from the Latin *apprehendere* (*ad*, to + *prehendre*, to seize). Apprehension harbors an ambiguity because the seizure it designates can be both active and passive. To apprehend means not only to grasp mentally but also to take into custody, and to anticipate with anxiety. Apprehension: a fearful or uneasy anticipation of the future, dread; a seizing or capturing, arrest; and the ability to understand or comprehend. Art breeds critical apprehension by cultivating what can be neither comprehended nor mastered.

This understanding of art cuts against the grain of much contemporary artistic practice. Art, like so much else today, has lost its way by following the trajectory from dematerialization through digitization to virtualization. As I have argued, the implicit presupposition of these developments is Hegel's appropriation of the self-reflexive structure of Kant's notion of inner teleology to form a speculative philosophy in which everything is supposed to be reconciled and integrated in a comprehensive and comprehensible whole. This line of analysis and its extension in twentieth- and twenty-first-century technologies privileges mind over body and vision over the other senses. If every apprehension can be comprehended, uncertainty gives way to certainty and calm confidence about a future that seems to have been programmed in advance. In such a world, art loses its critical edge. Like everything else, the work of art is instrumentalized and becomes an investment vehicle for wealthy hedge fund

FIGURE 1.2. Mark C. Taylor, *Response to Jeff Koons.*

managers to diversify their portfolios. Warhol's commodification of art becomes Jeff Koons's financialization of art. Rather than hawking his wares in department store windows and SoHo galleries, erstwhile commodities trader Koons markets floating basketballs and shiny party balloons through private equity funds initially designed by high-speed traders to sell virtual assets like the mortgage-backed securities that brought the global economy to the brink of collapse.[86]

When art becomes a security designed for investment in virtual financial markets that trade in signs of signs coded in self-generating algorithms and projected on screens, it becomes complicit in a system that is speeding toward collapse. To avoid this disaster, art must turn away from confidence men promising profitable returns and develop creative ways to help us come to our senses by gathering the remains of what the virtual condition represses. To begin this process, it is necessary to return to the point at which the philosophical foundation of modern art was first formulated.

Kant developed his interpretation of the autotelic structure of art at the time the traditional patronage system of church and aristocracy was breaking down and the modern art market was emerging. He distinguished low art from high art—low art is produced for the market and is intended to make a profit; high art, by contrast, is created for the appreciation of other artists rather than the market. High art or fine art is nonutilitarian and noninstrumental; its value is supposed to be intrinsic rather than extrinsic, that is, monetary or financial. Such art is not an investment and is not made with the expectation of a profitable return; to the contrary, it is created for its own sake. There is no financial justification for the investment of time, money, and resources necessary to produce such art; indeed, from the point of view of *homo oeconomicus*, such expenditure is senseless. For the artist, however, seemingly worthless remains and irrational excess lend the work its lasting value.

The insistence on intrinsic rather than extrinsic value creates a resistance to market forces that lends art its critical edge, which is always threatened from two directions. As I have shown, art can be appropriated by the system it is designed to resist as it has been in the commodification and financialization of art, or it can become so detached or withdrawn from the system of profitable exchange that it becomes irrelevant.

For art to maintain its critical function in the age of virtuality, it is necessary to recover its place "in the depths of the human soul" that Kant exposed in his critical philosophy. By mediating sensibility (passivity) and cognition (activity), the imagination exposes a gap that leaves consciousness and self-consciousness incomplete.

Descartes's philosophical revolution, whose far-reaching implications are still being felt, rests on two interrelated mistakes: first, the reduction of truth to certainty, which completely transforms the ostensibly objective world into a construction of creative subjects; and second, the claim that the mind (*res cogito*) and the body (*res extensa*) are separate and, in important ways, opposed. In his influential work *Descartes' Error: Emotion, Reason, and the Human Brain*, neuroscientist Antonio Damasio argues, "This is Descartes' error: the abyssal separation between body and mind, between the sizable, dimensioned, mechanically operated, infinitely divisible body stuff, on the one hand, and the unsizable, undimensioned, un-pushpullable, nondivisible mind stuff; the suggestion that reason, and moral judgment, and the suffering that comes from physical pain or emotional upheaval might exist separately from the body. Specifically: the separation of the most refined operations of mind from the structure and operation of a biological organism." To correct this error, it is necessary to recover the body and determine its role in the operation of the mind. "The comprehensive understanding of the human mind," Damasio insists, "requires an organismic perspective; . . . not only must the mind move from a nonphysical cogitum to the realm of biological tissue, but it must also be related to a whole organism possessed of an integrated body proper and brain and fully interactive with a physical and social environment."[87]

Kant's account of the imagination unexpectedly provides a bridge between eighteenth- and nineteenth-century philosophy and contemporary neuroscience. Apprehension, which,

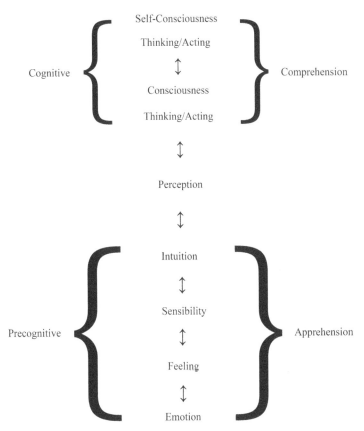

FIGURE 1.3.

we have seen, intersects with comprehension through the imagination, leaves an inescapable trace of bodily functions without which cognition is impossible. At the most rudimentary level, the process of schematization creates the distinction between subject and object without which consciousness and self-consciousness are impossible. The processes that produce apprehension are precognitive: they cannot be clearly articulated in concepts but can be figured in images that bear traces of what rational cognition excludes or represses.

Since apprehension exceeds comprehension, images cannot

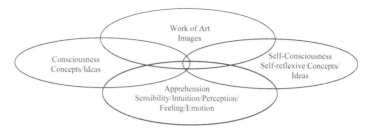

FIGURE 1.4.

be fully translated into concepts, and, thus, there are always remains to be gathered. These lingering remains are the future of art and, perhaps, of life itself. Though timely, this insight is not new; many of Hegel's colleagues and contemporaries rejected his claim that philosophy had replaced art and religion as the vehicle for truth. During the decisive decade of the 1790s, some artists, writers, poets, and philosophers argued that art, in fact, actually was displacing religion as the locus of humankind's spiritual striving. In different ways, they countered Hegel's logocentrism with figurative language and tropological twists and turns of art designed to express what is not semantically determinable. This approach is directly counter to Hegel's understanding of the self-reflexivity of language that grounds his system. "Because *language* is the product [*Werk*] of thought nothing can be said in it which is not general. What I *mean* is *mine*, belongs to me as this particular individual; but if language only expresses the general I cannot say what I *mean*. And the *Unsayable*, emotion feeling, is not the most excellent, the most true but rather the most insignificant, most untrue."[88]

The Unsayable cannot be articulated for two opposite reasons: either it is completely indeterminate, undifferentiated, and formless, or it is the radically differentiated singular that remains unrelated to anything other than itself. To break the repressive control of instrumental reason and the economic calculation it entails, it is necessary to refigure immaterial concepts as sensible images. During the last decade of the nineteenth century, writers and artists who rejected Hegel's claim that art is a thing of the past developed different styles to express what reason leaves out. Though their philosophical convictions differed, Schelling, Novalis, Hölderlin, Schiller, Friedrich and August Schlegel, Kierkegaard, and Schleiermacher agree that the task of art is to figure what cannot be comprehended in thoroughly rational language, which is limited by the opposition between subjectivity and objectivity. The common name for their different efforts is *poiesis*. This term does not refer to poetry in the usual sense of the term; rather it designates the creative use of language that fashions figures and creates forms instead of re-presenting what is already structured and coded. No longer referential, *poiesis* is performative—it is designed "to say" the Unsayable by torquing and twisting language, figures, and images to express what cannot be represented.

These poietic experiments established the notion of literature and art that became normative for modernism as well as the interpretation of writing (*écriture*) that lies at the heart of poststructural theory. Furthermore, the understanding of the bodily traces of language anticipates some of the most important insights of contemporary psychoanalytic theory. In her essay "From One Identity to the Other," Julia Kristeva, for example, suggests the far-reaching implications of this new understanding of language by drawing a distinction between semantic and semiotic aspects of discourse.

The semiotic process, which introduces errancy [*errance*] or fuzziness into language and, *a fortiori*, into poetic language is, from a synchronic point of view, a mark of the drive processes (appropriation/rejection, orality/anality, love/hate, life/death) and, from a diachronic point of view, stems from the archaisms of the semiotic body. Before recognizing itself as identical in a mirror and, consequently, as signifying, this body is dependent vis-à-vis the mother. At the same time instinctual and material, semiotic processes prepare the future speaker for entrance into meaning and signification (into the symbolic). But the symbolic (i.e., language as nomination, sign, and syntax) constitutes itself only by breaking with this anteriority, which is retrieved as "signifier," "primary processes," displacement and condensation, metaphor and metonomy, rhetorical figures—but which always remain subordinate—subjacent to the principal function of nomination-predication. Language as symbolic function constitutes itself at the cost of repressing instinctual drive.[89]

Kristeva's argument is an extension of Jacques Lacan's reading of Freud. In Lacan's calculation, the binary oppositions of structuralism are coded in digital programs that form the symbolic order, which constitutes only one layer of the unconscious. The symbolic order functions like a cybernetic system programming the data of experience. Every program, however, is incomplete because not all data (that is, everything that is given) can be processed. Therefore, there is a gap or hole in the unconscious that Lacan labels "the real." The real is a theoretical transcription of one of Freud's most important but least recognized insights. In an inconspicuous footnote in *The Interpretation of Dreams*, he admits, "There is at least one spot in every dream at which it is unplumbable—a navel, as it were, that is its point of contact with the unknown."[90] As the opening that traces the point of contact with the unknown, the real marks and remarks the gap that creates the space for the rhythmic pulsation of the drives, which are the psychic expression of the primal bodily functions. The dream of autonomy, which begins with Descartes's division of body and mind and reaches closure in the mirror play of speculative philosophy and its extension in the society of the spectacle, the culture of simulacra, and the virtual condition, here is exposed as a repressive fantasy. Lacan and his surrealist associates agree with the conclusions of today's neuroscientists—consciousness and self-consciousness are symptoms of bodily processes without which human life is impossible.

For many years, critics have dismissively argued that psychoanalysis is more art than science. Recently, however, some leading researchers have argued that neuroscience actually confirms many of Freud's most important insights about the bodily bias of thinking and reflection. If mind and body are inseparable, then pattern and stuff can never be separated, and, thus, consciousness and self-consciousness can never migrate from carbon to silicon. Furthermore, communication designed to be essentially linguistic, conceptual, and cognitive will always be incomplete and inadequate. Rather than decoding or translating images into concepts, the challenge is to create images that communicate on multiple levels by engaging all the senses.

Eric Kandel's account of the production and reception of works of art in terms of the latest insights of neuroscience both implicitly clarifies layers of the Freudian and Lacanian unconscious and exposes the irrepressible biological foundation of Kant's interpretation of the productive and reproductive functions of the imagination. Kandel makes his point by analyzing painting and, therefore, focuses on vision.

> The most remarkable aspect of visual perception is that most of what we see in the faces, hands, and bodies of other people is determined by processes that operate independently of the pattern of light falling on the retina. It depends on information processed from the bottom up—through low- and intermediate-level vision—that is then integrated with signals processed from the top down—from higher cognitive centers of the brain. It is the job of high-level visual processing to integrate the visual experiences from these two sources into a coherent whole. Top-down signals rely on memory and compare incoming visual information with prior experiences. Our ability to find meaning in a visual experience depends entirely on these signals.[91]

The bottom-up processes correspond to the apprehension of sensible intuition, and the top-down processes correspond to

the conceptualization of data through the program of categories of understanding (see fig. 1.3). In this way, the activity of
the imagination always *constructs* the world. However, this constructive activity always presupposes a more primordial passivity that *deconstructs* the notion of autonomous subjectivity.[92]

The apparent independence and autonomy of the subject are
subverted by a more radical heteronomy that can be repressed
but never entirely mastered. Far from being merely the delib-
erate construction of rational subjects, the world as we know it
emerges from data that cannot be completely programmed. The
givenness of sense experience, which never makes complete
sense, can create apprehension about a world that cannot be
penetrated or controlled. As Michel Serres suggests in his rich
book, *Five Senses: A Philosophy of Mingled Bodies*, "What we learn
in the middle of the night is that the world makes us flinch, and
that we would do anything not to hear it, to keep it far from us,
were it not for that tiny pinch of bitter but magnificent joy that
draws us to it. Our horror of sensations predisposes us towards
staying in our bunks, wrapped in words, dreaming."[93] This is not
the only response to a future that can be neither anticipated nor
prescribed. The world can also be apprehended as an incomprehensible gift, which, like Angelus Silesius's rose that is so dear to
Heidegger, is "without why." Always exceeding reason's grasp,
this gift is mediated by the body.

No one has done more to explain the genesis of bodily wisdom than Damasio. Kandel goes so far as to claim that Damasio's
empirical studies have "confirmed Freud's view that emotions
are an essential component of cognition and that they are essential for acting in accordance with reason."[94] Damasio develops
his position most clearly in *The Essential Feeling of Happiness:
Body and Emotion in the Making of Consciousness*. The emotions,
he argues, have an inescapable "biological core," which lends
them a primacy in mental life. "All emotions use the body as
their theater (internal milieu, visceral, vestibular and musculo-
skeletal systems), but emotions also affect the mode of opera-

tion of numerous brain circuits; the variety of emotional responses is responsible for profound changes in both the body landscape and for the brain landscape."[95] Always bearing traces of bodily process, images created by the imagination are essential to thinking but lie beyond the grasp of consciousness. Through the body, the mind extends into the world, and the world invades the mind. In other words, the body is not a closed system but is a porous organism open to and enfolded within the environment that nourishes it.

Maurice Merleau-Ponty describes the structure of this codependence as a chiasmus. "Chiasmus," he explains, "derives from the Greek *khiasmos*, which, in turn, comes from *khiazien*, meaning to mark with the letter X. In grammar, a chiasmus is a figure in which the order of words in one of two parallel clauses is the inverse of the other." In Christianity, X is the sign of the cross.

Merleau-Ponty develops his most complete analysis of the chiasmus in a chapter of *The Invisible and the Visible* entitled "*L'entrelacs — le chiasme.*" An *entrelacs* is an ornament consisting of two interlacing figures. When understood in terms of *l'entrelacs*, the chiasmus figures a complex structure of "implication," "enfoldment" (*enroulement*), and "envelopment"

FIGURE 1.5. Mark C. Taylor, *neXus.*

(*enveloppement*).[96] Within this chiasmic structure, bodies are intertwined to create a "tissue" of relations that he describes as "the flesh of things." "What we are calling flesh," Merleau-Ponty writes, "has no name in any philosophy. As the formative milieu of the object and the subject, it is not an atom of being, the hard in-itself that resides in a unique place and moment: one can indeed say of my body that it is not *elsewhere*, but one cannot say that it is *here* or *now* in the sense that objects are. . . . We must not think of the flesh starting from substances, from body and spirit—for then it would be the union of contradictories—but we must think of it . . . as an element, as the concrete emblem of a general manner of being." As the "formative milieu of subjectivity and objectivity," flesh is the domain of the imagination, and "the world is universal flesh."[97]

To answer this question of how the body's flesh can be comprehended, Merleau-Ponty turns to the work of art, or, more precisely, to painting. In an essay entitled "The Indirect Language," he argues that what is required is "a mode of communication which does not pass through objective evidence, a signification which does not refer to an already given object but constitutes and inaugurates its object—as such it would not be prosaic, because it awakens and rallies our whole power of expression and comprehension. Modern painting poses a quite different problem from that of the individual, namely, the question of knowing how one can communicate without the aid of a pre-established nature upon which all men's senses open and of knowing how there can be communication prior to communication and, finally, how there can be a reason before reason." The example Merleau-Ponty uses most often to illustrate the chiastic structure is visual—color and its perception. Color, he explains, is "a certain knot [*noeud*] in the woof of the simultaneous and the successive. It is a concretion of visibility, it is not an atom. The red dress a fortiori holds with its fibers onto the tissue or fabric of the visible, and thereby onto the tissue or fabric of invisible being. . . . Between the alleged colors and visibles, we would find anew the tissue or fabric that lines or doubles them, sustains them, nourishes them, and which for its part is not a thing, but a possibility, a latency, the *flesh* of things." The inter- weaving of universal flesh produces a "texture" that forms the "tissue or fabric of the visible." Perpetually alternating between warp and woof, this tissue is the textured fabric in which all things are interlaced. "My flesh and that of the world therefore involve clear zones, clearing, about which pivot their opaque zones, and the primary visibility . . . does not come without a second visibility, that of lines of force and dimensions, the mas- sive flesh without subtle flesh, the momentary body without a glorified body."[98] The body is porous rather than seamless and, therefore, the neXus that forms the tissue of reality has an empty center that can never be filled.

To express the flesh of the world, which is both beyond com- munication and the condition of the possibility of all communi- cation, Merleau-Ponty argues it is necessary to cultivate a dis- tinctive style that exceeds the limits of representation. "Style is what makes all signification possible. . . . If we really want to un- derstand the origin of signification, and unless we do, we shall not understand any other creation or any other culture, for we shall fall back upon the supposition of an intelligible world in which everything is signified in advance—we must give up ev- ery signification that is already institutionalized and return to the starting point of a nonsignifying world."[99] The imagination fashions that which cannot be reduced to an antecedent logic articulating the order of things. This interpretation of the cre- ative activity of the artist leads to an interpretation of style that is very similar to the notion of *poésie* initially advanced by post- Kantian writers and artists. As Jean-Luc Nancy and Philippe Lacoue-Labarthe demonstrate in their important book, *The Lit- erary Absolute: The Theory of Literature in German Romanticism*, leading figures in the Romantic movement thought that philos- ophy rather than art was a thing of the past.[100] Writing "phil- osophical fragments" designed to criticize Hegel's systematic speculative philosophy, Friedrich Schlegel declares, "poetry and philosophy should be made one."[101] This understanding of poetry grows out of his interpretation of the distinction between *Darstellung* and *Vorstellung* that Kant considers in the Third Critique. Rodolphe Gasché explains, "The issue is no longer how to depict, articulate, or illustrate something already present yet resisting discursive or figural expression, but of how something acquires presence—reality, actuality, effectiveness—in the first place. The question of *Darstellung* centers on coming into presence, or occurring, of the ideas."[102]

To present the unpresentable that shadows the coming into presence of all concepts and ideas, it is necessary to develop stylistic gestures that twist language in ways that create images that both figure and disfigure what they present. Innovative styles disrupt traditional ways of organizing experience and understanding the world. In one of his most influential fragments, Schlegel argues that the aim of Romantic poetry "isn't merely to reunite all the separate species of poetry and put poetry in touch with philosophy and rhetoric. It tries to and should mix and fuse poetry and prose, inspiration and criticism, the poetry of art and the poetry of nature; and make poetry lively and sociable, and life and society poetical."[103] So understood, poetry overflows the page and seeks to transform the world. It was left for Friedrich Schiller to draw the final conclusion to this line of argument in his *Letters on the Aesthetic Education of Man* (1794), where he argues that the challenge is to transform the world into a work of art. Schiller's manifesto marks the origin of the modern notion of the avant-garde, which has taken different forms during the last two-and-a-half centuries. For Schiller and his fellow Romantics, art becomes real in a social group, where individuals become themselves in beautiful organic communities whose living spirit they vitalize. As art becomes real and the real becomes artful, "is" and "ought" are reconciled and, at last, what is is what ought to be, and life becomes truly purposeless.

By reversing Hegel's effort to translate artistic *Vorstellungen* into philosophical *Begriffe*, Romantic artists and writers reveal Kant's "art concealed in the depths of the human soul." Since conceptualization and cognition are impossible apart from the activity of the imagination, imagocentrism turns out to be an abiding condition of logocentrism rather than just a phase that can be surpassed without remainder. In works like *Phenomenology of Perception* (1945), *Signs* (1960), and *The Visible and the Invisible* (1964), Merleau-Ponty uncovers the prereflexive structures and processes that consciousness and self-consciousness presuppose. More important, his interpretation of flesh overturns Cartesian dualism by exposing the inseparability of mind and body. These critical developments mark a decisive shift away from the linguistic turn that has preoccupied so many modern philosophers, humanists, and social scientists and toward an aesthetic turn that still remains incomplete. Though Romantics and phenomenologists recognize the impossibility of completely erasing sensible and material traces from clear and transparent concepts and ideas, they still privilege language. Romantics write poems, myths, and tales, and even Merleau-Ponty reveals a lingering linguistic bias when he entitles one of his influential books *The Prose of the World* (1969) in which he searches for "a reason before reason." The problem with all these stylistic gestures is that stones don't speak in words and, thus, their hieroglyphs cannot be deciphered and translated into prose that can be coded and stored in digital archives.

Many artists and, surprisingly, some scientists understand that to communicate what is prior to communication, words alone are not sufficient. As Damasio demonstrates, body and emotion play an essential role in making consciousness. It is, therefore, necessary to communicate with images and figures that touch the body by engaging all the senses. In this way, it becomes possible to bridge, which is not to say close, the gap separating subject and object, self and world, reader-viewer and work. To do this, philosophy must be taken off the page and art out of galleries and museums and transplanted into the world where abstract ideas can be incarnate in bodily and material processes. Not limited to the labor of artists, the work of art is never a finished product or object but always an open-ended practice that draws others into its ongoing process. The aim of art in the age of virtuality is to create conditions that make it possible to apprehend what cannot be comprehended conceptually. This art must be both performative rather than representational and interactive rather than detached. The creation of the work of art is not limited to the labor of artists but extends to participants. "Our response to art," Kandel explains, "stems from an irrepressible urge to re-create in our own brains the creative process—cognitive, emotional, and empathetic—through which the artist produced the work. . . . This creative urge of the artist and of the beholder presumably explains why essentially every group of human beings in every age and in every place throughout the world has created images, despite the fact that art is not a physical necessity for survival."[104] For art to be effective, it must be affective; that is to say, it must engage not only the eyes and mind but all the senses. By drawing participants into the work of art, it becomes possible to transform minds by exposing bodies to processes that can be neither grasped nor controlled.

While Kandel is right about the creativity involved in the production and response to the work of art, he is wrong to suggest that "art is not a physical necessity necessary for survival." As more and more people live their lives surrounded by screens in unreal real time, they lose touch with their bodies and the material world until life becomes senseless. When some of the most influential people shaping our future are guided by fantasies of life migrating from carbon-based biological organisms to silicon-based computational machines, and visions of super-intelligences evolving and colonizing the universe, it is possible that only art can save us. Art that matters reverses the trajectory that leads from dematerialization through digitization to virtualization by bringing us back to earth. Rather than transporting

FIGURE 1.6. Mark C. Taylor, *Bone Garden*.

disembodied minds and souls to a timeless realm, the art that is redemptive grounds those it grasps in a profound temporality that exceeds human comprehension. The media of this art are material and not immaterial—earth, water, fire, steel, bone, and, yes, stone. Far from being our own construction, the world this art reveals is a gift that is bestowed without reason. To receive this gift with humility is to give up the will to mastery by acknowledging human finitude, and to acknowledge this finitude is to accept mortality.

Posthumanism is antihumanism. From the myths of ancient gnostics to the secret codes and algorithms of today's neognostics, and from the caves of the Mideast to the deserts of Kazakhstan and Arizona, the effort to escape the body and gain immortality is profoundly nihilistic and threatens to destroy rather than extend life. To be human is to die and to know that you die; there is no life beyond—death is final. Liberation comes not from mastering or escaping death but from freely accepting it. Far from rendering life senseless, the embrace of mortality fills what little time remains for each person with infinite meaning. With disaster approaching, the urgent challenge is to gather the remains virtual culture leaves behind and fashion a realistic future filled with apprehension and hope.

NOTES

1. Don DeLillo, *Zero K* (New York: Scribners, 2016), 140–41, 256; epigram from 127. Hereafter references to this work are included parenthetically, with *Z* followed by the page number.

2. This phrase is a refrain that runs throughout DeLillo's *Underworld*.

3. For a discussion of DeLillo's interest in land art, see Mark C. Taylor, "'Holy Shit!': Don DeLillo, *Underworld*," in *Rewiring the Real: William Gaddis, Richard Powers, Mark Danielewski, and Don DeLillo* (New York: Columbia University Press, 2013), 156–249.

4. At one point, DeLillo echoes Saint Augustine's famous meditation on time in book 10 of his *Confessions*: "Time. I feel it in me everywhere. But I don't know what it is. . . . The only time I know is what I feel. It is all now. But I don't know what that means" (Z 15).

5. For a discussion of this work of art, see Mark C. Taylor, *Refiguring the Spiritual: Joseph Beuys, Matthew Barney, James Turrell, Andy Goldsworthy* (New York: Columbia University Press, 2012), 12–15.

6. Immanuel Kant, "What Is Enlightenment?," in *On History*, trans. Lewis White Beck (Indianapolis: Bobbs-Merrill, 1963), 3.

7. Immanuel Kant, *Critique of Judgment*, trans. James Meredith (New York: Oxford University Press, 1973), 2, 21.

8. For an informative account of the more recent role of images in consumerism, see Kathryn Lofton, *Consuming Religion* (Chicago: University of Chicago Press, 2017).

9. Andy Warhol, *The Philosophy of Andy Warhol* (New York: Harcourt Brace, 1975), 92.

10. "The Bilbao Effect," *Economist*, December 21, 3013, http://www.economist.com/news/special-report/21591708-if-you-build-it-will-they-come-bilbao-effect.

11. Warhol, *Philosophy*, 26.

12. *Report on the Construction of Situations*, http://www.bopsecrets.org/SI/report.htm.

13. *Report on the Construction of Situations*.

14. "Imagocentric" is my term, not Debord's. In the next section, I will consider the relationship between logocentrism and imagocentrism.

15. Guy Debord, *Society of the Spectacle* (Detroit: Black and Red, 1983). Hereafter references to this work are given parenthetically in the text, with S followed by the number of the aphorism.

16. *Report on the Construction of Situations*.

17. Martin Heidegger, "The Question of Technology," trans. William Lovitt (New York: Harper and Row, 1977), 27.

18. For further discussion of this point, see Mark C. Taylor and Esa Saarinen, *Imagologies: Media Philosophy* (New York: Routledge, 1994).

19. Jean Baudrillard, *Simulations*, trans. Paul Foss, Paul Patton, and Philip Beitchman (New York: Semiotext[e], 1983), 3.

20. Jean Baudrillard, *Symbolic Exchange and Death* (London: Sage Publications, 1993), 6–7.

21. Baudrillard, *Simulations*, 43.

22. Baudrillard, *Symbolic Exchange and Death*, 57.

23. For a more detailed analysis of these developments, see Mark C. Taylor, *Confidence Games: Money and Markets in a World without Redemption* (Chicago: University of Chicago Press, 2004).

24. https://en.wikipedia.org/wiki/Bitcoin.

25. Nick Bostrom, *Superintelligence: Paths, Dangers, Strategies* (Oxford: Oxford University Press, 2014), 17–18.

26. See Mark C. Taylor, *Speed Limits: Where Time Went and Why We Have So Little Left* (New Haven, CT: Yale University Press, 2014). In a recent development, the Securities Exchange Commission recently approved the proposal to launch a new stock exchange designed to reduce the speed of trading. The people responsible for this initiative are featured in Michael Lewis's popular *Flash Boys: A Wall Street Revolt* (New York: Norton, 2015). See Dave Michaels, "IEX Gains SEC Approval to Launch Exchange," *Bloomberg News*, June 17, 2016.

27. http://conferences.voxmedia.com/events/code-conference/.

28. http://www.newyorker.com/books/joshua-rothman/what -are-the-odds-we-are-living-in-a-computer-simulation.

29. For further elaboration of these developments, see Mark C. Taylor, *Abiding Grace: Time, Modernity, Death* (Chicago: University of Chicago Press, 2018).

30. Nick Bostrom, "Are You Living in a Computer Simulation?" *Philosophical Quarterly* 53, no. 211 (2003), http://www.simulation -argument.com/simulation.html.

31. Moravec teaches at Carnegie Mellon University, where he is a member of the Robotics Institute. For Moravec, the notion of brains in vats is not science fiction. He writes: "Picture a 'brain in a vat,' sustained by life-support machinery, connected by wonderful electronic links to a series of artificial rent-a-bodies in remote loca-

tions and to simulated bodies in virtual realities. Although it may be nudged from beyond its natural lifespan by an optimal physical environment, a biological brain evolved to operate for a human lifetime is unlikely to function forever. Why not use advanced neurological electronics, like that which links it with the external world, to replace the gray matter as it begins to fail? Bit by bit our failing brain may be replaced by superior electronic equivalents, leaving our personality and thoughts clearer than ever, though in time, no vestige of our original body or brain remains." Hans Moravec, *Robot: Mere Machine to Transcendent Mind* (New York: Oxford University Press, 1998), 169–70.

32. Jean Baudrillard, *The Ecstasy of Communication*, trans. Bernard Schutze and Caroline Schutze (New York: *Semiotext(e)*, 1987), 18.

33. Ihab Hassan, "Prometheus as Performer: Towards a Posthumanist Culture?," in *Performance in Postmodern Culture*, ed. Michael Benamou and Charles Caramella (Madison, WI: Coda Press, 1977), 212. For his reading of postmodern literature, see Ihab Hassan, *The Postmodern Turn: Essays in Postmodern Theory and Culture* (Columbus: Ohio State University Press, 1987).

34. Katherine Hayles, *How We Became Posthuman: Virtual Bodies in Cybernetics, Literature, and Infomatics* (Chicago: University of Chicago Press, 1999), 2–3.

35. In developing my account of Bostrom's background and the influences on his work, I have drawn on Raffi Khatchadourian's article, "The Doomsday Invention," *New Yorker*, November 11, 2015.

36. https://en.wikipedia.org/wiki/Transhumanism.

37. http://alcor.org/AboutAlcor/index.html.

38. https://www.fhi.ox.ac.uk/about/mission/.

39. Bostrom, *Superintelligence*, 22, 4.

40. In a provocative article entitled "Artificial Intelligence's White Guy Problem," Kate Crawford notes further problems with current applications of AI. "According to some prominent voices in the tech world, artificial intelligence presents a looming existential threat to humanity: Warnings by luminaries like Elon

Musk and Nick Bostrom about the 'singularity'—when machines become smarter than humans—have attracted millions of dollars and spawned a multitude of conferences. But this hand-wringing is a distraction from the very real problems with artificial intelligence today, which may already be exacerbating inequality in the workplace, at home, and in our legal and judicial systems. Sexism, racism, and other forms of discrimination are being built into the machine-learning algorithms that underlie the technology behind many 'intelligent' systems that shape how we categorize and advertise." Kate Crawford, "Artificial Intelligence's White Guy Problem," *New York Times*, June 25, 2016.

41. http://www.newyorker.com/magazine/2015/11/23/doomsday -invention-artificial-intelligence-nick-bostrom.

42. Bostrom, *Superintelligence*, 22.

43. Robin Hanson, *The Age of Em: Work, Love, and Life when Robots Rule the Earth* (New York: Oxford University Press, 2016), 6.

44. Bostrom, *Superintelligence*, 49.

45. Bill Joy, "Why the Future Doesn't Need Us," *Wired*, April 2000. In one of the more bizarre intersections I have ever noted, Ted Kaczynski's analysis of the ills of industrial society anticipates many of Joy's concerns. In Kaczynski's *Unabomber's Manifesto*, he writes, "If the machines are permitted to make all their own decisions, we can't make any predictions as to the results, because it is impossible to guess how such machines might behave. We have only to point out that the fate of the human race would be at the mercy of the machines. . . . As society and the problems that face it become more and more complex and machines become more and more intelligent, people will let machines make more and more of their decisions for them, simply because machine-made decisions will bring better results than man-made ones. Eventually a stage may be reached at which the decisions necessary to keep the system running will be so complex that human beings will be incapable of making them intelligently. At that stage the machines will be in effective control. People won't be able just to turn the machines off, because they will be so dependent on them that turning them off would amount to suicide." http://cyber.eserver.org/unabom.txt, 42.

46. Bostrom, *Superintelligence*, 99.

47. An article in the *Economist* entitled "The Return of the Machinery Question" examines the social and economic impact of expanding role of Artificial Intelligence. Just as people did two centuries ago, many fear that machines will make millions of workers redundant, causing inequality and unrest. Martin Ford, the author of two bestselling books on the dangers of automation, worries that middle-class jobs will vanish, economic mobility will cease and a wealthy plutocracy could "shut itself away in gated communities or in elite cities, perhaps guarded by autonomous military robots and drones." Others fear that AI poses an existential threat to humanity, because superintelligent computers might not share mankind's goals and could turn on their creators. Such concerns have been expressed, among others, by physicist Stephen Hawking and, more surprisingly, by Elon Musk, the billionaire technology entrepreneur who founded SpaceX and Tesla. Echoing Thomas Carlyle, Musk warns that "with artificial intelligence, we're summoning the demon." His Tesla cars use the latest AI technology to drive themselves, but Musk frets about a future AI overlord becoming too powerful for humans to control. "It's fine if you've got Marcus Aurelius as the emperor, but not so good if you have Caligula," he says. "The Return of the Machinery Question," *Economist*, June 25, 2016.

48. For an excellent profile of Andreessen, see Tad Friend, "Tomorrow's Advance Man: Marc Andreessen's Plan to Win the Future," *New Yorker*, May 18, 2015.

49. https://en.wikipedia.org/wiki/Technological_singularity.

50. Though usually associated with hippies and the back-to-the-land movement, Stewart Brand, editor of the *Whole Earth Catalog*, was an early and enthusiastic supporter of information technology. He saw a liberating potential in distributed and decentralized networks. His vision was very close to the outlook of the kids creating the information revolution in their garages down the street from Haight Ashbury.

51. https://docs.google.com/file/d/0B-5-JeCa2Z7hN1RfRDlqcXpVYzA/edit?pref=2&pli=1.

52. Verner Vinge, "The Coming Technological Singularity: How to Survive in the Post-Human Era," delivered at the VISION-21 symposium sponsored by the NASA Lewis Research Center and the Ohio Aerospace Institute (1993); published in the *Whole Earth Review*.

53. Quoted in Khatchadourian, "Doomsday Invention."

54. Bostrom, "Are You Living in a Computer Simulation?," 16.

55. Eric Charles Steinhart, *Your Digital Afterlives: Computational Theories of Life after Death* (New York: Palgrave, 2014), 7.

56. Steinhart, *Your Digital Afterlives*, 131.

57. Steinhart, *Your Digital Afterlives*, 216.

58. Ray Kurzweil, *The Singularity Is Near: When Humans Transcend Biology* (New York: Viking, 2005), 375.

59. Kurzweil, *The Singularity Is Near*, 389.

60. http://singularityu.org/.

61. Ray Kurzweil and Terry Grossman, *Fantastic Voyage: Live Long Enough to Live Forever* (New York: Penguin, 2005), 3.

62. Kurzweil, *The Singularity Is Near*, 371, 323.

63. http://www.grossmanwellness.com/iv-therapies?__hssc
=176124669.52.1465918562877&__hstc=176124669
.32330e83a4034f92c2bf7e4baedbca18.1465918562877.1465918562877
.1465918562877.1&__hsfp=3539773036&hsCtaTracking=dd186c0b
-616c-406e-8b0f-78b9938c93e1%7C4cbb9df0-daec-4c7d
-9094-3e57b07c6300.

64. Khatchadourian, "Doomsday Invention."

65. Kurzweil, *The Singularity Is Near*, 4, 29.

66. Friedrich Nietzsche, *The Gay Science*, trans. Walter Kaufmann (New York: Random House, 1974), 181.

67. Martin Heidegger, "The Question Concerning Technology," in *The Question Concerning Technology and Other Essays*, trans. William Lovitt (New York: Harper and Row, 1977), 27.

68. G. W. F. Hegel, *Hegel's Aesthetics: Lectures on Fine Arts*. Trans. T. M. Knox. (Oxford: Clarendon Press, 1975).

69. It is important to note that others, some of whom were his colleagues in Jena during the decisive decade of the 1790s, disagreed with him. In different ways, Schleiermacher, Schiller,

Hölderlin, and the Schlegel brothers maintained precisely the opposite. Art, they believed, played the role that previously had been reserved for religion.

70. Theodore Adorno, *Aesthetic Theory*, trans C. Lenhardt (New York: Routledge, 1986).

71. G. W. F. Hegel, *Science of Logic*, trans. A. V. Miller (New York: Oxford University Press, 1969), 736, 737, 759.

72. Baudrillard, *Ecstasy of Communication*, 130.

73. See Michel Serres's important *The Parasite* (Minneapolis: University of Minnesota Press, 2007). In French, *"le parasite"* means, among other things, interference or static.

74. Hegel, *Science of Logic*, 766.

75. Jacques Derrida, *The Truth in Painting*, trans. Geoff Bennington and Ian McLeod (Chicago: University of Chicago Press, 1987), 73, 35, 75.

76. Immanuel Kant, *Critique of Pure Reason*, trans. Norman Kemp Smith (New York: St. Martin's Press, 1965), 144.

77. Kant, *Critique of Pure Reason*, 181.

78. Dieter Henrich, *Between Kant and Hegel: Lectures on German Idealism*, trans. David Pacini (Cambridge, MA: Harvard University Press, 2003), 250, 264. Henrich offers the best analysis of this period of intellectual history. He correctly argues that the key to Hegel's entire system is his analysis of identity and difference in book 2 of the *Science of Logic*.

79. Henrich, *Between Kant and Hegel*, 255.

80. Kant, *Critique of Judgment*, quoted in Andrew Bowie, *Aesthetics and Subjectivity: from Kant to Nietzsche* (New York: Manchester University Press, 1990), 29.

81. Kant, *Critique of Pure Reason*, 183.

82. Eric Kandel, *The Age of Insight: The Quest to Understand the Unconscious in Art, Mind, and Brain—From Vienna 1900 to the Present* (New York: Random House, 2012), 444.

83. Jack Kerouac, *Dharma Bums* (New York: Penguin, 1976).

84. Annie Dillard, *Teaching a Stone to Talk* (New York: Harper, 2008), 113.

85. Derrida, *Truth in Painting*, 140–41.

86. See Mark C. Taylor, "The Financialization of Art," in *Refiguring the Spiritual: Beuys, Barney, Turrell, Goldsworthy* (New York: Columbia University Press, 2012). Figure 2 here is a plastic heart with a mouse skeleton inside. The reference is to Jeff Koons's "Hanging Heart" and Mickey Mouse sculptures.

87. Antonio Damasio, *Descartes' Error: Emotion, Reason, and the Human Brain* (New York: Penguin Books, 1994), 249–52.

88. Hegel, quoted in Bowie, *Aesthetics and Subjectivity*, 127.

89. Julia Kristeva, *Desire in Language: A Semiotic Approach to Literature and Art*, trans. Leon Roudiez (New York: Columbia University Press, 1980), 136.

90. Sigmund Freud, *The Interpretation of Dreams*, trans. James Strachey (New York: Avon Books, 1965), 143n.

91. Kandel, *Age of Insight*, 305–6.

92. This insight has led to the recent emergence of what has been labeled "affect theory." See, e.g., Brian Massumi, *Politics of Affect* (New York: Polity, 2015); Paul Redding, *The Logic of Affect* (Durham, NC: Duke University Press, 1991); and Melissa Gregg and Greg Seigworth, *The Affect Reader* (Durham, NC: Duke University Press, 2010).

93. Michel Serres, *Five Senses: A Philosophy of Mingled Bodies*, trans. Margaret Sankey and Peter Cowley (New York: Continuum, 2008), 134.

94. Kandel, *Age of Insight*, 369. It is important to note that this insight undercuts Kant's claim that fine art is disinterested. Theodor Adorno underscores the importance of this point. "In the context of Kant's philosophy, the idea of a beautiful object possessing a kind of independence from the sovereign ego must seem like a digression into intelligible worlds. The source from which art antithetically originates, as well as the content of art, are of no concern to Kant, who instead posits something as formal as aesthetic satisfaction as the defining characteristic of art. His aesthetics presents the paradox of a castrated hedonism, of a theory of pleasure without pleasure. This position fails to do justice either to

artistic experience wherein satisfaction is a subordinate moment in a larger whole, or to the material-corporeal interests, i.e. repressed and unsatisfied needs that resonate in their aesthetic negations— the works of art—turning them into something more than empty patterns." Adorno, *Aesthetic Theory*, 16.

95. Antonio Damasio, *The Feeling of What Happens: Body and Emotion in the Making of Consciousness* (New York: Harcourt Brace, 1999), 51–52.

96. Maurice Merleau-Ponty, "Intertwining: The Chasm," *The Visible and the Invisible*, trans. Alfonso Lingis (Evanston, IL: Northwestern University Press, 1968), 131–55; and Maurice Merleau-Ponty, *Phenomenology of Perception*, trans. C. Smith (London: Routledge and Kegan Paul, 1978), 149.

97. Merleau-Ponty, *The Visible and the Invisible*, 147, 137.

98. Merleau-Ponty, *The Visible and the Invisible*, 56, 148, 73.

99. Merleau-Ponty, *The Visible and the Invisible*, 58.

100. Jean-Luc Nancy and Philippe Lacoue-Labarthe, *The Literary Absolute: The Theory of Literature in German Romanticism*, trans. Philip Barnard and Cheryl Lester (Albany: State University of New York Press, 1988). Nancy and Lacoue-Labarthe's analysis makes it clear that the deconstructive interpretation of writing (*écriture*) can be traced to the account of poésie and literature developed by the Romantics.

101. Friedrich Schlegel, *Philosophical Fragments*, trans. Peter Firchow (Minneapolis: University of Minnesota Press, 1991), no. 115.

102. Rodolphe Gasché, "Foreword: Ideality in Fragmentation," in Schlegel, *Philosophical Fragments*, xx.

103. Schlegel, *Philosophical Fragments*, no. 116.

104. Kandel, *Age of Insight*, 393.

ABOVE US, ONLY SKY

Mary-Jane Rubenstein[1]

Imagine all the people living life in peace.

JOHN LENNON, "Imagine"

Today, the same spirit beckons us to begin new journeys of exploration and discovery, to lift our eyes all the way up to the heavens, and once again imagine the possibilities waiting in those big, beautiful stars if we dare to dream big.

DONALD TRUMP, 2017

"I CHOOSE TO GO TO THE MOON!"

The revelation wasn't as well-produced as one might expect. With an unreliable sound system, poorly timed slides, and either a wonky teleprompter or a profound deficiency in extemporaneous speaking, the omnipresent technoprophet Elon Musk held a late-autumn press conference to introduce the man who had just bought every seat aboard his speculative lunar orbiter, the BFR (or "Big F*ing Rocket").[2] In other contexts, Musk is known as the CEO and chief architect of Tesla, Inc., cofounder of PayPal, and cofounder of Neuralink, which seeks to accelerate the transhuman revolution through implantable brain-computer interfaces (BCIs). But in this setting, Musk was

speaking as founder and CEO of the private aerospace manufacturer, SpaceX, whose stated mission is to make (trans-)human-
kind "a multi-planet species and true spacefaring civilization"
by opening space travel to civilians.[3]

Having failed to secure government funding through NASA
or the US military, SpaceX turned to the private sector to finance
its research and development. And on September 17, 2018, Musk
stood before a few hundred awkwardly positioned investors,
reporters, and technophiles to provide a stilted update on the
progress of the rocket (he's hoping for a 2023 launch) and the
details of its design (largely inspired by *The Adventures of Tin-
tin*[4]) before summoning onstage "the first private citizen that's
gonna go into deep space."[5] Accompanied by neither musical
flourish nor light display but greeted nonetheless by enthusiastic applause, out bounced the forty-something fashion designer
Yusaku Maezawa who grinned, waved, introduced himself as a
Japanese national, and thanked his audience before announc-
ing, "Finally, I can tell you that *I choose to go to the moon!*"[6]

However updated the circumstances, this particular declaration self-consciously echoed the refrain of an address that
John F. Kennedy delivered at Rice University in 1962. Both com-
mending and commanding the scientific advancement that
might finally propel the United States into outer space, President Kennedy declared, "We choose to go to the moon. We
choose to go to the moon in this decade and do the other things,
not because they are easy, but because they are hard." To be sure,
Kennedy was aware that this reason might seem like very little
reason at all, and he went on to compare his own justification
to that of Everest-explorer George Mallory when asked why he
wanted to climb the mountain that would eventually kill him:
"Because it is there," Mallory replied. Similarly, Kennedy concluded, in a strained metaphoric extension, "space is there, and
we're going to climb it."[7]

Of course, the "there-ness" of space is hardly a sufficient
explanation for America's formidable financial and ideologi-

cal investment therein. And indeed, at less prominent places in his address, Kennedy concedes that the real motivation behind "our" having chosen the moon is American control over the "sea" of space. Just as terrestrial peace has allegedly depended on American dominance of the water and air, paraterrestrial peace will depend on American dominance of outer space. "Space science," Kennedy explains, "like nuclear science and all technology, has no conscience of its own. Whether it will become a force for good or ill depends on man, and only if the United States occupies a position of pre-eminence can we help decide whether this new ocean will be a sea of peace or a new terrifying theater of war." The promise the United States makes to the whole world is peace, harmony, and "the progress of all people," secured by means of its benevolent oversight of otherwise dangerous technological development. "Yet," Kennedy qualifies, "the vows of this nation can only be fulfilled if we in this nation are first, and therefore we intend to be first."[8] Modern ears may catch in this injunction an eerie precursor to the forty-fifth president's "America first" strategy—an imperialist nationalism that may lose its cosmopolitan sheen as the decades wear on, but which can be found even in Kennedy's earliest imperatives to get America off the planet. On October 10, 1960, then-Senator Kennedy explained to voters still reeling three years after Sputnik that "if the Soviets control space they can control earth, as in past centuries the nation that controlled the seas dominated the continents. . . . We cannot run second in this vital race. To insure peace and freedom, we must be the first."[9]

When Yusaku Maezawa channeled the language of JFK's "choosing the moon" in Musk's 2018 press conference, he also renewed the former president's logic of benevolent primacy. After professing a lifelong admiration for American boldness and ingenuity, Maezawa responded to the question he imagined was on everybody's mind: "Many of you may be wondering, *why* do I want to go to the moon? *What* do I want to do there? And most of all, why did I purchase *the entire BFR*? Entire BFR! Very huge!" Because, Maezawa explained, he began to think it would be extremely "valuable" to be *first*—namely, "the first private passenger to go to the moon."[10] Here, then, is a collective imperial dream individualized, "first-ness" conferred not on the "we" of the militarized nation-state but on the "I" of the private speculator able to pay some astronomical sum to achieve it. And in further keeping with Kennedy's vision, Maezawa goes on to imagine the universal harmony his preeminence might ensure: "At the same time [that I thought about the value of being the first], I thought about how I can give back to the world, and how this can contribute to world peace. This is my lifelong dream" [applause].[11]

With the invocation of this dream, Maezawa announces a departure—at least an intended departure—from the American imperial script. Maezawa seeks not to conquer the moon, but to admire it: "With utmost love and respect for the moon, our planet's constant partner"—note the linguistic and affective dissonance with political, military, and technological rhetoric—"I named this project #DearMoon." His "dear" encoding at once an epistolary addressee, a beloved object of affection, and an expensive financial investment, Maezawa's imagined journey aims to secure peace on the earth it escapes. And to catalyze such peace, Maezawa endeavors not to secure aeronautic hegemony but rather to awaken the global imagination. In this spirit, Maezawa offers a further revision of Kennedy's tagline: "I choose to go to the moon—*with artists!*" [cheering, applause].[12]

Over the course of his brief address, Maezawa's artistic vision is more sketched than filled in, marked by unanswered questions and vague, extravagant possibilities. But the idea, it seems, is to instill a global imaginary by means of extraordinary images—to awaken our love of this world through otherworldly perspectives on it. "What if [Jean-Michel] Basquiat had gone into space and had seen the moon up close or saw the earth in full-view? What masterpiece would he have created?"[13] Maezawa's implication is that a bird's (or god's)-eye view of our earth and its "constant partner" might confer upon the artist a kind of superhuman vision—a capacity to see our world as rare, fragile, and most importantly, united. And his assumption is that any work of art conceived from such heights would be a de facto "masterpiece," establishing the supremacy of the artist not only over merely terrestrial artists but over the object itself: the artist who can see the earth from beyond earth becomes, in a sense, its master.[14]

Having collided again with mastery, we find ourselves closer than we might have imagined to the old Cold War promise of peace secured through sovereignty—rendered this time in an aggressively countercultural key. This time, the masters will not be the political, military, and scientific elite, but rather the pop-cultural elite. "Jean-Michel Basquiat," intones Maezawa. "Andy Warhol. Pablo Picasso. John Lennon. Michael Jackson. Coco Chanel."[15] The designer gives no principle of selection behind his list of artists, but what they all share—apart from their being nearly all male and unexceptionally dead—is a prophetic-revolutionary aspiration: an attempt to imagine the world otherwise and build it up in brick, canvas, dance, vinyl, fabric, and song. What they also all share is an afterlife of mass production, which has drawn each of them—either willingly or in spite of themselves—into the torrential circulations of consumer capital, assimilating their otherworldly visions into the relentless mechanisms of the world as it is.

In the case of Basquiat—the Haitian–Puerto Rican New York graffiti artist turned neo-expressionist who constantly sought new ways to assail colonialism, capitalism, and American antiblackness—Maezawa arguably accelerated his assimilation in May 2017 when he bought the artist's *Untitled* (1982) for $110.5 million. As critic Ben Davis explains in an exhibition notice, "Basquiat's centering figure here is a human head, boiled down to a caricatured symbol of itself. It's squashed and flattened, the back of the skull bulging out to the side. You could say that, with its gaping mouth and popping eyes, it becomes a depiction of how painful it is to be reduced to a symbol."[16] The palate is vibrant, even electric; the strokes are bold and untidy; the genre a mash-up of street art and European "masters"; and the effect an inescapable implication of the viewer in the absurd, violent order of things.

It is therefore painfully ironic that Maezawa's immense admiration of the painting led him to pay highest price ever commanded by a piece of art made in the United States, after "winning" an online Sotheby's auction on his smartphone. Here too channeling JFK's channeling of George Mallory, Maezawa said in an interview following the sale that he bought the painting because he "decided to go for it."[17] Characteristically, there is magnanimity in this gesture of tautological bravado; in addition to buying the Basquiat because it was *there*, Maezawa explained that this acquisition would allow people around the world to encounter this tremendous painting for themselves: "I want to share that experience with as many people as possible."[18] And true to his word, Maezawa is lending the painting to art institutions until it finds its permanent home at a museum he intends to build in Chiba, Japan, to house the collection he has amassed from the proceeds of his retail clothing business.[19] As with his lunar journey, however, Maezawa's vision of art-for-all is mediated at every turn by self-promotion and massive expenditure. Meanwhile, the critical intervention of the artwork itself—the unequivocal communication of fear, immense pain, and anti-black racism in Basquiat's *Untitled* (1982)—is swept right back into the economics of racist exploitation it sought to expose.

"As you can see," said Maezawa at the SpaceX press conference, opening the lapels of his blazer, "I am wearing a Comme des Garçons t-shirt, featuring Jean-Michel Basquiat." Basquiat, he explained, was the artist he wanted above all to take with him on Musk's rocket. Unfortunately, "he passed away already," along with each of Maezawa's other heroes. Who, then, will paint, style, film, and sing the world from outer space? Maezawa hasn't yet decided. Their only qualifications, it seems, will be popularity and disciplinary diversity: "top artists," he promises,

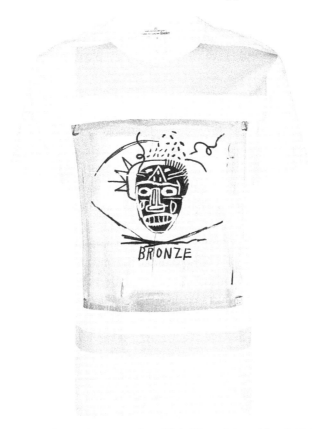

FIGURE 2.1. *Comme des garçons*, Jean-Michel Basquiat graphic print t-shirt, $150.00.

"who will represent our planet from various fields, including painters, sculptors, photographers, musicians, film directors, fashion designers, architects, etc."[20] When he finds them, their charge will be to gaze upon "the moon up close, the earth in full-view" and then to create, upon returning to earth, "works that reflect this experience." And ultimately Maezawa's expectation is that "these masterpieces"—there's that word again—"will inspire the dreamer within all of us."

Throughout Maezawa's address and the ensuing question-and-answer period, it remains frustratingly unclear what exactly such works might inspire "us" to dream, or, indeed, how such dreaming might contribute to the broader and even hazier vision of "world peace." But the appeal to dreamwork calls to mind the aesthetic mappings of Friedrich Nietzsche, who in *The Birth of Tragedy* proposes dreaming as the mode of "the Apolline" (whereas intoxication is the mode of the Dionysiac).[21] Apollo, god of the sun, who circles the earth and sees it entire, is of course the namesake of the NASA missions that eventually landed US astronauts on the moon. Apollo's vision is one of mastery, regulation, totality, and control—which again stands in dazzling tension with the Dionysiac unruliness of the artists Maezawa tends to revere. Indeed, an Apollonian tone dominates the #DearMoon promotional video that ends his formal presentation. Opening with light-skinned earthly children gazing up at the stars, the video builds to a simulation of the earth "rising" over the moon while a blonde, white, female-appearing person stares at it from a minimalist spacecraft, the earth reflected in the blue iris of her eye. Above all, it is the image of the earth, these visuals suggest, that will spur the imagination of the artist: "What will they feel," asks a deep-voiced movie-trailer narrator, "when they . . . see the earth in full-view? And what will they *create*? Their works will certainly become a legacy for humankind. An awe-inspiring, global, universal art project is about to begin. Dear—*moon*."[22]

One early questioner, a reporter from a Japanese newspaper, tested the contours of this cosmopolitanism by asking why Musk chose a Japanese citizen for his inaugural flight to the moon. "*He* chose *us*," Musk interrupted, before ceding the floor to the questioner again. "Oh, okay," the reporter replied. "But . . . what's your message behind the first passenger [being] a Japanese citizen, instead of [a] U.S. citizen, or the rest of the world?" Thinking perhaps of the postwar collaboration between former enemies—of the template it might provide for international or postnational reconciliation—or perhaps even asking Musk to concede that such lunar journeys would be limited at least for a while to the absurdly wealthy inhabitants of overde-veloped nations like Japan and the United States, the reporter asked, "What's your message to the rest of the world through this announcement?"

Musk was flummoxed. Maezawa's nationality had abso-lutely nothing to do with it. "Well, um, he, um, is the, I think, the bravest person and the most willing to do so, and he was—the best adventurer, I think [Maezawa nods energetically]. He stepped forward to do it. . . . We are honored that he would choose us. Aaand," Musk finally added, "and because he is pay-ing a lot of money—we're not disclosing the amount—but he is paying a lot of money. . . ." Considering the financial and even bodily risk of such an adventure, Musk concluded, "you have to be a very brave person to do that."[23] There is, in other words, no message at all. No internationalist intention; just an exchange between private individuals, whose courage can be measured in financial output. Over the course of the press conference, then, Maezawa's Japaneseness, along with Musk's South-Africanness, both disappear into the false universal of American-style capi-talism and cowboy-frontier frenzy.

This eclipse of the political stands at odds not only with the commitments of Maezawa's artistic heroes but also with his stated goal of "world peace," whose contours at least one member of the audience kept trying to envision. "How did you react," asked a reporter from a major American news network, "when you learned that Maezawa wanted to bring *artists* to the moon?" Here, too, Musk seemed completely unprepared, stalling and shifting on his feet before rattling off details about rocket safety, food supplies, and the immense capacity of his ab-solutely gargantuan rocket. Later, in response to another ques-tion, Maezawa offered a lone clarification: "art," he said, "makes people smile, brings people together."[24] So the most this press conference tells us about the Apollonian dreamwork of #Dear-Moon is that it seeks to inspire a calm sort of pleasure, and that it has something to do with *unity*—whatever that means.

What I'd like to suggest in this brief undertaking is that, far from being radical, revolutionary, or even new, this dream of global unity through Apollonian vision—of a collective imagination ignited by extraterrestrial images—is a tragic reanimation of an old imperial fantasy. Rooted in the Constantinian era but flowering in the Age of Exploration, the effort to represent the whole earth visually is inextricably bound to the imperial effort to own and control it. As Denis Cosgrove argues, the entirety of European modernity operates by means of "simultaneously gazing upon the world and mastering it," obsessed as this era is with mapping, charting, traveling, and "settling."[25] Launched by the Doctrine of Discovery, propelled by Manifest Destiny, projected back across the seas in the wars of the twentieth century, and blessed in all these adventures by a God (re-)made in its image, the United States becomes the terrestrial consummation of this colonial collusion between image and imagination. Finally, the Christianized militarism or militarized Christianity that weaves itself throughout US history extends itself along a brand-new axis in the humanitarian nationalism of the Apollo missions—specifically, in NASA's quest to make America *first* "for the benefit of all mankind."[26]

Named theologically and conducted evangelically, the Apollo "missions" ended up producing the two "most-disseminated photographs in history"[27]: *Earthrise* (1968)—in which our planet appears to ascend, partially shaded, above the foregrounded surface of the moon—and *AS17-148-2272* (1972), informally titled *Blue Marble*, which captures the earth as a blue, white, green, and brown sphere centered on the southern cone of Africa, capped in snow and ice, and suspended in what Buckminster Fuller called "a quality of blackness never before experienced."[28]

The moment they were snapped, these images were credited with having changed forever "our" perspective on humanity and the planet we share.[29] They immediately prompted calls for environmental stewardship and an end to war. At the same time, these images had been enabled materially by the technological

FIGURE 2.2. *Earthrise*, 1968. Photo credit: NASA.

ravaging of the earth and military one-upsmanship they were suddenly called upon to contest. And so even as they conveyed the fragility, uniqueness, and unity of the earth, they also communicated its smallness, triviality, and susceptibility to total domination in the hands of whoever manages to see the whole thing from beyond it.[30]

Cosgrove has called these competing visions of the planet "whole-earth" and "one-world," the former connoting naturalism and environmental advocacy while the latter connotes the neoliberal, globalized order to which the Apollo era also gave rise.[31] The former term gets its name from Stewart Brand's back-to-the-land *Whole Earth Catalog* whose first issue, printed in the fall of 1968, bore a composite cover image of the earth taken by the ATS-3 satellite, a photograph Brand had petitioned NASA to release so that it might inspire works of ecological and social justice. As Andrew Kirk retells it, "Brand felt sure that

FIGURE 2.3. *AS17-148-2272*, 1972, also known as *Blue Marble*. Photo credit: NASA.

if people could view their planet from space, it would change 'everything.'"[32] By contrast, the latter term connotes neoliberal economics, the corporate victory over nation-states, and the capitulation of everything that *is* to market forces. Cosgrove explains the distinction thus: "One-world is a geopolitical conception coeval with the European and Christian sense of *imperium*. . . . Whole-earth is, by contrast, an environmentalist conception that appeals to the organic and spiritual unity of terrestrial life."[33] Think fossil fuels versus compost collectives; media conglomerates versus transcendental meditation; mushroom cloud versus mushroom foragers.

Despite their obvious dissimilarities—tonally, interpersonally, ethically—it is important to note that both of these visions insist on seeing the planet as what Plato's *Timaeus* calls "a single, complete whole."[34] In each framework, the multiplicity of terrestrial life can (and ought) ultimately to be assembled into a frictionless unity, whether mechanically or organically connected. Moreover, the "organic" option is hopelessly technological, having been enabled by the technomilitary apparatus that allows us to see the "whole earth" from space in the first place (or, indeed, to get the word out online about our neighborhood farmers' markets, print the reusable bags, and pay the local vendors with our watches and phones). Building on Cosgrove's analysis, Benjamin Lazier has therefore asked whether the two visions might be less "competing" than they are "complicit": could it be, he asks, "that Whole Earth and mushroom cloud, Gaia and globalization, are just two sides of a coin?"[35] What if the drive to "save" the earth by learning to see it entire is just a humanistically palatable cover for the imperial fantasies that demand, produce, and realize themselves by means of such holistic pictures? What sorts of aerocolonial operations are currently conditioning the possibility of Maezawa's clearly earnest imaginings of a "world peace" brought about by images of the earth?

"THE EARTH IN FULL-VIEW"
IMAGINE THERE'S NO HEAVEN

"If John Lennon could have seen the curvature of the earth from space," asks Maezawa, "what kind of songs would he have written?" Of course, depending on what "seeing" means, one might answer that John Lennon *did* see the earth from space. He had access not only to the composite satellite image reproduced on the *Whole Earth Catalog* and numerous photos taken by the Apollo missions but also to video footage of an (admittedly grainy) "lunar sunrise" through the live telecast of the Apollo 8 mission on Christmas Eve, 1968. Viewed by an estimated billion

FIGURE 2.4. *The Whole Earth Catalog*, volume 1 (Fall 1968).

other earthlings,[36] this was the event that produced the photograph *Earthrise*.[37] Of course, Lennon was clearly not a *passenger*
on these journeys to the moon. But he would have been able to
see—again, along with anyone else at the time who had access
to television, newspapers, and magazines—"the moon up close,
the earth in full-view" by means of these omnipresent images.
And Lennon's clearest musical expression of the antiwar, social

FIGURE 2.5. AT&T logo, 2019.

justice, and environmentalist movements that these pictures helped fuel—along with the Cold War politics that generated them in the first place—was "Imagine," a song that he once designated as "virtually the *Communist Manifesto*, even though I'm not particularly a Communist and I do not belong to any movement."[38]

Written in 1971 with Yoko Ono, "Imagine" envisions the world from Apollonian heights.[39] The first verse empties out "heaven" and "hell," replacing them with the human gaze that now operates, scientifically and artistically, from their ceded terrain. The verse goes on, much like whole-earth photography, to dissolve past and future into the pseudo-eternal stillness of "living for today." Having carved out an atemporal atopia, the song then proceeds to imagine the eventual dissolution of human divisions and even distinctions—specifically, of nation, war, religion, class, and gender. The resulting "brotherhood of man"—not even identifiable as "communist," as Lennon later clarified—becomes a monistic "all," a unified, motionless, colorless "people / Living life in peace." Finally, in keeping with its Apollonian operation, the chorus acknowledges and even celebrates its vision as a *dream*: the sort that might ravish others into its agreement so that the possible becomes actual, "and the world will live as one."

For Nietzsche, the Apollonian dream is just that—a comforting "illusion" covering up the mess of lived experience.[40] In the case of "Imagine," the sleight-of-hand does not, of course, obscure the obvious disasters of two world wars, McCarthyism, Korea, Vietnam, the Chicago Riots, the Paris Riots, or the assassinations of Malcolm X, Martin Luther King, John F. Kennedy, Robert Kennedy, and even Lennon himself. One might even say that each of these reflects holographically the racist violence that became the clear, escalating object of Ono's and Lennon's protest. These events—or else their fractal reduplications in the decades that have followed—need to sit somewhere close to the auditor's surface for the song to register at all. Rather, what the song obscures is the violence that "unity" itself can enact: the complicity, for example, of "color-blindness" in racism, of "secularism" in Islamophobia and anti-Semitism, or indeed of the whole-earth vision in the tentacular reach of global capital.

One would only need to scan the array of cheap "Imagine" merchandise available online—some of it silk-screened by self-employed artisans but most of it made in sweatshops under excruciating conditions—to appreciate consumerism's capacity to dull the edges of its sharpest critiques. Ideologically, however, we can see the sinister side of Ono-Lennon's indistinct "Oneness" at work in the 2011 Twitterstorm over CeeLo Green's torchy New Year's Eve performance of "Imagine" in Times Square. "Nothing to kill or die for," sang the child of two Baptist ministers, "if all religion is true."[41] Incensed commentators (almost none of whom mentioned Ono) called the revision a complete betrayal of Lennon and his message. One called out the hypocrisy of singing "Imagine" "in a fur coat and expensive jewelry," while changing the lyrics "to be pro-religion."[42] As far as "the internet" was concerned, CeeLo's action was ignorant at best and abusive at worst, the atheist equivalent of a sacrilege. And, as such, it provoked levels of outrage frankly indistinguishable from religious offense.

"Yo I meant no disrespect by changing the lyric guys!" CeeLo tweeted back. "I was trying to say a world where u could believe what u wanted that's all."[43] But the Lennonites were unconvinced by CeeLo's elision of the difference between unity and difference (which is to say, between homogeneity and multiplicity, or "no religion" and "all religion[s]"), so he deleted his clarification a few hours after posting it. The consensus seemed to be, as the *Guardian*'s Sean Michaels insisted a few days later, that "Lennon's original lyrics *don't praise pluralism* or interchangeable religious truths—they damn them."[44] And indeed, "damning pluralism" is precisely the danger of the vision of unity that both conditions and emerges renewed from the Apollo missions. The only way to see the earth as an undivided whole is to wipe away most of the stuff that makes it the place we live. And so it is possible, Hannah Arendt suggests, that the modern-secular age, "which began with a turning-away . . . from a god who was the Father of men in heaven, [might] end with an even more fateful repudiation of an Earth who was the Mother of all living creatures under the sky."[45]

EVERYBODY WANTS TO RULE THE WORLD

The National Aeronautics and Space Administration (NASA) was established in 1958, one year after the two Sputnik launches that humiliated US nationalists.[46] Speaking as Senate majority leader, Lyndon Johnson led the charge to create such an institution by tying the conquest of space into the history of the conquest of the globe. "The Roman Empire controlled the world because it could build roads," he explained. "Later—when men moved to the sea—the British Empire was dominant because it had ships. In our age we were powerful because we had airplanes. Now the Communists have established a foothold in outer space."[47] The breakdown of parallelism in Johnson's final sentence makes the message as clear as it is unspoken: if the United States wants to rule the world, it is going to have to build rockets that can extend its terrain extraterrestrially—and it's going to have to do so faster and better than anyone else.

Johnson's unmitigated imperialism is notably tempered in the resulting National Aeronautics and Space Act (April 1958), which opens, "The Congress hereby declares that it is the policy of the United States that activities in space should be devoted to peaceful purposes for the benefit of all mankind." To be sure, the very next sentence qualifies significantly the act's commitment to "all mankind" by charging NASA with securing "the general welfare and security of the United States," but nowhere is Johnson's hegemonic quest mentioned explicitly. Rather, the nascent "civilian agency" is directed toward "the preservation of the role of the United States as a leader"—*a* leader, not *the* leader—"in aeronautical and space science and technology and in the application thereof to the conduct of peaceful activities within and outside the atmosphere."[48] As we have already seen, it is with JFK's presidential campaign two years later that this legislation's vision of peace and cooperation finds integration with Johnson's insistence on American primacy. To return to that text, we find Kennedy opening with an unacknowledged citation of Johnson: "If the Soviets control space they can control earth," he writes, "as in past centuries the nation that controlled the seas dominated the continents." Immediately, however, he softens the hegemonic appeal: "This does not mean that the United States desires more rights in space than any other nation," he cautions, before bringing this genteel concession to a nationalist finish: "But we cannot run second in this vital race. To insure peace and freedom, we must be first."[49]

As promised, Kennedy carried this commitment into his presidency. Just months after taking office—in the wake of the twin accomplishments of the Soviet Yuri Gagarin's orbiting the earth (April 12, 1961) and the American Alan Shepard's achieving suborbital travel (May 5, 1961)—Kennedy returned to the crucial terrain of "space" before a joint session of Congress. "If we are to win the battle that is now going on around the world between freedom and tyranny," he declared, thinking above all of the escalating situation in Vietnam, "it is time . . . for this nation to take a clearly leading role in space achievement, which in many ways may hold the key to our future on earth." Considering the Soviets' "many months of leadtime," Kennedy endeavored to speed up American progress with a deadline. Requesting the appropriations to fund such a project, he announced, "I believe that this nation should commit itself to achieving the goal, before this decade is out, of landing a man on the moon and returning him safely to the earth."[50] And although he would not be there to see it, in the wake of the April 1967 crash of the Soviet Soyuz 1 rocket and the December 1968 lunar orbit of Apollo 8, Kennedy's injunction was finally carried out on July 20, 1969, when the Apollo 11 mission landed Neil Armstrong and Buzz Aldrin on the surface of the moon before delivering them four days later into Hawaiian waters.

It is no accident that NASA chose for its splashdown the site of America's first full-fledged colonial appropriation.[51] As Johnson and Kennedy both insisted, the struggle to "control space" was indeed a new chapter in the long Western endeavor to "control the earth," so why not stage the victory in newly possessed waters? Indeed, just as the intra-European race to "settle" Africa, the Americas, and South Asia had secured national hegemony by extending those nations outward, the space race promises to confer earthly control upon the nation that extends itself upward. As Donald Trump explained in his 2020 creation of the "Space Force" as a new branch of the US military, "Space is the world's new war-fighting domain. Among grave threats to our national security, American superiority in space is absolutely vital. And we're leading, but we're not leading by enough, and very shortly we'll be leading by a lot."[52] "Space," in other words, is a means toward earthly sovereignty. But it is also an end in itself: a vast, perhaps infinite,[53] three-dimensional "frontier" filled with lands that humans might use and inhabit, expanding the terrain of the earth itself. In short, the Apollo missions that laid the groundwork for today's Space Force assumed the mantle of the long Western colonial adventure, simultaneously securing US dominion over earth and sky.

In *The Myth of the Eternal Return*, Mircea Eliade theorizes any nation's appropriation of foreign lands as a "cosmogonic act," which is to say a repetition of that nation's creation story. The conquerors act like their gods, turning the "chaos" of the discovered land into an ordered cosmos. This repetition is enacted above all by ritual; as Eliade explains, "When possession is taken of a territory—that is, when its exploitation begins—rites are performed that symbolically repeat the act of Creation: the uncultivated zone is first 'cosmicized,' then inhabited."[54] Now as with much of the work of the social sciences' founding fathers (Durkheim, Geertz, Freud), Eliade's analysis might illuminate more clearly the culture that produced it than the non-Western societies he claims more often to be interpreting. Whether or not his analysis tells us anything helpful about ancient India, Egypt, Babylon, China, Iran, or Turkey; twentieth-century Australia, Madagascar, Polynesia, Native America, or South Africa; "every Oriental city," or indeed the interchangeability of any of these regions with most of the others, it certainly tells us a great deal about the Western imperial project that *produced* this totalizing knowledge. The West *did*—and does—tend to reenact its creation story ritualistically when it claims new territory. For example, as Patricia Seed has shown, "colonial rule over the New World was initiated through largely ceremonial practices—planting crosses, standards, banners, and coats of arms—marching in processions, picking up dirt, measuring the stars, drawing maps, speaking certain words, or remaining

silent."⁵⁵ Such ceremonies operate analogically to divinize the
colonizer: just as God is god of the creation he delivers from
chaos, so does the colonizer become god over the colonized land
and its inhabitants, turning the whole alleged mess into an ordered world.

The Apollo mission produced two high-profile cosmogonic
acts that immediately implanted themselves within American and even global audiovisual memory. The first took place
during the 1968 lunar orbit of Apollo 8. Calculated to coincide
with Christmas Eve, when a majority of Americans would be
home with their extended families awaiting something mirac-
ulous, this journey around the moon introduced earthlings to
various mountains, craters, and cracks before culminating in
the gradual appearance of the earth over its dusty surface: a vision of *terra cognita* from this new *terra incognita* that made all
of it look strange. "I hope that all of you back on earth can see
what we mean when we say it's a rather foreboding horizon—a
rather dark and, uh, unappetizing place." A place that left one
longing for a little bit of light: "We are now approaching, uh,
lunar sunrise," astronaut Bill Anders said,

> and for all the people back on earth, the crew of Apollo 8 has a
> message that we would like to send to you: "In the beginning,
> God created the heaven and the earth. And the earth was with-
> out form, and void, and darkness was upon the face of the deep.
> And the spirit of God moved upon the face of the waters. And God
> said, 'Let there be light,' and there was light."⁵⁶

Taking turns, the three astronauts intoned the first ten verses of
Genesis, right through the separation of the light from the darkness, the waters from the waters, and the land from the seas:
"and God saw that it was good" (Genesis 1:10).

As it turns out, the choice of this particular reading was almost as chaotic as the lunar terrain it was called upon to cos-
micize. Before the launch, NASA's chief public affairs officer

Julian Scheer had informed astronaut Frank Borman that the rocket was scheduled to circle the moon on Christmas Eve. "We figure more people will be listening to your voice than that of any man in history," said Scheer. "So we want you to say something appropriate." As Christopher Potter narrates the ensuing scramble, Borman first asked a publicist, "Simon Bourgin, Science Policy Officer at the US Information Agency for advice. [Bourgin] in turn asked a journalist, Joe Laitin; a Christian who searched the New Testament without finding anything that struck him as suitable. [Laitin] asked his wife, and she said, 'Why don't you begin at the beginning.'"[57] And in the beginning—at least for a secular-Christian America—was Genesis 1.

As Anders, Borman, and Lovell took turns reading the Revised Standard Version of the text, which Borman had photocopied onto fireproof paper, these haphazard conditions of ritual assemblage disappeared behind the calm, reverential tone of the astronauts' voices. The men were both humbled and in charge, both praising their God and assuming his role in the universe. After all, the text they intoned claims the "image" of God (three times) for humanity—at least for those humans within the cosmogonic lineage of Genesis—granting them "dominion . . . over every living thing that moves upon the earth."[58] Staged at the beginning of the Christian liturgical year, the performative reading of Apollo 8 therefore both asserts and extends the American nation's divine inheritance. Granted in Genesis 1, Christianized in the Great Commission,[59] and mobilized during the Age of Exploration, (male, Christian) human dominion is projected in the Apollo missions onto the nonliving, nonearthly surface of the moon—even out, as we shall see, into the endless terrain of deep space.

NASA's second cosmogonic act was, of course, Apollo 11's ceremonial planting of an American flag on the moon. Tying the nation more explicitly to its colonial creation story than to the Genesis narrative (with which it is nonetheless entangled), the flag's erection recapitulated the land claims that progressively assembled the United States out of stolen terrain.[60] Granted, the flag could not quite mark the moon as legal property. As the United Nations' 1967 Outer Space Treaty insists, "outer space is not subject to national appropriation by claims of sovereignty."[61] Symbolically, however, the "stars and stripes" marked the moon in which they stood as fundamentally American terrain. To return to Eliade, the flag serves in colonial contexts as an *axis mundi*: a "sacred pole" the god or hero uses to transform an "uninhabitable" land "into a world" by connecting the regions of heaven, earth, and underworld.[62] When Aldrin and Armstrong planted the flag on the moon, they arguably abolished these distinctions altogether (*imagine there's no heaven*), lifting the territory of the earth up (or down) into a zone that, in almost any other mythological context, would constitute a different ontological plane altogether. As in the reading of Genesis 1, then, the ceremonial planting of an American flag on the moon both repeats and extends the mythic creation of cosmos out of chaos, bringing order even to the undifferentiated, otherworldly landscape of the moon.

"For the pole to be broken denotes catastrophe," writes Eliade; "it is like 'the end of the world,' reversion to chaos."[63] Aldrin and Armstrong seem to have intuited some of the dangers of ritual failure, weaving a metal rod into the fabric of the flag ahead of time so that it would appear to "wave" in the airless "wind." They hadn't, however, anticipated the recalcitrance of the lunar surface. "Armstrong broke into a sweat as he struggled to push the flagpole into the ground," writes Potter. "There was nothing between dust and solid rock."[64] Over the course of nearly three-and-a-half minutes, the footage shows the two men futzing over the flag—rearranging its position, manipulating its fabric, and even trying to kick some dust into a little mound to hold the sacred pole in place, beach-vacation style.[65] Meanwhile, Michael Collins orbited the surface in the command module NASA had named *Columbia* to mark the analogous voyages of 1968 and 1492. Alone in space, he called home.

"*Columbia*," comes the reassuring voice over the line, "this is Houston, reading you loud and clear." Collins provided an update: "I believe they're setting up the flag now." Houston seemed bemused. Of course they were setting up the flag. The whole world could see it, except for one of the guys who was actually there. "I guess you're about the only person around who doesn't have TV coverage of the scene," said Houston. "That's alright," Collins replied from his lonely circles, "I don't mind a bit. [Pause.] How is the quality of the TV?"

> "Oh, it's beautiful, Mike; it really is."
> "Aw, geez, that's great . . . is the lighting halfway decent?"
> "Yes, indeed; they've got the flag up now. You can see the stars and stripes on the lunar surface."
> "Beautiful; just beautiful."[66]

Having done everything they could think of to secure the flag, Aldrin and Armstrong bounce-walked away, hoping to the emptied heavens it would stay in place. The moment their lunar module blasted off to rejoin the *Columbia*, the flag fell over,[67] but that was okay. They'd gotten the *picture*. An early instance of "doing it for the 'gram," Collins's exchange with Houston is testimony to the importance of the picture as such: it didn't matter that he couldn't see the event in person as long as the TV quality was okay, as long as the lighting was "halfway decent." The very fact of there *being* a picture to see prompted Collins to call it "beautiful" (twice), even without having seen it. From this ritual-colonial perspective, then, all that really matters is the fact of the image—the there-ness of the now infinitely replicable picture of two American heroes conquering the lunar chaos with their *axis mundi*.

As proof of the imperial importance of the image, one might cite the recent online kerfuffle over Damien Chazelle's 2018 film, *First Man*, starring Ryan Gosling. The film stages a mythic reenactment of the 1969 lunar landing but leaves out the specific scene of Aldrin's and Armstrong's flag-planting. Responding to the ensuing bafflement and criticism, Gosling defended Chazelle's directorial decision, saying the moonwalk had been a "human achievement" rather than a specifically American achievement, "transcend[ing] countries and borders." This, Gosling continued, was the way "Neil" understood himself— not as an "American hero," but as resting on the shoulders of "the 400,000 people" of countless nationalities "who made the mission possible."[68] Of course, Gosling conceded, "I'm Canadian, so might have a cognitive bias."[69]

Florida Senator Marco Rubio wasn't buying it. "This is total lunacy," he tweeted in response. "The American people paid for that mission, on rockets built by Americans, with American technology & carrying American astronauts. It wasn't a UN mission." The response to Rubio's correction was overwhelmingly critical, ridiculing the senator for his unabashed jingoism and his misdirected anger. "Glad you're feeling outraged about this," tweeted one respondent, "and not, say, the several recent mass shootings in your state."[70] In a dramatic plot reversal, however, Buzz Aldrin himself weighed in a few days later, posting two pictures of the flag-planting, marked by a series of nationalist hashtags.[71] Although he did not mention the film specifically, the message was clear: the images should have been there. Here they were again, circulated once more with feeling so the whole world would know this was an American mission. And the internet fell silent. No one would dare contradict Buzz.

"OH MY GOD! LOOK AT THAT PICTURE OVER THERE!"

Visually speaking, the most enduring inheritance of the Apollo missions is that modest pair of endlessly circulated photographs: *Earthrise* (Apollo 8; 1968) and *AS17-148-2272*, or *Blue Marble* (Apollo 17; 1972). The first was caught as the Apollo 8 crew first saw the earth peeking out from behind the moon. "Oh my God!" Frank Borman reportedly cried. "Look at that

Buzz Aldrin ✅
@TheRealBuzz

#proudtobeanAmerican #freedom #honor #onenation #Apollo11
#July1969 #roadtoApollo50

♡ 46K   11:43 PM - Sep 2, 2018   ⓘ

💬 18.5K people are talking about this   ＞

FIGURE 2.6. Buzz Aldrin Twitter post, September 2, 2018.

picture over there! Here's the earth coming up. Wow, is that
pretty!"[72] The resulting image (fig. 2.7), which usually gets ro-
tated 90 degrees in reproduction so the earth tops the moon (see
fig. 2.2), shows our planet emerging sideways, still shaded by
its "constant partner." The moon in this image is a drab, gray
foreground that forces the eye to fixate on the brilliant blues,
browns, and whites of earth.

"Look at that picture," Borman exclaimed, moments before
either he or Anders grabbed the camera and pushed the shutter
release.[73] As Kelly Oliver has argued, Borman's effusion demonstrates that "the Earth had become a *picture* even before the photo
was taken."[74] She is thinking here of Martin Heidegger, who in
1938 began to argue that "the modern age" is marked above all
by its conception of the world as "picture." "World picture, when
understood essentially," he explains, "does not mean a picture of
the world, but the world conceived and grasped as a picture"—
that is, as contained (or, in Heidegger's language, *enframed*) by

FIGURE 2.7. *Earthrise,* in original orientation. Photo credit: NASA.

the human subject "who represents and sets it forth."[75] All that *is* is now reducible to human representation, manipulation, and control, so that *"the world stands at man's disposal as conquered."*[76] When Borman sees the earth through the circular glass window of the command module (fig. 2.8) and calls it a picture, he is unconsciously encapsulating the whole technomilitary metaphysic that encapsulates the world as such, testifying to those values and practices that have conquered the earth to the point of allowing him to escape it. The earth is "pretty"—Anders went on to compare it to a Christmas tree ornament[77]—a feminized,[78] manageable icon of itself. As Buzz Aldrin would boast half a year later, "the earth was eventually so small I could blot it out of the universe by holding up my thumb."[79]

FIGURE 2.8. The command module from which the crew of Apollo 8 saw the "picture" of earth. Photo credit: Smithsonian Institution. Online at https://www.smithsonianmag.com/smithsonian-institution/how-apollo-8-saved -1968-180970991/.

This "tokenization and trivialization" of the earth from space operates in keeping with Cosgrove's one-world paradigm—with its tireless drive to connect, control, and monetize every inch of the earth. This particularly sinister ethos is energetically obscured, however, by the lofty whole-earth rhetoric that immediately followed *Earthrise*'s planetary enframing.

Just one day after Apollo 8's *"Earthrise"* transmission, on Christmas morning of 1968, the *New York Times* published a grandiose front-page "reflection" by the poet and former Librarian of Congress Archibald MacLeish, subtitled "Riders on Earth Together, Brothers in Eternal Cold." In just a few paragraphs, MacLeish summarizes the entirety of "human" existence, dividing it into three major eras. First, there was the European medieval period (the author says nothing of the tens of thousands of years that preceded it, or of the multitudes of human communities to which it doesn't apply), which viewed human beings "as creatures at the center of the universe."[80] Being the favored product of an omnipotent God, "they ruled and killed and conquered as they pleased." Then, once the Copernican Revolution reached its apex in Einstein and Hubble, the earth became just "a small, wet, spinning planet," the center of nothing at all, "at the edge of an inconsiderable galaxy in the immeasurable distances of space." So the vision was reversed but the outcome was the same: having been decentered both cosmically and theologically, "men began to see themselves, not as God-directed actors at the center of a noble drama, but as helpless victims of a senseless farce where . . . millions could be killed in world-wide wars or in blasted cities or in concentration camps." Whether Ptolemaic or Copernican, then, the self-perception of "humanity" has endorsed its untrammeled violence—until now.

"In the last few hours," MacLeish proposes, "the notion may have changed again. For the first time in all of time men have seen the earth—seen it from the depths of space; seen it whole and round and beautiful and small."[81] It seems important at this point, if Scroogelike, to point out that neither the billion Christmas Eve viewers nor the Apollo crew members themselves had actually seen the earth "whole." However disorienting, however astonishing, *Earthrise* renders the earthly sphere a softened, overstuffed semicircle—the planetary equivalent of a waxing (or waning) gibbous moon. Even *Blue Marble*, which offers an unshadowed, "full" view of the earth (see fig. 2.3), still only shows one side of it. In short, until humanity manages to develop four-dimensional vision, *no one* will see the planet "whole" (as Arendt phrased it in the throes of the space race, "the only true Archimedian point would be the absolute void behind the universe"[82]). MacLeish's point, however, is that "we" have suddenly glimpsed the earth from beyond it, and that a few hours in, this unprecedented[83] image was already in the process of transforming "us" existentially. "No longer that preposterous figure at the center, no longer that degraded and degrading victim off at the margins of reality and blind with blood, man may at last become himself."[84] And by "himself," MacLeish means a harmonious, collective humanity that has outgrown both God and war: a single species that can at long last live in peace.

Frank Borman was struck with a similar vision of oneness the moment he saw the earth from space. "When you're finally up at the moon looking back at earth," he told *Newsweek*, "all those differences and nationalistic traits are pretty well going to blend and you're going to get a concept that maybe this is really one world and why the hell can't we learn to live together like decent people."[85] The irony, as Oliver points out, "is that Borman claims that he only accepted the mission because as a military officer he wanted to 'win' the cold war."[86] So either we have discovered another instance of global vision covering over global aggression, or we have a classic conversion story: the American military hero sees his home planet from afar and suddenly renounces both nationalism and war. Although the present author will clearly support the former interpretation, Archibald MacLeish would certainly support the latter. In his view, Apollo's brand-new image of the earth had unveiled a brand-new imagination: an Ono-Lennon-like unity of "brothers who know now that they are truly brothers." Now that humans could see their home from beyond it, they had gained a new vision of themselves as "riders on the earth together, brothers on that bright loveliness in the eternal cold."[87]

Much like "Imagine," however, this Apollonian vision attains the unity it commends by sweeping away differences of race, gender, class, and religion—assembling them all into an undifferentiated, false male universal. In MacLeish's case, the collective is also aggressively Euro-American, bearing a strictly Western history. However post-Copernican, his humanity is moreover recentered, even all-powerful, owing nothing to the gods; making no mention of animal, vegetable, or mineral life; and at its enlightened apotheosis "riding on" the earth as if Earth were a racehorse at best and a motorcycle (or spaceship) at worst. In short, MacLeish's humanitarian imagination is predicated on the eradication of biotic difference on the one hand and the objectification of earth on the other, rendering our planet a lifeless, silent underwriter of Western Man's all-important quest to "become himself."

For Heidegger, the transformation of world into picture is concomitant with the establishment of "man" as the sole measure and ruler of *what is*. "What is," explains Heidegger in his notoriously tortuous prose, "in its entirety, is now taken in such a way that it first is in being and only is in being to the extent that it is set up by man, who represents and sets it forth. . . . [Man] gives the measure and draws up the guidelines for everything that is."[88] "Man" becomes "subject," in other words, by becoming the ultimate arbiter of what is and what's allowed to be. Think, for example, of the light pollution that blots out the stars; the fracking that takes mountains out of existence; or the carefully delineated territory that settler-American "man" has set aside as state and national parks, simultaneously removing indigenous nations to be enframed in reservations. In effect, this "man" recosmicizes the cosmos, saying with his singular god to everything "chaotic"—meaning all that isn't himself—"thus far shall you come, and no farther."[89] According to Heidegger, such technocolonial power over everything that *is* ends up establishing "man" as the most important thing—perhaps even the only thing—in existence. In thus gaining "himself," however, "man" loses the very world he thinks he owns. "I do not know whether you were frightened," said Heidegger in a 1976 interview, "but I at any rate was frightened when I saw pictures coming from the moon to the earth. We don't need any atom bomb [to destroy the earth]. The only thing we have left is purely technological relationships. This is no longer the earth on which man lives."[90] And if it is the case, as Arendt argued in 1958, that "the earth is the very quintessence of the human condition,"[91] then the human who becomes "man" by seeing, mastering, and then losing the earth becomes something other-than-human: a departicularized "brother" at best and pseudodivine master of the universe at worst.

And yet, the photos that terrified Heidegger continue to be screened onto children's books, organic socks, holistic magazines, hemp tote bags—as if they might somehow save us from the forces that produce them. Why is this the case? What is it we *want* from these images of earth? In the late 1960s, it was an end to war; that is, again, an end to the very apparatus through which they emerged. With the dawn of the 1970s, concretized in the first Earth Day and accelerated by the 1972 release of *Blue Marble*, pictures of the earth from space were also increasingly marshaled in support of the nascent environmental movement. Naturalists, biologists, poets, teachers, and activists ventured that the uniqueness and fragility of Earth as revealed in this photo—our lonely planetary suspension in a seemingly infinite darkness—would surely inspire viewers to deal more kindly with their surroundings. Especially considering the seeming insignificance of humanity from extraterrestrial heights (even the autocratic Richard Nixon asked, "What could bring home to us more the limitations of the human scale than the hauntingly beautiful picture[s] of our earth seen from the moon"[92]; after all, as Hans Blumenberg marveled, these photographs bear "no trace of human beings, as if there had never been men, his works, his refuse at all!"[93]), we should probably learn to live in harmony not just with one another but with the more-than-human world, as well. In this spirit, James Lovelock and Lynn Margulis began to argue in the early 1970s that the earth was an autocreative, self-sustaining macro-organism of which humans were just a negligible part.[94] Lovelock's numerous books feature versions of both *Earthrise* and *Blue Marble*, whose joint message seems clear. As Carl Sagan infamously said of the latter, it "underscores our responsibility to deal more kindly with one another, and to cherish the pale blue dot, the only home we've ever known."[95]

Poised as we are on the brink of ecological collapse and caught as humanity remains in the throes of endless war, it goes without saying that these aeronautic images of the earth have not managed to realize the whole-earth dream they allegedly inspire. Either that or, to return to Lazier, the whole-earth imagination is actually "technologically complicit" with the planetary destruction it so energetically opposes.[96] We see such complicity most clearly in what Donna Haraway calls our tragicomic "cosmofaith in technofixes";[97] that is, in those lofty dreams of seeding clouds over growing deserts, hypercooling the ice caps, shooting trash into space, converting large cities to "clean" nuclear power, and so on. But we also see it in the quieter, more suburban conflation of "environmentalism" with middle- and upper-class consumer practices: buying organic produce from Jeff Bezos,[98] throwing the unrecyclable packaging into the recycling bin, shopping for mass-produced items on Etsy, or driving one of Elon Musk's Teslas. Even the "earth system science" that generates our most well-intentioned monitors of climate change and mass extinction is built on the satellite data funded by the military apparatus.[99] At every turn, we find Whole-earth created, managed, and dispensed by One-world, an entanglement that calls into question both the effectiveness and the basic integrity of the former. As James Cone asks, "do we have any reason to believe that the [white, Euro-American, overdeveloped] culture most responsible for the ecological crisis will also provide the . . . resources for earth's liberation?"[100]

The problem, as Oliver has argued, is that the whole-earth and one-world frameworks both reflect "totalizing and globalizing ideologies that promote managing the earth or mastering it."[101] Both of them insist on seeing the world as *one*, a vision available only from an Apollonian perspective. In other words, whether the aim is to rule the world or "save" it, these extraterrestrial images of the earth instill in their viewers a divine imagination. "We are as gods," proclaims the first issue of the *Whole Earth Catalog* (the one covered in that composite satellite image), "and we might as well get good at it."[102] These, to speak frankly, are supposed to be the good guys. But as we have seen from Johnson and Kennedy through Lennon and the

Apollo missions, however benevolent it may seem, the effort to
imagine the world as *one* consistently deifies a particular kind of
humanity—that is, wealthy, white, Euro-American Christian
(but secular!) "man" who, as Sylvia Wynter argues, confuses
himself for "the human" in the first place[103]—while collapsing
the rest of the world into the category of "resources."

The world stands at man's disposal as conquered.

WHY CAN'T WE BE *THERE*?
DREAMING THE FINAL FRONTIER

From the moment Lyndon Johnson argued for the establishment of NASA, America's adventure in space has been explicitly tied to its settler-colonial past. The "sea" of space is likened
in this perennial narrative to the transatlantic crossing and the
astronauts to Columbus, boldly setting sail for *terra incognita*.
Or, in an updated register, space becomes the "wild" terrain of
the North American continent while the astronauts incarnate
Davy Crockett, extending the reach of the "civilized" world
in his immensely butch fashion. Bill Anders gave voice to this
analogy in an interview after Apollo 8: "To me," he explained,
"and I think to many Americans, there has always been a sense
of exploration and a sense of frontier. The Appalachian Trail,
the wide Missouri, Antarctica—they were there, and men came
to conquer them and to benefit from them. Now space was our
frontier."[104] Once again, we might note the way the there-ness of
space mysteriously endorses its possession, here encapsulated
in the analogy to the American West. As we will see, Anders was
not the first to configure space as a frontier, and any Star Trek
fan knows he was certainly not the last. The phrase is ubiquitous
to the point of seeming empty of meaning; indeed, its endless
repetition both enacts and masks the ideological work of "space,
the final frontier."

As Catherine Newell has shown, it was nostalgia for the frontier that drummed up the public support Congress needed to

pass the 1958 National Aeronautics and Space Act.[105] The frontier, she argues, serves as a foundational myth for America—
that is, a creation narrative that consolidates "Americans" as
such, establishing them as a unique, unified people chosen by
their creator above all other nations. This myth therefore tends
to reemerge in earnest during times of national crisis. In particular, Newell tracks the intensification of frontier nostalgia
during the Cold War, threatened as Americans thought they
were with the collapse of their political, economic, and religious
world. "Over and against the specter of Communism," writes
Newell,

> America's frontier myth told America's cherished principles
> back to itself . . . equality, free enterprise, individualism, pragma-
> tism, optimism, and faith in God's purpose for their lives. As the
> Cold War escalated, this iteration of the American frontier myth
> became entrenched in popular culture, and played out again and
> again in movies, on the radio, and television, as in Disney's Davy
> Crockett series. And as the 1950s expanded into the 1960s, the
> myth of the frontier in the old west became reanimated in the
> frontier of outer space.[106]

And the agent behind this reanimation was none other than the
Animator himself: Walt Disney.

Unearthing a history of scientific, military, and artistic entanglement, Newell traces the midcentury fascination with
rockets, Martians, and lunar colonies to the 1955 creation of Disneyland in Anaheim, California. Just a year earlier, Disney had
almost finished the plans for the four "lands" of his embryonic
theme park. Fantasyland, Adventureland, and Frontierland
were all set, "but for the final space, Tomorrowland, Disney
discovered he had no story."[107] One of his animators suggested
he look to a 1952 issue of *Collier's* magazine (fig. 2.9), whose
cover showed a rocket blasting across the horizontal plane of
the earth and promised, "Man Will Conquer Space Soon," and

FIGURE 2.9. The *Collier's* issue that inspired Disney's Tomorrowland.

which laid the groundwork for Lyndon Johnson's congressional address by insisting that "the U.S. must immediately embark on a long-range development program to secure for the West 'space superiority.' If we do not, somebody else will. That somebody else very probably would be the Soviet Union."[108]

The chief contributor to this issue was none other than Wernher von Braun, the former Nazi rocket engineer granted amnesty in 1945 in exchange for his scientific service through the then-secret CIA initiative, Operation Paper Clip. In a lead article that designates space as "the last frontier," von Braun insists that, given sufficient funding and "determined effort," the United States could build a space station within the next ten to fifteen years. Moreover, he suggests that such a space station would simultaneously grant terrestrial dominance to the United States *and* constitute "a long step toward uniting mankind."[109] Much like his ideological descendants Musk and Maezawa, von Braun spends no time explaining *how* his vision will enact the unity it promises, instead spending pages on pages on the material and operational specifics of the proposed space station. The components of such a thing would of course need to be carried into space by rockets, whose design von Braun had initiated for Adolf Hitler, but which he now seemed happy to perfect for Harry Truman. As the magazine's front matter explains, "At forty, [von Braun] is considered the foremost rocket engineer in the world today. He was brought to this country from Germany by the U.S. government in 1945."[110] And Disney seemed to share his government's conviction that von Braun's scientific supremacy rendered his political misfirings unimportant. So he relied almost entirely on von Braun to provide the imaginative vision for Tomorrowland. To be sure, the rockets needed a bit of aesthetic work. They were, in short, "ugly."[111] But the ever-malleable von Braun readily tweaked his design to make the rockets more palatable to Disney's imagined audience. Once the new design was in place, von Braun also served as professor-expert for Disney's two immensely popular promotional-instructional videos on the impending human "conquest of space."[112]

When he finally broke ground, Disney positioned his von Braun-inspired Tomorrowland directly opposite Frontierland, architecturally affirming America's aeronautic future as the ideological inheritance of its frontier past. The juxtaposition held particular resonance for—and was likely inspired by— von Braun, who understood the aeronautic *mission* as a simultaneously political, military, and religious task. "Not long after his surrender to US forces in Germany," explains Newell, "von Braun became a born-again Christian. . . . The two causes—space exploration and Christianity—were joined in his mind as a calling from God. With a profound sense of 'manifest destiny,' von Braun felt humans were called by God to leave Earth and explore the galaxy, to travel to other planets and to spread the truth of the Gospel to other worlds."[113] "Man's conquest of space" would, in other words, be for the good of space itself. Just as the Europeans had brought Christian civilization to the ends of the earth, von Braun's formerly Nazi rockets would bring it out to earths without end.

According to Richard Francaviglia, Walt Disney's power over the American imagination was enacted through the images that reflected and shaped it. "Image was substance," he suggests, "and whoever controlled that image wielded . . . the power to affect *views of the past* and *visions of the future*."[114] Disney's videos and latter-day sacred spaces have allowed Americans to *see* the world as it allegedly was and will be, and, thus seeing it, to will it as such. As we can see in the case of Disneyland, space-longing and frontier nostalgia co-constitute one another; the fantasy of "conquering space" reduplicates the mythology of primordial conquest, so that America's extraterrestrial imperialism reaffirms the truth and even inevitability of its terrestrial supremacy. And this popular imperial imagination was all in place in time for Sputnik—which is to say just in time for Johnson to sound the alarm, Kennedy to set the deadline, Congress to redirect funds, and Apollo astronauts to read the "Christian" Bible and plant the American flag. Americans were ready to get behind the space race—not, as Newell argues, because they were imagining a more effective defense system, but because they were imagining themselves as ultramodern Davy Crocketts. "In America's popular imagination," she explains, "space was not filled with nuclear cannons hovering in low orbit or laser guns trained on Moscow; space was populated by *them*, by regular people who were going to transplant their suburban lifestyles to the moon."[115] Of course, the people to whom this fantasy was available were those who *had* suburban lifestyles—those with the paid vacation and televisions to deliver the images that fed the extraterrestrial imagination. Those, in other words, whom the frontier fantasy had rewarded, as distinct from those whom it had displaced; those who had the luxury to imagine the Columbian inheritance as "freedom" and "justice" rather than genocide and enslavement.

ANTICOLONIAL SOUNDINGS

We find a countermovement to white, middle-class space fantasies in the early rumblings of Afro-futurism, sounded above all by the experimental jazz musician Sun Ra. A war resister who abandoned what he considered the "slave name"[116] he'd been assigned at birth in favor of one that connected him to a noble Egyptian past and a "pure solar" future,[117] Sun Ra called his band the Omniverse Arkestra after its intention to transport its listeners from a violent, doomed world (hence the "ark") to an infinite ("omni-") soundscape of other possibilities. As Paul Youngquist explains, "Sun Ra took it on himself and his music not to demand freedom and equality in this world but to create . . . even better worlds to come."[118]

Like the "new frontier" rhetoric of white aeronautic fantasy, Afro-futurism draws a homology between sea and space. But the perspective, of course, is inverted. Rather than extending into space the work of those "bold" explorers who ravished the lands they allegedly found, Afro-futurists read the space race back into the ship holds of the Middle Passage. As Kodwo Eshun proposes, the transatlantic slave trade was *already* an "alien abduction," a forced transportation into a murderous world. What artists like Sun Ra imagine, then, is a full appropriation of the means of transport, a relocation for those who have never belonged to this world anyway. "It's in music," writes Eshun, "that you get this sense that most African-Americans owe *nothing* to the status of the human. . . . there's this sense of the human as being a really pointless and treacherous category."[119] The "human," after all, is a constitutively antiblack construction, especially in America. As Alexander Weheliye reasons, "once your animal characteristics have been measured against human ones in the pages of the plantation ledger, desiring the particular image of humanity on the other side of this very ledger seems, to put it mildly, futile."[120]

Vaulting over the category that continues to oppress black Americans, Sun Ra transvalued subhumanity into posthumanity. Claiming to have come from Saturn ("it isn't an allegory," writes Eshun; "he really did come from Saturn"[121]), Sun Ra composed pieces like "We Travel the Spaceways," "Space Is the Place," and "Rocket Number Nine (Take off for the Planet Venus)" to carry listeners off to a better world—a world to which they might actually belong.[122] "Second stop is Jupiter," cry the Arkestra's space-train musician-conductors, "Second stop is Jupiter." Deliberately atonal, these pieces interrupt Western expectations of scale, melody, harmony, and rhythm, genuinely *doing* something (or somewhere) else. This music, Ra insisted, was "*from* outer space."[123] He had learned it from his home planet and from numerous interstellar journeys. In Ra's words, "Superior beings definitely speak in other harmonic ways than the earth way because they're talking something different, and you have to have chord against chord, melody against melody, rhythm against rhythm: if you've got that, you're expressing something else."[124] To mark this "something else," Sun Ra and his Arkestra furthermore wore regal-comical spacelike costumes (metal plates, cloaks, and headpieces signifying their Egyptian-interstellar futurepast); experimented with new sound technologies like synthesizers and tape delay; and incorporated musical styles from every corner of the globe including, yes, Disneyland.[125]

Like Disney, Ra sought to capture the imagination of his audience vis-à-vis the vast terrain of extraterrestrial space.

Unlike Disney, however, Ra sought to transvalue rather than recapitulate the transatlantic and transcontinental journeys of Euro-American imperialism. For Disney and his scientist-collaborators, America's future in space would revive "the great age of exploration and conquests, when Columbus, Magellan, Vasco da Gama and the Cabots found and claimed new worlds for their royal sovereigns. . . . These colorful adventurers, hunting for treasure and glory"[126] would serve as a prototype for American astronauts, blazing new paths for the honor of the old imperium. For Ra, by contrast, the journey into space would provide an *escape* from the order of conquest. His musicians were not *conquistadores* from the old imperial world but rather liberators from it. They were guides to what Pentecostal philosopher Ashon Crawley might call "otherwise worlds"[127] of genuine peace and freedom—worlds, as the Movement for Black Lives is currently enabling us to imagine, without prisons or militarized police forces. Worlds like Ra's, whose *harmony* only sounds like "noise" from the perspective of those who demand uniformity, confusing multiplicity with chaos.

One might be tempted to locate the difference between Disney and Ra—or between imperial and counterimperial imagineering—in their respective sensory registers: the former operating by means of the removed, masterful faculty of *vision* and the latter operating in the more immersive medium of *sound*, so readily convertible with *touch*.[128] But of course, Disney's project works sonically and tactilely as well as visually, and Ra's sonic tactilism is at least assisted by striking visuals. So although one might perhaps hold out hope for a sonic reorientation of our visual captivation,[129] the difference between Disney's world-replication and Ra's world-transformation seems primarily to lie in their respective aesthetics of unity and multiplicity, or sameness and difference: between the white fantasy of bringing sofas, TVs, and Ovaltine to the moon and the black-liberationist effort to live otherwise. The Disney fantasy reduplicates this exploitative, genocidal world *out there* everywhere, forever, whereas Ra attempts to think, hear, and play "other worlds" as such—worlds that depend on collaboration rather than stolen labor, joy rather than subjugation, and playful difference rather than enforced unity. As Ra often intoned in a spoken-word interlude,

> Imagination is a magic carpet ride
> On which we soar to distant lands and climes
> And even go beyond the moon to any planet in the sky.
> If we are here . . . [whole band joins in]
> WHY CAN'T WE BE *THERE*?[130]

Imagination, in other words, was real for Ra. It did real things; it transported dehumanized people to otherwise worlds. As Ra wrote in the liner notes for the Arkestra's 1959 album, *Jazz in Silhouette*, "In tomorrow's world, men will not need artificial instruments such as jets and space ships. In the world of tomorrow, the new man will 'think' the place he wants to go, then his mind will take him there."[131] In other words, Ra's imagination was *the force itself*, rather than the effervescent means toward the more literal (and totally unimaginative) end of actually boarding ships to plunder the resources of some new land, now that the old one was all used up; to plant colonies to destroy the otherness of worlds by making them all just like this one.

AND I THINK IT'S GONNA BE A LONG, LONG TIME
EVERYONE'S GONE TO THE MOON

On March 26, 2019, just a few months shy of the fiftieth anniversary of Aldrin's and Armstrong's moonwalk, Vice President Mike Pence directed NASA, under the authority of the president, to ensure that the United States be the first nation to return to the moon. "Just as the United States was the first nation to reach the moon in the twentieth century," said Pence, "so too will we be the first nation to *return* astronauts to the moon in the twenty-first century." Giving the gathered scientists, policy makers, and investors five years at most to get back to the moon, Pence was uncompromising about the importance of making America first (again). "Let me be clear," he stated. "The first woman and the next man on the moon *will both be American astronauts*, launched by American rockets from American soil" [applause]. Without even a touch of internationalist or humanitarian qualifiers, however disingenuous they might be, Pence held a strictly nationalist, ultra-authoritarian line culminating in an uncompromising message. "The President has directed NASA and Administrator Jim Bridenstine to accomplish this goal," stated Pence, unsmiling and narrowing his eyes, "by any means necessary."[132]

Even for those attuned to the active colonial tendency of neoliberalism to assimilate all resistance, Pence's appropriation of Malcolm X here is shocking.[133] In 1964, the liberationist introduced this phrase as the "motto" of his Pan-Africanist Organization of Afro American Unity (OAAU), demanding "the complete independence of people of African descent . . . by any means necessary."[134] In 2019, Pence now claims it as a Machiavellian assertion of the right of the sovereign to protect his ever-fragile sovereignty, especially in the face of the aeronautic advancement of China, Israel, and India alongside the old Russian enemy.[135] "In order to succeed," Pence insists, "we must focus on the mission over the means." What this jettisoning of "means" means for the vice president is that government agencies, which is to say NASA and the Defense Department, will need to consider "every option" for getting America moonward as soon as possible, including "private industry." The irony, of course, is that private industry transcends national boundaries, threatening the very governmental sovereignty that now turns to it in desperation for protection. Elon Musk, for example, holds three different passports. His aerospace manufacturer SpaceX, although headquartered in California, holds contracts with Kazakhstan as well as the United States and is currently competing for contracts with Europe. More importantly, SpaceX and other publicly traded rocket companies are funded by private investors around the globe, including, of course, Yusaku Maezawa, who dreams of a peace secured through the collaboration of finance capital with a government built on genocide and enslavement, fueled by the systematic assault of the earth, and secured through appalling inequality, murder at the border, and endless wars abroad.

As far as Pence goes, his dreams are more explicitly in keeping than Maezawa's—or Kennedy's, for that matter, or even von Braun's—with the mechanisms of their advancement. In short, Pence seeks not to heal the world but to subdue it. He reveals this vision above all toward the end of his address when he begins to channel the millennial strategy of "shock and awe," conceived under Bill Clinton as a means of attaining "rapid dominance" and deployed to notoriously disastrous ends under George W. Bush.[136] "America," Pence proclaims, "will once again *astonish* the world with the heights we reach, the *wonder* we achieve."[137] The nations will be so overawed, they won't even try to compete. America, they will see, has made it to the moon. Again.

Two days after Pence issued his stern directive, the *Washington Post* ran a bemused editorial entitled, "Mike Pence, Boldly Sending America Back to Where Man Has Gone Before."[138] Six weeks later, President Trump incurred similar mockery by tweeting that "Under my administration, we are restoring @NASA to greatness and we are going back to the Moon, then Mars."[139] Even Fox News was underwhelmed, its business anchor Neil Canuto tweeting back, "Didn't we do this moon thing quite a few decades ago?" It took Trump three weeks to respond, which he eventually did by blaming NASA for *its* backwardness. "For all of the money we are spending," he wrote, "NASA should NOT be talking about going to the Moon—We did that 50 years ago. They should be focused on the much bigger things we are doing, including Mars (of which the Moon is a part), Defense and Science!"[140]

The foundations of this frankly confusing statement of goals
were laid two years earlier, in June 2017, when Trump signed
an executive order reestablishing the defunct National Space
Council (NSC). As chair of this body, which American astrono-
mer Lucianne Walkowicz has called "an ineffectual bureaucratic
film . . . a kind of vestigial membrane attached to the office of
the President,"[141] Mike Pence directed NASA to focus its energies
on "returning humans to the Moon for long-term exploration
and utilization, followed by human missions to Mars and other
destinations."[142] This directive reversed the policy of the Obama
administration (itself a reversal of the policy of the Bush administration), which had instructed NASA to forego a return to the
moon and work on getting to Mars. As Barack Obama said in a
2010 speech at the Kennedy Space Center in the presence of Buzz
Aldrin, "Now, I understand that some believe that we should
attempt a return to the surface of the Moon first, as previously
planned. But I just have to say pretty bluntly here: We've been
there before. Buzz has been there. There's a lot more of space to
explore, and a lot more to learn when we do."[143]

So why this administrative toggling? What is at stake in pri-
oritizing the moon over Mars, or vice versa? As Walkowicz explains, these particular celestial bodies have become "the two
favorite political footballs of interplanetary exploration, each
with their own fervent base of advocates. Fans of the Moon,"
who include George W. Bush, Newt Gingrich, Trump, and
Pence, "often argue that a permanent base on the Moon is an
essential stepping stone in our eventual journey to Mars, although no one has yet connected the dots as to how that specifically might happen." Lunar advocates nod to Mars in order to
avoid the accusation that their big dream has already been realized. But their primary goal is to get back to the moon—and to
stay there this time. As Walkowicz argues, there is at this point
very little to be learned scientifically from another trip to the
moon; this is the reason Mars advocates like Obama have been
reluctant to spend upward of $100 billion to put human beings

back on the lunar surface. What we *can* get from the moon, however, is "a strategic outpost for national security"[144] and a source of "material resources"—in particular, "water, which can be processed into rocket propellant."[145] To be sure, returning to the moon will be expensive, but this is the reason moon advocates like Trump and Pence are calling on private industry to help America get back there first. What's in it for private industry and their investors? Ownership of whatever they're able to mine there—thanks to a bipartisan bill Obama signed into law in 2015, granting American aeronautic corporations like Planetary Resources and Moon Express the right to own and sell whatever they manage to mine from celestial bodies.[146] (One can only imagine how Arendt might intensify her post-Sputnik reflection upon hearing such news: "If I were the moon," she told Karl Jaspers in 1957, "I would take offense."[147])

Just a year into his presidency, Donald Trump issued his Space Policy Directive-1, which in his words "marks an important step in returning astronauts to the moon . . . for long-term exploration and use. This time," he insists, "we will not only plant our flag and leave our footprint, we will establish a foundation for an eventual mission to Mars. And, perhaps someday, to many worlds beyond."[148] As Trump explains it, the reason for this imperative to seek out, use, and inhabit other worlds lies in the very essence of the nation he leads—namely, "the pioneer spirit." Drawing on the now-familiar analogy between sea and space, Trump reminds his audience that "after braving the vast unknown and discovering the new world, our forefathers did not merely sail home. . . . They stayed, they explored, they built, they guided, and through that pioneering spirit, they imagined all of the possibilities that few dared to dream." Similarly, American astronauts will stay in space, take whatever they find there, and "imagine" more or less what non-Native, English-speaking, white Americans and their Euro-descended transplants like Musk and von Braun have been imagining since the fifties— that is, this life here, out there on any cosmic body we manage to land on. *This* imperial order, projected into the heavens; *these* earth-destroying technologies, fracking the moon and nuking Mars;[149] *this* remaking of whatever we find in our own image, scattering our trash in the meantime through the endless run of space.[150]

FIRST WE TAKE MANHATTAN

Trump's directive to get back to the moon has found an energetic recipient in NASA, whose then-administrator Jim Bridenstine pledged the agency's full compliance in immediate response to Pence's "by any means necessary" speech.[151] Over the next few months, NASA rolled out a website called "Moon to Mars" that explains the connection between these two bodies, rendering a little less mysterious Trump's above-cited tweet about the moon's being "a part" of Mars. As NASA explains it, the moon plays two crucial roles in getting us to Mars: first, it will teach humans how to live off-earth, serving as a kind of bunny slope for the Martian black diamond.[152] What's puzzling about this claim is that "we" already know how to live in space. In fact, one of the astronauts present at the signing of Trump's Space Policy Directive-1 was Peggy Whitson, who had just spent 665 days on the International Space Station (ISS)—which is to say, living in space. It is hard to imagine what the moon would teach scientists about strategies for extraterrestrial survival that the ISS hasn't already taught them, other than ways for the United States to operate in space without any formal responsibility to other nations.

The second role the moon will play in forging a path to Mars is far more believable than the first. The moon, NASA tells us, has stuff we want. As the "Moon to Mars" website testifies, "We believe the poles of the Moon hold millions of tons of water ice. That ice represents power. It represents fuel. It represents science." Without mentioning the shareholders positioned to make untaxed millions from the extraction and sale of this "fuel," NASA focuses on the potential in lunar water to localize production. "The farther humans venture into space," the website explains, "the more important it becomes to manufacture materials and products with local resources. . . . We will print, manufacture, and build as much as we can with materials found on the Moon."[153] The question no one seems to be asking is what right the US government and private companies *have* to the water and minerals they find on the moon. To clarify, the question has indeed been asked (and answered) in a legal register, with Obama's 2015 Commercial Space Launch Competitiveness Act granting ownership over extraterrestrial "resources" to whoever manages to grab them first. But it hasn't been asked *ethically*—at least not by anyone to whom Pence, NASA, or Moon Express seems to be listening.[154] Who says that the moon's water is anyone's but the moon's? And has Mars invited human beings to come colonize it?

In September 2018, Lucianne Walkowicz hosted a public forum at the Library of Congress called "Becoming Interplanetary: What Living on Earth Can Teach Us about Living on Mars."[155] Speakers included artists, musicians, scientists, anthropologists, and science fiction writers, all of whom interrogate the goal of "terraforming" Mars—that is, of turning it into a humanly habitable planet, or, in the language I've been proposing, of re-creating it in the image of imperial "humanity." Media interviews with the participants reveal three major areas of concern. The first calls out the recklessness of using Mars as a "backup planet,"[156] which is to say, as an excuse to ignore or even accelerate the escalating ecological crisis on Earth in favor of moving the species elsewhere. (This is the line of thinking that allows NASA pilot Joseph Cooper to proclaim in 2014 film *Interstellar*, "Mankind was born on earth. It was never meant to die here," and his colleague Dr. Amelia Brand to explain, "We're not meant to save the world; we're meant to leave it."[157]) Besides, if the earth is any indication, humans seem to be better at ruining their planetary homes than making them more habitable. So even if it were an admirable strategy, it would not be a particularly good bet.

The second major concern of the "Becoming Interplanetary" speakers is with the integrity of Mars itself. As Walkowicz reminds us, Mars has its "own history"—either biotic or abiotic—which terraforming activities will erase entirely.[158] Moreover, as astrophysicist and intersectional feminist Chanda Prescod-Weinstein reasons, "Perhaps life hasn't developed [on Mars] yet. Perhaps life may develop in the future. Will our interactions with Mars preclude that possibility? Do we have the right to make that choice for the ecosystem?"[159]

Both of these interventions begin to voice the speakers' third collective concern, which is to say the colonial replications enacted in the contemporary aeronautic imagination. Just as the conquistadores and pioneers believed they had the right to take, use, destroy, and remake whatever they "found" in the allegedly empty Americas, so is private industry now claiming the right to extract whatever it finds in the new *terra nullius* of space. Moon Express cofounder and CEO Bob Richards made and even celebrated this connection when he compared the 2015 Commercial Space Launch Competitiveness Act (CSLCA) to the 1862 Homestead Act, which gave indigenous lands to white settlers for unregulated "development." "I think this will be a big deal from a historical perspective," said Richards, confident that speculators would be far likelier to invest in the space market now that they were assured ownership of extraterrestrial water and minerals. Like the Homestead Act, he said, the CSLCA is sure to become a "fantastic spur to development."[160]

Prescod-Weinstein worries that this sort of reasoning replicates not only past but present violences and inequalities. "Can we be trusted," she asks rhetorically, "to be in balance with Mars if we refuse to be in balance with Earth? Can we be trusted to be equitable in our dealings with each other in a Martian context if the U.S. and Canadian governments continue to attack indigenous sovereignty, violate indigenous lands, and engage in genocidal activities against indigenous people?"[161] For terraforming advocates, however, the comparison is a false one. To be sure, founder of the tax-exempt Mars Society Robert Zubrin acknowledges the unsavory imperial history that has globalized the earth. Nevertheless, he argues, the eventual human development of Mars will be a totally different game—as long as there really is no intelligent life on Mars (but who, one might ask, sets the standards of intelligence? Or of life, for that matter?). "On Mars," Zubrin asserts, "we have a chance to create something new with clean hands. We're not going to Mars to steal other people's property, we're going to Mars to create—not just property but a society."[162] To avoid confusion with terrestrial imperialism, Zubrin refuses to use the word "colony" in reference to eventual human habitations on Mars, preferring the word "settlement"—as if that word carries no traces of genocidal violence in the Americas, Australia, the West Bank, South Africa, or Hawai'i.

Although still ignored in political speeches, press releases, and investor updates, this effort to speak differently has found a few advocates on numerous sides of the terraforming debate. Like Zubrin, Walkowicz worries that the "language of colonization" carries with it a terrestrial history we have no business reenacting in space. Unlike Zubrin, they are also critical of the word "settlement," fearing it both erases and authenticates the violation of indigenous peoples. Perhaps to make sure the speaker is actually thinking, Walkowicz suggests "using a couple of extra words," such as "humans living on Mars."[163] Even NASA has begun to change some of its language to encourage "inclusivity," specifying in its updated Style Guide that, "In general, all references to the space program should be non-gender-specific (e.g. human, piloted, unpiloted, robotic, as opposed to manned or unmanned)."[164] The question, however, is how far language and inclusiveness will go toward creating new standards of conduct, or toward *actually* imagining worlds otherwise.

The problem of linguistic tokenism is perhaps nowhere more apparent than in the newly baptized NASA program: the one that will get us to the moon to stay, to build "a space economy built on mining, tourism, and scientific research," and to help eventually colonize Mars. If the twentieth-century mission was named Apollo after the all-seeing terrestrial circumnavigator, the twenty-first-century mission will be named Artemis, his twin sister and the goddess of the moon. Divorced from any lived religious practice that might, say, *revere* the moon, this thealogical remnant (NASA refers to her in the past tense[165]) lends a divine, feminist patina to the forthcoming adventure in strip-mining. Artemis will absolutely host a woman astronaut,[166] NASA promises, as if this woman's mere presence on the ship will make Artemis any less of a hyperphallic endeavor. Extending the inclusion intersectionally, one of the downloadable promotional posters for the Artemis mission represents the Commander of the Gateway—the orbiting space station that will be able to navigate anywhere above the lunar surface—as a woman with Afro-textured hair, floating above the lunar surface she commands, alone and in charge.

On a "Decolonizing Mars" panel at the "Becoming Interplanetary" conference, the music producer, rapper, and science studies scholar Enongo Lumumba-Kasongo, who records under the name Sammus, suggested that "representation" is insufficient to the task of decolonizing space exploration. The mere presence of black, indigenous, and female bodies on "piloted" rather than manned "missions" (*that* term is remarkably uninterrogated) will not ensure the just treatment of celestial bodies or their microbial or macro-organic life forms. "We have to push for not just representation," explains Lumumba-Kasongo, "but a genuine understanding of other world views."[167] Models for such understanding can be found, she suggests, in Afro-futurist music, fiction, and art. And indeed, as we saw with Sun Ra, such work does endeavor to think, sound, and live other worlds *as such*, rather than "other worlds" as infinite reduplications of the one we've got. The challenge is to mobilize such work in a way that it actually speaks to the space-crazed billionaires, some of whom think they're already listening. After all, Basquiat was an Afro-futurist, and now he's on a sweatshop-made t-shirt drumming up investment in SpaceX, whose CEO is currently angling

FIGURE 2.10. NASA promotional poster. Online at https://www.nasa.gov /specials/moon2mars/img/M2M_Gateway_Poster.pdf.

to help NASA help Trump colonize the moon, and then Mars, and then whatever else they manage to land on and exploit.[168]

ANOTHER WORLD IS IMPROBABLE

In "Black Nihilism and the Politics of Hope," Afro-pessimist philosopher Calvin Warren elucidates the dangers of faith in "the Political."[169] Such faith asserts, all evidence to the contrary, that murderous racism is losing ground in the United States, that "things" are getting "better," and that some charismatic president will one day (soon!) secure genuine freedom and equality for black Americans. But these political promises are structurally impossible, Warren argues, because in the United States especially, "the political" is *constitutively* antiblack. "The American dream," he insists—thinking of "safe" neighborhoods, "good" schools, and of escalating profits for plantation owners, slaveholders, CEOs, and shareholders—"is realized through black suffering" (217). Even the Civil Rights Movement, especially as Martin Luther King Jr. imagined it, positioned black Americans as "suffering servants," charged to withstand endless violence for the sake of an ideal political order, an ever futural "beloved community."[170] For Warren, then, the only possible "disposition" for those who seek "justice, redress, and righteousness" is nihilism (232). Not the passive nihilism of quiet, sofa-bound despair, but the "active nihilism" that seeks to destructure the political as such (233). In the face of the liberal assurance that "another world is possible," Warren insists that other worlds invariably reduplicate this same, unbearable world. Every effort to configure "worlds" otherwise—whether here or there, imagined or actual—has "inevitably reconstituted and reconfigured the anti-blackness it tried to eliminate" (239). Warren therefore looks with Franz Fanon to "*end the world itself*," which is to say, to "destroy the field of all possible solutions" (239).

Cornel West has criticized black nihilism for encouraging "a self-destructive disposition to the world."[171] For Warren, however, it is the world itself that is cold-hearted—the world, along with its infinitely promised, infinitely deferred "other worlds," each of which reduplicates the death-dealing order it says it's departing from. Hence Basquiat's labor raking in millions for Sotheby's, or "Imagine" bludgeoning the black musician who modestly reimagines it, or Janis Joplin in a Mercedes-Benz ad, or Jesus of Nazareth endorsing Wernher von Braun who inspires Walt Disney who boosts the Cold War one-upsmanship that produces the whole-earth imaginary enabled by the one-world dominion to which it everywhere capitulates. Another world is increasingly improbable.

On February 6, 2018, SpaceX launched its "Falcon Heavy" rocket, which marked its capacity to deliver spacecraft extraterrestrially by propelling a Tesla Roadster convertible, piloted by a white-space-suited robot, into elliptical orbit around the sun.[172]

Engineers predict the Roadster will circle our star for no more than "a few tens of millions of years," at which point it will crash either into Venus or Earth,[173] unless some asteroid has mercy on all of us and incinerates it ahead of time into a more useful form of mass energy. When asked what possessed him to launch a Tesla into space—all that steel, plastic, and underpaid labor tossed off the planet like a gum wrapper out a car window— Elon Musk said he had to launch *something*, and that the usual candidates, like blocks of steel or concrete, would have been "boring. Of course, anything boring is terrible."[174] He wanted to launch something that was "fun, and that people could identify with . . . that felt like you could maybe be there." Besides, he said the whole spectacle "was a tribute to David Bowie," whose alien messiah Starman provides the robot-astronaut's namesake.[175] And there goes another visionary.

In the meantime, Yusaku Maezawa is still on the lookout for living artists who might join him on a trip to the moon, see the earth entire, and help bring about world peace. "If I ask you," Maezawa asks the investors and reporters, "please don't say no!"

FIGURE 2.11. Elon Musk's "Starman" against the Pale Blue Dot. Screenshot from SpaceX livestream.

It's a joke, but the sort that makes one wonder whether Maezawa might be having a hard time finding passengers. Indeed, the two artist conversations featured on the #DearMoon website both end in refusals: Ringo Starr has no interest in going to the moon (he couldn't even last all that long in India), and Damien Chazelle and Ryan Gosling say they're happy just to *pretend* to reenact Armstrong's journey from the safety of Earth.[176] Even Musk isn't sure he wants to make the lunar journey, responding when asked directly that Maezawa "did suggest that maybe I would join on this trip, I don't know."

> "Yeah, yeah, yeah," Maezawa chimes in. "Please."
> "Maybe we'll both be on it," shrugs Musk.[177]

Yeah, maybe.

But even if Maezawa does manage to get a diverse cohort of willing geniuses onto his rocket, it's still not clear how their Apollonian visions will do anything other than distract the rest of us from the real work of strip-mining and extraterrestrial colonialism with which they're entangled. Such visions might even make us feel okay about the whole enterprise. "Look at all those diverse humans," we'll marvel; "united toward a common goal."

In a radio interview, Walkowicz takes a moment to reflect on the persistently false humanitarian reflex of space-racers. As they explain to NPR's Guy Raz,

> People will just casually say, "well! We're going to go to Mars and then! Then we will look back at the earth and you know, world peace will break out and (laughs) all these wonderful things will come to pass; we'll *really* understand our place in the universe." Okay . . . we actually already did that—you know, we already sent people to space and took a picture of the earth. Did human nature suddenly (laughs) suddenly change right after that?[178]

We've already seen the whole earth in full view, and it's caused us time and again to recycle the same imperial imaginings under the guise of peace and harmony. Fifty years later, the Apollonian vision of the world as picture, of all that is, united and interconnected, is sending the worst of us hurtling head-long into an endless journey of intergalactic plunder while it buckles the rest of us in place like Musk's hapless Starman, that would-be messiah who sees the same world appearing on every horizon despite his best efforts to imagine another one. Starman is out there *for us*, says Musk; we should see ourselves in that robonaut, as if we "could maybe be there." But in a sense, there we already are: posthuman and useless, stuck forever with visual repetitions of the same broken promise, and lamenting along with that other doomed Bowie hero, "Planet earth is blue, and there's nothing I can do."[179]

NOTES

1. For the contemporary framing of this piece, I am entirely indebted to Patrick Guariglia. For her work on the colonial history of

the space race, I am grateful to Helen Handelman. I have also bene-fited immensely from conversations with Claire Grace, Lori Gruen, Meredith Hughes, Kenan Rubenstein, and Sheeja Thomas. Winfield Goodwin has read a draft and provided invaluable suggestions.

2. "The 'B' stands for 'big;' the 'R' is for 'rocket.' In public, Gwynne Shotwell, SpaceX's president, states its full name as 'Big Falcon Rocket.' Mr. Musk and the company's news releases have re-mained ambiguous about what the 'F' stands for" (Kenneth Chang, "With Moon as His Muse, Japanese Billionaire Signs up for SpaceX Voyage," *New York Times*, September 18, 2018.

3. Yusaku Maezawa and Elon Musk, *First Private Passenger on Lunar Bfr Mission*, https://youtu.be/zu7WJD8vpAQ, September 17, 2018.

4. Eric Berger, "Big Fiscal Reality: NASA Isn't Going to Pay for the Bfr, So Musk Charts a New Course," *Vox*, September 18, 2019.

5. Musk's choice of the relative pronoun "that" over "who" in this situation seems already to alter the humanity of his aspira-tional extraterrestrial. Maezawa and Musk, *First Private Passenger*.

6. Maezawa and Musk, *First Private Passenger*.

7. John F. Kennedy, *Address at Rice University on the Na-tion's Space Program*, September 12, 1962; https://youtu.be/WZyRbnpGyzQ.

8. Kennedy, *Address at Rice University*.

9. John F. Kennedy, "If the Soviets Control Space, They Can Control Earth," *Missiles and Rockets* (October 10, 1960): 12. With thanks to Helen Handelman for having first directed my attention to this text.

10. Maezawa and Musk, *First Private Passenger*. If Maezawa does, indeed, become the first private passenger to orbit the moon, he will not have been the first private passenger to travel into *space*; as Kenneth Chang explains, "So far, seven people have paid for a trip to space, riding on a Russian Soyuz rocket for short stays at the In-ternational Space Station. (One person, Charles Simonyi, has made two trips.)" (Kenneth Chang, "Meet Spacex's First Moon Voyage Customer, Yusaku Maezawa," *New York Times*, September 17, 2018.

Maezawa had been looking into the Russian space tourism firm Space Adventures before he settled on SpaceX (Chang, "With Moon as His Muse").

11. When asked how much he had paid for "the entire BFR," Maezawa looked uncomfortable and gestured to Musk, who refused to disclose the amount, but who called it "a very significant deposit" (Maezawa and Musk, *First Private Passenger*).

12. Maezawa and Musk, *First Private Passenger*.

13. Maezawa and Musk, *First Private Passenger*.

14. For Martin Heidegger, the conquering of the world "as picture" is concomitant with the establishment of humanity as the measure of all that is.

15. Maezawa and Musk, *First Private Passenger*.

16. Ben Davis, "How a One-Painting Show Lets You Get inside the Brilliant Young Basquiat's Head," *Artnet News* (February 8, 2018); https://news.artnet.com/exhibitions/lets-talk-about-this -one-basquiat-painting-at-the-brooklyn-museum-1218755.

17. See Motoko Rich and Robin Pogrebin, "Why Spend $110 Million on a Basquiat? 'I Decided to Go for It,' Japanese Billionaire Explains," *New York Times*, May 26, 2017. Note the resonance in the logic of this title with JFK's Mallory-inspired "because it is there."

18. Colin Dwyer, "At $110.5 Million, Basquiat Painting Becomes Priciest Work Ever Sold by a U.S. Artist," *National Public Radio* (May 19, 2017).

19. Alex Martin, "Zozotown Founder Yusaku Maezawa Follows Eclectic Path," *Japan Times*, April 1, 2018); https://www .japantimes.co.jp/news/2018/04/01/business/corporate-business /zozotown-founder-yusaku-maezawa-follows-eclectic-path/# .XQvNGNNKjOQ.

20. Maezawa and Musk, *First Private Passenger*.

21. Friedrich Nietzsche, "The Birth of Tragedy," in *The Birth of Tragedy and Other Writings*, ed. Raymond Geuss and Ronald Speirs (Cambridge: Cambridge University Press, 1999), 14, 17.

22. #DearMoon, "Promotional Video" (2018); https://www .youtube.com/watch?time_continue=133&v=LPyyXeyVfGI.

23. Maezawa and Musk, *First Private Passenger*.

24. Chang, "With Moon as His Muse."

25. On Constantine's use of a sphere as "imperial emblem," see Denis Cosgrove, "Contested Global Visions: One-World, Whole-Earth, and the Apollo Space Photographs," *Annals of the Association of American Geographers* 84, no. 2 (June 1994): 272.

26. United States Senate and United States House of Representatives, "National Aeronautics and Space Act of 1958," sec. 102(a); https://history.nasa.gov/spaceact.html.

27. Kelly Oliver, *Earth and World: Philosophy after the Apollo Missions* (New York: Columbia University Press, 2015), 1.

28. R. Buckminster Fuller, "Vertical Is to Live—Horizontal Is to Die," *American Scholar* 39, no. 1 (1969–70): 36.

29. See, e.g., Archibald MacLeish, "A Reflection: Riders on Earth Together, Brothers in Eternal Cold," *New York Times*, December 25, 1968.

30. As Yaakov Garb has argued, "the ubiquitous media portrayals of the Earth [show it] as surrounded and contained, conquered and controlled, rendered into a dead artifact, mapped into a barren rectilinear monolith, and trivialized into a mere plaything." Yaakov Jerome Garb, "Perspective or Escape? Ecofeminist Musings on Contemporary Earth Imagery," in *Reweaving the World: The Emergence of Ecofeminism*, ed. Irene Diamond and Gloria Feman Orenstein (1990), 265.

31. See Cosgrove, "Contested Global Visions."

32. Andrew G. Kirk, *Counterculture Green: The Whole Earth Catalog and American Environmentalism* (Lawrence: University Press of Kansas, 2007), 41.

33. Cosgrove, "Contested Global Visions," 289–90.

34. Plato, "Timaeus," in *Timaeus and Critias*, ed. Thomas Kjeller Johansen (New York: Penguin Books, 1977), 31a-b.

35. Benjamin Lazier, "Earthrise; or, the Globalization of the World Picture," *American Historical Review* 116, no. 3 (June 2011).

36. NASA, "Apollo 8, the Second Mission: Testing the Csm in Lunar Orbit (21 December–27 December 1968)," *Nasa History*: https://history.nasa.gov/SP-4029/Apollo_08a_Summary.htm.

37. See https://www.youtube.com/watch?v=1aIfoG2PtHo&t=435s.

38. Cited in John Blaney, *Lennon and McCartney: Together Alone* (London: Jawbone Press, 2007), 52.

39. John Lennon and Yoko Ono, "Imagine," *Imagine* (London: Apple Records, 1971).

40. Nietzsche, "The Birth of Tragedy," 15–17.

41. https://www.youtube.com/watch?v=HC4MD16fmjc.

42. Cited in Sean Michaels, "Cee Lo Green Criticised for Changing Lyrics to John Lennon's Imagine," *Guardian*, January 3, 2012; https://www.theguardian.com/music/2012/jan/03/cee-lo-green -john-lennon.

43. Lauren Moraski, "Cee Lo Green Sparks Controversy over Lyrics Change," *CBS News* (January 2, 2012); https://www.cbsnews .com/news/cee-lo-green-sparks-controversy-over-lyrics-change/.

44. Michaels, "Cee Lo Green," emphasis added.

45. Hannah Arendt, *The Human Condition* (1958; Chicago: University of Chicago Press, 1998), 2.

46. Sputnik 1 launched on October 4, 1957, and Sputnik 2 on November 3, 1957—this time with a dog on board. "Within days," writes Sheila Jasanoff, "the outlines of a U.S. space program were under discussion" (Sheila Jasanoff, "Heaven and Earth: The Politics of Environmental Images," in *Earthly Politics: Local and Global in Environmental Governance*, ed. Sheila Jasanoff and Marybeth Long Martello [Cambridge, MA: MIT Press, 2004], 40.)

47. Chris Gainor, *To a Distant Day: The Rocket Pioneers* (Lincoln: University of Nebraska Press, 2008), 163.

48. US Senate and House of Representatives, "National Aeronautics and Space Act of 1958," sec. 102(a) and sec. 102(c)(5).

49. Kennedy, "If the Soviets Control Space, They Can Control Earth."

50. John F. Kennedy, "Special Message to the Congress on Urgent National Needs," May 25, 1961; https://www.jfklibrary.org /archives/other-resources/john-f-kennedy-speeches/united-states -congress-special-message-19610525.

51. Having destroyed the Hawaiian kingdom in the late nineteenth century, the United States went on immediately to use it for

commercial and military purposes. Once the region was occupied by a majority of non-Native voters, the United States incorporated it as a state in 1959. On the relationship between capitalist endeavors, military expansion, and the colonization of Hawai'i, see Julia Flynn Siler, *Lost Kingdom: Hawaii's Last Queen, the Sugar Kings, and America's First Imperial Adventure* (New York: Grove Press, 2013). On the current controversy over the construction of the Thirty Meter Telescope on Mauna Kea, see Bryan Kamaoli Kuwada, April 3, 2015, https://hehiale.wordpress.com/2015/04/03/we-live-in-the-future-come-join-us/; and Joseph Anthony Salazar, "Multicultural Settler Colonialism and Indigenous Struggle in Hawai'i: The Politics of Astronomy on Maua a Wākea" (University of Hawaii at Manoa, December, 2014).

52. Associated Press in Washington, "Donald Trump Officially Launches US Space Force," *Guardian*, December 29, 2019; https://www.theguardian.com/us-news/2019/dec/21/donald-trump-officially-launches-us-space-force.

53. On the possible spatial infinity of our universe (not to mention the multiverse of which it may or may not be a part), see Mary-Jane Rubenstein, *Worlds without End: The Many Lives of the Multiverse* (New York: Columbia University Press, 2014), 156–59, 212–13.

54. Mircea Eliade, *The Myth of the Eternal Return: Cosmos and History*, trans. Williard R. Trask (Princeton, NJ: Princeton University Press, 2005), 9–10.

55. Patricia Seed, *Ceremonies of Possession in Europe's Conquest of the New World, 1492–1640* (Cambridge: Cambridge University Press, 1995). With thanks to Helen Handelman for having pointed me toward this source. For her interpretation of the cosmogonic act of the Apollo missions as an attempted *creatio ex nihilo*, see Helen Jewell Handelman, "A Trip to the Moon: Lunar Fantasies and Earthly Supremacy" (Wesleyan University, 2016).

56. https://www.youtube.com/watch?v=1aIf0G2PtHo&t=435s.

57. Christopher Potter, *The Earth Gazers: On Seeing Ourselves* (New York: Pegasus Books, 2018), 293.

58. Genesis 1:26–28 (RSV).

59. "Go therefore and make disciples of all nations, baptizing them in the name of the Father and of the Son and of the Holy Spirit, teaching them to observe all I have commanded you" (Matthew 28:19–20 [RSV]). In the logic of this charge, the commanded become the commanders: just as Christ is to Christians, so are Christians to non-Christians.

60. Patricia Seed has unearthed countless such rituals. I will cite just a few here: "Landing on the soil of the Bahamas on October 12, 1492, Christopher Columbus planted the royal banners of the king and queen (Ferdinand and Isabel). . . . In several of their journeys to the New World, Frenchmen claimed the region for the crown by planting a cross, a pillar, or a royal standard. . . . To discourage other Europeans . . . from claiming a region, Dutchmen planted their arms near Philadelphia (where the threat was Swedish) and on Cape Cod and at the mouth of the Connecticut River (where the menace was English)." Seed, *Ceremonies of Possession*, 1, 56, 166.

61. The United Nations Office for Outer Space Affiars, "Treaty on Principles Governing the Activities of States in the Exploration and Use of Outer Space, Including the Moon and Other Celestial Bodies," 1967; http://www.unoosa.org/oosa/index.html. Ironically, my browser tells me this UN site is "insecure."

62. Mircea Eliade, *The Sacred and the Profane: The Nature of Religion*, trans. Williard R. Trask (New York: Harcourt Brace, 1987), 33, 36–37.

63. Eliade, *The Sacred and the Profane*, 33.

64. Potter, *Earth Gazers*, 321.

65. https://www.youtube.com/watch?v=IBqbi-zly10.

66. https://www.youtube.com/watch?v=IBqbi-zly10. The trip-hop group Lemon Jelly samples the audio transcript from Apollo 11, including the Houston-Collins exchange, in their song "Space Walk": https://www.youtube.com/watch?v=u5VR05MBUXY.

67. Potter, *Earth Gazers*, 321.

68. Travis Clark, "Neil Armstrong Movie 'First Man' Omits the American Flag Being Planted on the Moon, and Star Ryan Gosling

Defend[s] the Decision," *Business Insider*, August 30, 2018; https://www.businessinsider.com/neil-armstrong-movie-first-man-omits-american-flag-on-moon-gosling-defends-2018-8.

69. David Moye, "Marco Rubio Slams U.S. Flag Omission in 'First Man,' and Twitter Users Pounce," *Huffington Post*, August 31, 2018; https://www.huffpost.com/entry/marco-rubio-first-man-american-flag_n_5b8984d3e4b0511db3d83483.

70. Moye, "Marco Rubio."

71. Ashley Collman, "Buzz Aldrin Tweets Photos of Neil Armstrong Planting the American Flag on the Moon Amid Controversy the 'First Man' Movie Omitted the Scene," *Business Insider*, September 4, 2018; https://www.businessinsider.com/buzz-aldrin-first-man-flag-controversy-tweet-2018-9.

72. Alan Taylor, "Photos: 50 Years since Apollo 8 Showed Us *Earthrise*," *Atlantic*, December 20, 2018; https://www.theatlantic.com/photo/2018/12/photos-50-years-since-apollo-8-showed-us-earthrise/578674/.

73. On the photo's contested authorship, see Taylor, "Photos."

74. Oliver, *Earth and World*, 3.

75. Martin Heidegger, "The Age of the World Picture," in *The Question Concerning Technology and Other Essays* (New York: Harper and Row, 1977). Originally published in Heidegger's 1952 *Holzwege* collection, this essay began as a 1938 Freiburg lecture called "The Establishing by Metaphysics of the Modern World Picture."

76. Heidegger, "Age of the World Picture," 133; emphasis added.

77. Jasanoff, "Heaven and Earth," 42.

78. "As the planet Earth's cloud-bewreathed, sapphire-watered blueness was dramatically displayed against the x-trillions of time years of nothingness . . . America's senior TV commentator exclaimed, 'There she is—floating there!'" Fuller, "Vertical Is to Live—Horizontal Is to Die," 36.

79. Cited in Karen Litfin, "The Gendered Eye in the Sky: Feminist Perspectives on Earth Observation Satellites," *Frontiers: A Journal of Women Studies* 18, no. 2 (Autumn 1997): 40.

80. MacLeish, "Riders on Earth."

81. MacLeish, "Riders on Earth."

82. Hannah Arendt, "The Conquest of Space and the Stature of Man," *New Atlantis* 18 (Fall 2007 [1963]): 53.

83. Scrooge again: "we" had had satellite photos for over a decade as well as a composite photograph of the "whole earth" since 1966. See note 32 above.

84. MacLeish, "Riders on Earth."

85. Borman, cited in Cosgrove, "Contested Global Visions," 282.

86. Oliver, *Earth and World*, 14.

87. A few days later, *Time* magazine echoed MacLeish's annunciation, proclaiming Borman, Lovell, and Anders "the indisputable Men of the Year" for having revealed "the fundamental unity of man" (Cosgrove, "Contested Global Visions," 284). Citing MacLeish's "Riders on the Earth," the article proclaims the dawn of "a new age, one that will inevitably reshape man's view of himself and his destiny" (TIME). Between the *New York Times* and *Time*, it suddenly seemed clear that Apollo 8's vision of the whole earth had ushered in a new age of global understanding.

88. Heidegger, "Age of the World Picture," 129–30, 134.

89. Job 38:11 (RSV).

90. "'Only a God Can Save Us': Der Spiegel's Interview with Martin Heidegger (May 31, 1976)," *Philosophy Today* 20 (Winter, 1976): 277.

91. Arendt, *The Human Condition.*

92. Richard Nixon, *Public Papers of the Presidents of the United States: Richard Nixon, January 20–December 31, 1969* (Washington, DC: Government Printing Office, 1969), 434.

93. Hans Blumenberg, cited in Lazier, "Earthrise," 612.

94. For the evolution of Lovelock's and Margulis's thought, and on the differences between Lovelock's monism and Margulis's pluralism, see Mary-Jane Rubenstein, *Pantheologies: Gods, Worlds, Monsters* (New York: Columbia University Press, 2018), 188–30.

95. Carl Sagan, cited in Oliver, *Earth and World*, 17–18.

96. Lazier, "Earthrise," 608.

97. Donna Haraway, *Staying with the Trouble: Making Kin in the Chthulucene* (Durham, NC: Duke University Press, 2016), 3.

98. On Bezos's own aspirations toward space exploration, see https://www.businessinsider.com/jeff-bezos-interview-axel -springer-ceo-amazon-trump-blue-origin-family-regulation -washington-post-2018-4?mod=article_inline.

99. Litfin, "Gendered Eye," 29.

100. James Cone, "Whose Earth Is It Anyway?," *Cross Currents* (2000): 43.

101. Oliver, *Earth and World*, 22.

102. Stewart Brand, "We Are as Gods," in *Whole Earth Catalog* (Fall 1968): 1.

103. Sylvia Wynter, "Beyond the Word of Man: Glissant and the New Discourse of the Antilles," *World Literature Today* 63, no. 4 (1989): 645.

104. Bill Anders, in Gene Farmer and Dora Jane Hamblin Farmer, *First on the Moon: A Voyage with Neil Armstrong, Michael Collins, and Edwin E. Aldrin, Jr.* (Boston: Little, Brown, 1970), 202.

105. Catherine Newell, "The Strange Case of Dr. Von Braun and Mr. Disney: Frontierland, Tomorrowland, and America's Final Frontier," *Journal of Religion and Popular Culture* 25 (Fall 2013): 427.

106. Newell, "Strange Case," 417.

107. Newell, "Strange Case," 418.

108. "What Are We Waiting For?," *Collier's* (March 22, 1952): 23.

109. Wernher von Braun, "Crossing the Last Frontier," *Collier's* (March 22, 1952): 25–26 24.

110. "What Are We Waiting For?," 23.

111. See Newell, "Strange Case," 420.

112. Newell estimates that "nearly a quarter of Americans watched 'Man in Space,' and that percentage possibly came closer to fifty . . . when the same episode was rebroadcast in early 1956. An even larger audience tuned in to watch the second installment, 'Man and the Moon,' on 28 December of the same year" ("Strange Case," 421.) An online clip of the former can be found at https://www.youtube.com/watch?v=2fautyLuuvo; most of the latter can be found at https://www.youtube.com/watch?v=eXIDFx74aSY.

113. Newell, "Strange Case," 420.

114. Richard Francaviglia, "History after Disney: The Signifi-

cance of 'Imagineered' Historical Places," *Public Historian* 17 (Autumn 1995): 74.

115. Newell, "Strange Case," 427.

116. John F. Szwed, *Space Is the Place: The Lives and Times of Sun Ra* (New York: Da Capo, 1998), 4.

117. "That is my music playing the kind of world I know about. It's like someone else from another planet trying to find out what to do . . . a pure solar world" (Sun Ra cited in Paul Youngquist, *A Pure Solar World: Sun Ra and the Birth of Afrofuturism* [Austin: University of Texas Press, 2016], 9.)

118. Youngquist, *A Pure Solar World*, 3.

119. Kodwo Eshun, *More Brilliant Than the Sun: Adventures in Sonic Fiction* (Interlink, 1999), 175, 193.

120. Alexander G. Weheliye, "'Feenin': Posthuman Voices in Contemporary Black Popular Music," *Social Text* 20, no. 2 (Summer 2002): 24.

121. The quotation continues, "I try to exaggerate that impossibility, until it's irritating, until it's annoying, and this annoyance is merely a threshold being crossed in the readers' heads, and once they unseize, unclench their sensorium, they'll have passed through a new threshold and they'll be in my world" (Eshun, *More Brilliant Than the Sun*, 193).

122. Sun Ra and His Myth Science Arkestra, "We Travel the Spaceways," *We Travel the Spaceways* (Chicago: El Saturn Records, 1967); Sun Ra, "Space Is the Place," *Space Is the Place* (Beverly Hills, CA: Blue Thumb Records, 1972); Sun Ra, "Rocket Number Nine," *Space Is the Place.*

123. Sun Ra, cited in William Sites, "Radical Culture in Black Necropolis: Sun Ra, Alton Abraham, and Postwar Chicago," *Journal of Urban History* 38, no. 4 (2012): 599; emphasis added.

124. Sun Ra, cited in Youngquist, *A Pure Solar World*, 69–70.

125. Composed mainly of improvised versions of favorite Disney tunes, the Arkestra's tribute album is entitled *Second Star to the Right: Salute to Walt Disney.*

126. Oscar Schachter, "Who Owns the Universe?," *Collier's* (March 22, 1952): 36.

127. Ashon T. Crawley, *Blackpentecostal Breath: The Aesthetics of Possibility* (New York: Fordham University Press, 2016), 192.

128. "There is," writes Eshun, "a big transference to tactility wherever sound gets subdermal" (Eshun, *More Brilliant Than the Sun*, 181).

129. See, e.g., Julian Henriques, *Sonic Bodies: Reggae Sound Systems, Performance Techniques, and Ways of Knowing* (New York: Continuum, 2011); Alexander G. Weheliye, *Phonographies: Grooves in Sonic Afro-Modernity* (Durham, NC: Duke University Press, 2005).

130. Sun Ra, cited in Sites, "Radical Culture in Black Necropolitics," 708.

131. Cited in David Stowe, "From Ephrata (F-Ra-Ta) to Arkestra," *Esoterica*; http://www.esoteric.msu.edu/VolumeV/Arkestra.htm.

132. NASA, "Fifth Meeting of the National Space Council," March 26, 2019; https://www.youtube.com/watch?v=ZQkoFuNWXg8.

133. Furthering this bald-faced revelation of the space program's racialized past, present, and future, Trump announced less than a year later that his newly created Space Force and the Air Force would be "separate but equal" entities. See Betsy Klein, "Trump: Space Force and Air Force Will Be 'Separate but Equal,'" *CNN* (June 18, 2018); https://www.cnn.com/2018/06/18/politics/trump-space-force-air-force/index.html.

134. Malcolm X, "By Any Means Necessary," speech for the *Organization for Afro American Unity*, June 28, 1964; https://www.youtube.com/watch?v=WBS416EZsKM.

135. "Mike Pence, Boldly Sending America Back to Where Man Has Gone Before," *Washington Post*, March 28, 2019.

136. Harlan K. Ullman and James P. Wade, *Shock and Awe: Achieving Rapid Dominance* (Washington, DC: Center for Advanced Concepts and Technology, 1996).

137. "Mike Pence," *Washington Post*; emphasis added. With thanks to Maggie Greaves for pointing me toward this source.

138. "Mike Pence," *Washington Post*.

139. Donald Trump, cited in Brian Resnick, "Trump's Confusing Tweet About 'Mars (of Which the Moon Is a Part),' Explained," *Vox*,

June 7, 2019; https://www.vox.com/science-and-health/2019/6/7
/18656865/trump-moon-mars-tweet-artemis-whaaa.

140. Resnick, "Trump's Confusing Tweet."

141. Lucianne Walkowicz, "The Interplanetary Political Football
of Space Exploration," *Scientific American*, October 23, 2017; https://
blogs.scientificamerican.com/observations/the-interplanetary
-political-football-of-space-exploration/.

142. NASA, "Nasa Statement on National Space Council Policy
for Future American Leadership in Space," October 5, 2017; https://
www.nasa.gov/press-release/nasa-statement-on-national-space
-council-policy-for-future-american-leadership-in.

143. Barack Obama, cited in Kenneth Chang, "One Small Tweet
for Trump, One Giant Question for Nasa's Moon Plans," *New York
Times*, June 7, 2019; https://www.nytimes.com/2019/06/07/science
/trump-moon-nasa.html.

144. Walkowicz, "Interplanetary Political Football."

145. Mike Wall, "New Space Mining Legislation Is 'History in the
Making,'" *Space.com*, November 20, 2015; https://www.space.com
/31177-space-mining-commercial-spaceflight-congress.html.

146. United States Congress, "U.S. Commercial Space Launch
Competitiveness Act," November 25, 2015; https://www.congress
.gov/bill/114th-congress/house-bill/2262/text. For a distillation
and explanation of the bill vis-à-vis space mining, see Wall, "New
Space Mining."

147. Arendt, cited in Lazier, "Earthrise," 62n2.

148. Donald J. Trump and Michael Pence, "Remarks by President
Trump and Vice President Pence at Signing Ceremony for Space
Policy Directive—1," December 11, 2017; https://www.whitehouse
.gov/briefings-statements/remarks-president-trump-vice
-president-pence-signing-ceremony-space-policy-directive-1/.

149. I'm not making it up. Elon Musk's plan to "terraform"
Mars—that is, to turn it into a planet like earth—involves "warm-
ing it up" by attacking the frozen poles with nuclear bombs. See
Loren Grush, "Elon Musk Elaborates on His Proposal to Nuke
Mars," *Verge*, October 2, 2015; https://www.theverge.com/2015/10

/2/9441029/elon-musk-mars-nuclear-bomb-colbert-interview
-explained.

150. On the estimated 20,000 pieces of human trash orbiting the
earth, see NASA, "Space Debris and Human Spacecraft," September 26, 2013; https://www.nasa.gov/mission_pages/station/news
/orbital_debris.html. On the human detritus not decaying on the
lunar surface, including spacecraft, family photos, wet wipes, and
bags of the astronauts' urine, vomit, and feces, see Megan Garber,
"The Trash We've Left on the Moon," *Atlantic*, December 19, 2012;
https://www.theatlantic.com/technology/archive/2012/12/the
-trash-weve-left-on-the-moon/266465/. On the recent effort to
glorify this detritus as archaeological treasure, see United States
Senate Bill 1694: "One Small Step to Protect Human Heritage in
Space Act," introduced May 23, 2019; https://www.govtrack.us
/congress/bills/116/s1694/text.

151. "You have given us a charge today and it is right on time,
and I want to say thank you for that vision and leadership. Our
agency, NASA, is gonna do everything in its power to meet that vision, to meet that deadline, uh, and you have my full commitment
to achieving that" (Jim Bridenstine, NASA, "Fifth Meeting of the
National Space Council").

152. "The moon is a testbed for Mars. It provides an opportunity
to demonstrate new technologies that could help build self-
sustaining outposts off Earth" (NASA, "Explore Moon to Mars").

153. NASA, "Explore Moon to Mars."

154. In 2008, NASA published an "Astrobiology Roadmap"
that began to consider the ethical problems of encountering and
engaging not only life forms but also ecosystems on other planets. In 2015, it published a revised version called "Astrobiology
Strategy," "with the role of ethics still acknowledged but pushed
into the margins, consigned to a single paragraph in a document
almost exclusively given over to science conceived of in terms
which are functional to the discovery of life." As astroethicists
James Schwartz and Tony Milligan explain, "there is a reasonable
concern that ethics may be a source of unhelpful constraints which

could stand in the way of the emerging space economy" (James S. J. Schwartz and Tony Milligan, "Introduction: The Scope and Content of Space Ethics," in *The Ethics of Space Exploration*, ed. James S. J. Schwartz and Tony Milligan [New York: Springer, 2016], 6.)

155. "Becoming Interplanetary: What Living on Earth Can Teach Us about Living on Mars," public forum, Library of Congress, 2018; https://www.decolonizemars.org/becoming-interplanetary.

156. Walkowicz herself has been the most outspoken critic of this strategy. See Lucianne Walkowicz, "Let's Not Use Mars as a Backup Planet," *TED* talk, March 2015; https://www.ted.com/talks/lucianne_walkowicz_let_s_not_use_mars_as_a_backup_planet?language=en.

157. Christopher Nolan, *Interstellar*, (2014).

158. Lucianne Walkowicz in Doris Elin Salazar, "The Ethics of Mars Exploration: Q&A with Lucianne Walkowicz," *Space.com*, August 2, 2017; https://www.space.com/37679-lucianne-walkowicz-talks-mars-ethics.html. For early work on the "inherent value" of celestial bodies and the ethics of terraforming, see Eugene C. Hargrove, ed., *Beyond Spaceship Earth: Environmental Ethics and the Solar System* (San Francisco: Sierra Club Books, 1986); Alain Pompidou, "The Ethics of Space Policy," *United Nations Educational, Scientific, and Cultural Organization* (2000), https://unesdoc.unesco.org/ark:/48223/pf0000120681. As the latter declares, "Earth and Space are not ours. They are treasures, real and symbolic, which we owe to ourselves to safeguard for our descendants" (ii).

159. Chanda Prescod-Weinstein, cited in Ryan F. Mandelbaum, "Decolonizing Mars: Are We Thinking about Space All Wrong?," *Gizmodo*, November 20, 2018; https://gizmodo.com/decolonizing-mars-are-we-thinking-about-space-explorat-1830348568. For a defense of Martian value based on its inherent beauty, see Sean McMahon, "The Aesthetic Objection to Terraforming Mars," in *Ethics of Space Exploration*, ed. Schwartz and Milligan.

160. Wall, "New Space Mining."

161. In Mandelbaum, "Decolonizing Mars."

162. In Meghan Bartels, "Should We Colonize Space? Some

People Argue We Need to Decolonize It Instead," *Newsweek*, May 25, 2018; https://www.newsweek.com/should-we-colonize -space-some-people-argue-we-need-decolonize-it-instead-945130.

163. In Nadia Drake, "We Need to Change the Way We Talk about Space Exploration," *National Geographic*, November 9, 2018; https://www.nationalgeographic.com/science/2018/11/we-need-to -change-way-we-talk-about-space-exploration-mars/.

164. NASA, "Style Guide for Nasa History Authors and Editors," August 2012; https://history.nasa.gov/styleguide.html.

165. Artemis, they explain, "*was* the twin sister of Apollo and goddess of the Moon in Greek mythology" (NASA, "Explore Moon to Mars").

166. Artemis "personifies our path to the Moon as the name of NASA's program to return astronauts to the lunar surface by 2024, including the first woman and the next man" (NASA, "Explore Moon to Mars").

167. Enongo Lumumba-Kasongo, in Mandelbaum, "Decoloniz-ing Mars." For an argument in favor of the "intrinsic value" of ex-traterrestrial microbes, see Charles S. Cockell, "The Ethical Status of Microbial Life on Earth and Elsewhere: In Defence of Intrinsic Value," in *Ethics of Space Exploration*, ed. Schwartz and Milligan.

168. On Saturday, May 30, 2020, SpaceX made private-industrial history by launching a rocket from the Kennedy Space Center carrying NASA astronauts Robert Behnken and Douglas Hurley, who docked a day later at the International Space Station. On NASA's relation to SpaceX prior to this event, see Eric Berger, "Bfr Now? In New Starship Details, Musk Reveals a More Practical Approach," February 1, 2019; and Brian Resnick, "Trump's Hasty Plan to Get Americans Back on the Moon by 2024, Explained," *Vox*, June 14, 2019; https://www.vox.com/science-and-health/2019/5/22 /18623177/nasa-artemis-moon-2024-trump-bridenstine-explained.

169. Calvin Warren, "Black Nihilism and the Politics of Hope," *CR: The New Centennial Review* 15, no. 1 (Spring 2015): 232. Subse-quent references will be cited internally.

170. See, e.g., Martin Luther King Jr., "An Experiment in Love,"

in *A Testament of Hope: The Essential Writings and Speeches of Martin Luther King, Jr.*, ed. James M. Washington (1958; San Francisco: HarperSanFrancisco, 1986); and Martin Luther King Jr., "Suffering and Faith," in *A Testament of Hope: The Essential Writings and Speeches of Martin Luther King, Jr.*, ed. James M. Washington (1960; San Francisco: HarperSanFrancisco, 1986).

171. Cornel West, *Race Matters* (New York: Vintage, 1994), 23.

172. Mike Wall, "A Year after SpaceX's 1st Falcon Heavy Launch, Starman (and Tesla) Sail On," *Space.com*, February 6, 2019; https://www.space.com/43242-spacex-falcon-heavy-starman-tesla-launch-anniversary.html. For a comparative map of the roadster's orbit with that of Ceres and four major planets, see www.whereisroadster.com.

173. Mike Wall, "Elon Musk's Tesla Roadster Headed for Earth or Venus Crash (in a Few Million Years)," *Space.com*, February 15, 2018: https://www.space.com/39704-elon-musk-tesla-roadster-earth-venus-crash.html.

174. Brett Molina, "How Elon Musk Cleverly Used the Starman to Promote His Car Brand (Tesla)," *USA Today*, February 9, 2018; https://www.usatoday.com/story/tech/news/2018/02/09/how-elon-musk-cleverly-used-starman-promote-his-car-brand-tesla/319798002/.

175. Maezawa and Musk, *First Private Passenger*. Incidentally, David Bowie played Nikola Tesla in Christopher Nolan's 2006 film *The Prestige*.

176. The interviews can be found at https://dearmoon.earth/interview/ringostarr/ and https://dearmoon.earth/interview/firstman/.

177. Cited in Chang, "With Moon as His Muse."

178. Guy Raz, "The Next Frontier," *TED Radio Hour* (December 21, 2018); https://www.npr.org/programs/ted-radio-hour/674248681/the-next-frontier.

179. David Bowie, "Space Oddity," *David Bowie* (London: Trident Studios), 1979.

FACIAL RECOGNITION

Thomas A. Carlson

> In an age of identity theft and virtual realities, the face has remained one of the last traces of human selfhood. When faces become masks we can change at will, where does the fake end and the real begin?
>
> MARK C. TAYLOR

> A truth I've come to know was being driven home, that your sight does not exist in your eyes. Sight exists in your mind and heart.
>
> JOHN DUGDALE

On April 12, 1961, Soviet Air Force pilot and cosmonaut Yuri Gagarin became the first human being to fly into outer space, making one complete orbit of the earth in his capsule on the spacecraft Vostok 1. That same year, the ethical thinker and phenomenologist Emmanuel Levinas published not only his first major philosophical work, *Totality and Infinity: An Essay on Exteriority*,[1] but also a brief essay—"Heidegger, Gagarin, and Us"—that reflects on the significance of cosmonaut Gagarin's singular human achievement in relation to Martin Heidegger's philosophy. Levinas and Heidegger both see in humanity's technologically enabled entry into space a radical kind of uprooting,

but they understand the meaning of such uprooting in fundamentally different ways. As Mary-Jane Rubenstein notes in her
essay here, Heidegger was "certainly frightened [*erschroken*]"
when he saw "photographs of the earth taken from the moon.
We don't need an atom bomb at all; the uprooting of human beings is already here [*die Entwurzelung des Menschen ist schon da*].
We now have only purely technological relations [*rein technische
Verhältnisse*]. It is no longer an earth on which human beings
live today."[2] While Heidegger is not commenting here specifically on Gagarin but on the Apollo photographs that Rubenstein
discusses in her essay, he would surely see already in Gagarin's
achievement yet another sign that nothing in the cosmos can
now escape the reach of our technological "enframing" (*das
Gestell*), a sign that, by leaving the earth and looking back upon
it as he does, Gagarin participates in the "fundamental event
of the modern age" that is "the conquest of the world as picture."[3] Differing sharply from Heidegger, Levinas posits a close
kinship between the uprooting systems of modern technology
that enabled Gagarin's spaceflight, on the one hand, and, on the
other, an ethical sensibility that Levinas finds in Judaism. On
Levinas's reading, Judaism and modern technology are similar in that they stand equally, and pointedly, at odds both with
what Levinas disgustedly calls "the pagan recesses of our Western souls" and with a related Christianity that has "conquered
humanity" because it "continues to give piety roots, nurturing
itself on landscapes and memories culled from family, tribes,
and nations."[4]

From a perspective that recurs influentially in theories of
secularization from Max Weber to Peter Berger, Levinas contends that, "like technology," Judaism "has demystified the universe. It has freed Nature from a spell. Because of its abstract
universalism, it runs up against imaginations and passions. But
it has discovered man in the nudity of his face." The claim is not
only provocative but also polemical, bringing to its final point
the essay's sharp attack on Heidegger's existential phenom-

enology and on Heidegger's related analyses of technology. Seeing operative in Heidegger's construal of our existence as "Being-there" (*Dasein*) or "Being-in-the-world" an attachment to nature, landscape, and place that "is the very splitting of humanity into natives and strangers," Levinas takes the real lesson of Gagarin's flight to be this: technology goes beyond the alternatives of enrootedness and exile, it "wrenches us out of the Heideggerian world and superstitions surrounding *Place*. From this point on, an opportunity appears to us: to perceive men outside the situation in which they are placed, and let the human face shine in all of its nudity."[5] In this way, Levinas sees in Gagarin's standing-beyond the earthly world an opening to something crucial about the ethical relation as Levinas understands it: the other person, and more specifically the face of the other person, is ethically significant—and calls me to responsibility—not thanks to that person's situation within the context or horizon of any given world but rather through a radical transcendence of, or absolution from, any such context or horizon. Indeed, for Levinas it is the ethical face-to-face between persons that lends any eventual significance to the world—and not a world and its structures of significance that would allow a face to appear.

As Rubenstein's essay richly signals, Levinas may have been overly optimistic in his thought that technological systems so closely bound up with our imperialistic, militaristic, and racist politics and economics could ever have transported a man "outside" of horizons. But Levinas's intuition that the significance of modern technology concerns the human face in some notable way remains an important one, and it can lead us to ask: What of technology and the human face today, nearly six decades after Gagarin's flight and Levinas's provocative reflection on it? How do things stand today in the interplay between technology and this aspect of our existence—the face—where we might hope to see one another, and where we might hope to be seen, as distinctively human?

SEEING AND BEING SEEN TECHNOLOGICALLY

It may be understatement to say that our experience both of seeing and of being seen are today undergoing—thanks to new technologies of image production, reproduction, recording, storage, transmission, and so on—transformations we can barely begin responding to because we can barely imagine them, even as they seem increasingly and radically to reshape our world and experience. At the level of seeing, to note one current example, the production of "deep fake" videos and their dissemination on a global scale at the speed of light are now becoming as easy and as common as word processing.[6] Consequently, we are involved increasingly—and often unknowingly—in modes of seeing that take as perfectly real what is, in fact, utterly fictitious. Notable especially for their "face swap" function, deep fakes make use of "real people, real faces" and "close to photorealistic footage" in order to present us with "entirely unreal events."[7] Deep fakes are common in the seemingly (and only seemingly) benign realms of entertainment and consumer culture, where they can indeed be good for a laugh (witness, for example, Steve Buscemi's face integrated seamlessly with the body and voice of Jennifer Lawrence[8]). But deep fakes have far more troubling uses and potentials in such realms as news, politics, and warfare. A logic of warfare is in fact operative at the center of the deep fake technology itself, which derives its name from the process of artificial intelligence's "deep learning," where computer programs learn and evolve in and through their own operation. In this particular case, the "learning" transpires within a "generative adversarial network" or GAN, which stages a kind of battle between two programs: one generative, working to create images that will not be detected as fake, and one discriminating, working to detect and eliminate the generated fakes; as the generative program is repeatedly challenged by the discriminating, it learns how to refine its deceptions, and as the discriminating program is repeatedly challenged by fakes, it learns ever better to detect

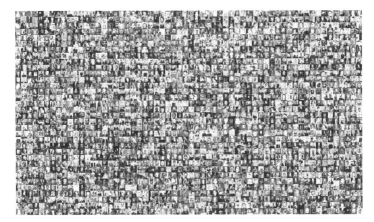

FIGURE 3.1. A visualization of 2,000 of the 100,000 identities included in the MS-Celeb-1M dataset distributed by Microsoft Research. License: Open Data Commons Public Domain Dedication. MegaPixels describes itself as "an art and research project investigating the ethics, origins, and individual privacy implications of face recognition datasets created 'in the wild.'" https://megapixels.cc/datasets/msceleb/.

them. As each program tries to outdo the other—rapidly running billions of rounds—and the generative program responds ever more effectively to the challenges of the discriminating, the images likely to fool us grow ever more lifelike and convincing. The seeming reality, and personality, of the images thus derive from and grow deeper thanks to the operation and interaction of wholly impersonal programs. A long-standing confidence in photography or video's ability to secure—and expand—our access to the real thus becomes a ground upon which the purely simulated image can disseminate as truth what is in fact a lie. However, as we ourselves grow increasingly aware of the possibility that every image we see may be a deep fake, such a distinction itself between truth and lie grows difficult to hold on to. We might see in this difficulty not just a technological counterpart to but an active and distinctive part of our current politics and related cultures, in which the lie—visual as well as verbal—becomes so pervasive that more and more people grow unable, or unwilling, to maintain, or even entertain, any distinction between real and fake.[9]

It is perhaps no mistake that the uncanny power of the deep fake is centered around the face swap and the voice: those dimensions of the human person we often take to be most real, and most intimate to the person's uniqueness—the aspect through which, as Levinas never tires of insisting, the person calls to us, even accuses us, in her singularity. And in related fashion, it is probably no mistake that one of the most profound, and for many people one of the most troubling, transformations underway today with our technologically mediated *being seen* focuses likewise on the face: the advancement and spread of "facial recognition" systems that subject us increasingly to a new mode of being seen—always and everywhere—that we ourselves cannot see. In those systems, we, while in reality singular persons, are "recognized" and "identified" not in our personal singularity, and by other singular persons, but by means of impersonal machines and programs that "see" us through the deployment of massive data sets and statistical calculation. In one of its disturbing uses recently in the news, facial recognition technology has been introduced into the classroom in order to monitor students through machine readings of their faces and thus to judge their levels of interest, engagement, responsiveness, and the like, as if in an effort to demonstrate the reality and truth of DeLillo's fiction ("All the sensors in the room that are watching you, listening to you, tracking your habits, measuring your capabilities"[10]). Even more disturbing are the uses of surveillance and facial recognition technologies within the security state and contemporary policing, where racial biases programmed into these systems may well perpetuate or expand deadly forms of dehumanizing injustice.[11] The fact that our faces specifically are involved, or indeed enframed, in these systems of surveillance seems important to explaining the relatively high levels of discomfort and resistance recently expressed in relation to them. For setting aside the fact that we are dealing in this particular case with the human face, we have, socially and culturally speaking, already massively given in—even eagerly given ourselves over—to the reality that the lives we lead by digital means (which means increasingly most every aspect of life) are subjected through and through, and in ways we don't even realize, to surveillance, storage, and eventual sale in the capitalist marketplace. Social psychologist Shoshana Zuboff and others quite rightly argue that ours has become an age of "surveillance capitalism,"[12] wherein our very life experience, or what once may have been called our private life, becomes a raw material appropriated—largely without our permission—by a very small number of others who convert that material into capital. The chance of profit within this realm of surveillance is tied notably to the calculative and predictive power of the surveillance system. Thoroughgoing surveillance of our behavior, and a recording of its past, prove financially valuable insofar as they yield predictive power in relation to our behavior's future. The logical extreme of such predictive calculation would be actual control of that behavior itself. As Zuboff succinctly observes, "it is no longer enough to automate information flows about us; the goal now is to automate us."[13] Or as Mark Taylor puts it here in "Gathering Remains," the screens through which digitized and coded images circulate today "reverse the direction of the gaze by looking at the people looking at them. Rather than humans manipulating images on screens, algorithms and codes control the lives of the people who created them."[14]

SUBSTITUTION AND MORTAL CAPABILITY

No philosopher in the twentieth century was more prescient than Heidegger with respect to the driving obsession in modern thought and its technological culture with the kind of predictive calculation that Zuboff's troubling analysis highlights. If the two recent technological transformations I've noted with respect to our seeing and being seen are especially telling in relation to political, economic, social, and cultural conditions where privacy, individuality, and personality seem threatened or effaced, Heidegger can help us to appreciate the senses in which they involve a general, seemingly unlimited, logic of the substitute. In its digital mediations, every single face we see today may be a fake, and not that of the unique person we believe; and all real faces, though each singular and personal, are threatened with capture and containment, universally, by pervasive systems of surveillance that remain frighteningly impersonal—to the point that the term "personalization" itself names what in fact "defiles, ignores, overrides, and displaces everything about you and me that is personal."[15] As Taylor's incisive analysis here suggests, such a perversion and eclipse of the personal with respect to the face manifests in distilled form something characteristic more broadly of our current "metaphysics of the code": "if natural, social, economic, and cultural formations are constituted by digital code, then all images and signs are fungible, i.e., they are commutable or interchangeable and can be combined with and translated into each other."[16] By contrast, then, to the Levinas who could see in our technological systems a liberation of the face in its nudity, we today find the face captured and exploited, and endlessly replaced or exchanged, within economically and politically charged technological frames that threaten to efface its singularity and thus muffle its ethical call.

Such an effacement of the personal could be read as a latter-day variant on a paradox that Heidegger points to already within his analyses of the modern metaphysics undergirding scientific technology, where an eclipse of the individual person in her uniqueness stems from the calculating self-assertion of our very human subjectivity—which reduces not only the world but also the human subject to the status of object (or which, as he later sees things, dissolves even objectivity within an all-encompassing "standing reserve"). As Heidegger puts it in his 1938 "Age of the World Picture" ("Die Zeit des Weltbildes"), "in the planetary imperialism of technologically organized man, the subjectivism of man attains its acme, from which it will descend to the level of organized uniformity and there firmly establish itself. The uniformity becomes the surest instrument of total, i.e., technological rule over the earth. The modern freedom of subjectivity vanishes totally in the objectivity commensurate with it."[17] Under the calculating gaze of modern technology, all beings come to appear as objects apart from which human subjectivity stands in a relation of willful and totalizing self-assertion, but that self-assertive project comes to subject even the human individual to its objectifying gaze. Human self-assertion can thus be understood as central to a project of mastery and control that ultimately undermines itself, as the will to control finally runs out of control. In Heidegger's view of the matter, the tendency of our modern, technological self-assertion toward uniformity and control involves a logic of substitution or equivalence that happens to suit quite well the dynamics of ever-accelerating production, consumption, and replacement within capitalist markets that come to span the globe: as "the object-character of technological dominion spreads itself over the earth ever more quickly, ruthlessly, and completely," the "humanness of man and the thingness of things dissolve into the calculated market value of a market" that "trades in the nature of Being" and thus subjects all beings to calculation, even or especially when numbers are not needed.[18] In this way, the calculation of markets is founded in a logic of the replacement, substitute, or fake that Heidegger takes to be distinctive of modern thought and culture more broadly, where technoscientific rationality "replaces the frailties of things by the thought-contrived fabrications of calculated objects. These objects are produced to be used up. The more quickly they are used up, the greater becomes the necessity to replace them even more quickly and more readily. What is lasting in the presence of objective things is not their self-subsistence within the world that is their own. What is constant in things produced as objects merely for consumption is: the substitute—*Ersatz*" (WPF, 129–30; 308).

As Taylor emphasizes in his essay here, extending insights that play centrally in Heidegger, modern humanity's project of rational-technical mastery—and its reduction of all being to an objectivity amenable to market calculations—should be understood to involve a flight from the transience and loss that remain, nonetheless, inherent to our mortal existence. An important discussion of modernity's technological flight from mortality—in Heidegger's text "What Are Poets For?"—is guided by poet Rainer Maria Rilke's claim that our modernity is a destitute time. That destitution is multilayered. Our time is destitute, Rilke and Heidegger alike suggest, thanks to a default of God that we—like those who encounter the madman in Nietzsche's marketplace[19]—cannot even recognize as default (WPF 91; 269). But then, at another level, our time is destitute less because God is dead and more "because mortals are hardly aware and capable of their own mortality" (WPF 96; 274). As Taylor's work has been insisting for decades now, to think through the death of God is not to set our humanity in the place of God, such as might the techno-utopian aspiration to transcend our mortality; it is rather to rethink the human in a manner that acknowledges, and even affirms, its essential mortality.

But how is it that we, mortals, have grown incapable of our own mortality? We have grown so not only insofar as the gaze of rational-technical calculation seeks to transcend the limits and conditions of our finitude; we have grown so also (and this is essentially related) insofar as the gaze of rational-technical calculation eclipses what Heidegger, drawing on Rilke and Pascal, evokes as a thinking of the heart. As contrasted with the calculating rationality of modern metaphysics in the lineage of Descartes, such a thinking of the heart would disclose, and attend to, the frailty of things in their uniqueness and the mortality of persons in their singularity—which are both eclipsed increasingly by the ever spreading, ever accelerating, and seemingly endless movement of production, consumption, and replacement within our technological systems, mass culture, and related market economies. "At nearly the same time as Descartes," Heidegger reminds us, "Pascal discovers the logic of the heart as over against the logic of calculating reason. The inner and invisible domain of the heart is not only more inward than the interior that belongs to calculating representation and therefore more invisible; it also extends further than does the realm of merely producible objects. Only in the invisible innermost of the heart is man inclined toward what there is for him to love: the forefathers, the dead, the children, those who are to come" (WPF 127–28; 306).

UNDERSTANDING AFFECTION (OR: LOVING DESTRUCTION)

As this reference to a thinking of the heart might suggest, and despite the common assumptions and assertions of readers troubled by perceived ethical and erotic failures in Heidegger's thinking, Heidegger points recurrently in his writing and teaching to the heart's disclosive power—to the role of affection, broadly, but also of love quite specifically, in opening our worlds and in sustaining our engagement with the world. The references that Heidegger makes to the role of heart or love in our encounter with the world are not trivial or passing, either. In fact he links heart and love to terms as central to his thinking as "thinking" itself. For example, his important text from the early 1950s, published as "What Is Called Thinking?" and based on his first teaching after the Second World War, defines thinking as the thankfulness and devotion of a "taking to heart" (*beherzigen*) that "lets be." And in some of his earliest teaching, he explicitly ties love to a concept as fundamental as "understanding": while *Being and Time* contends in one of its most central developments that "all sight is grounded primarily in understanding [*alle sicht primär in Verstehen grundet . . . ist*],"[20] an important lecture course from 1919–20, *Basic Problems of Phenomenology*, while setting ground for *Being and Time*, asserts in its concluding session that "understanding is in *love* [*In der **Liebe** ist Verstehen*]."[21]

By "understanding"—as the primary ground of all sight—
Heidegger means our primordial, pre-theoretical capacity to
move about and live our lives in a world that is always already
familiar and of concern to us in its meaning. Within that familiarity and concern, the world is given not as an object of theoretical contemplation or logical analysis (which are always
secondary operations, founded on, and abstracted from, this
more fundamental familiarity and concern), but as the context
of significance in which we are always already making sense of
our lives—practically and experientially—through the projection and pursuit of the various possibilities opened to us by our
Being-in the particular world that is ours. Placing "love" in ap-
position to this being "able to go along with—being familiar,"
Heidegger takes love "as motive ground of the phenomenological understanding." (BP 142; 185)

The construal and practice of philosophy that accompanies
this understanding of understanding—as grounded in love—is
one driven by a need "for the fullness of life": "Every genuine
philosophy," Heidegger comments while evoking philosophy's
affective ground, "is born out of the *need* for the fullness of
life and not out of a pseudo problem in epistemology or out of
a basic question of ethics" (BP 115; 150). Observing that such
pseudoproblems are especially prevalent "in the philosophy
of religion, not to mention the pseudo problems of theology
and apologetics" (BP 121; 158), Heidegger goes on to claim that
their overcoming or avoidance requires what he calls—echoing
Luther and foretelling Jacques Derrida—a "destruction." Inspired and informed in no small part by Luther's effort to free
Christian believers from the rigidified categories of late medieval scholasticism and thus to return the Christian experience
to its original existential sense, Heidegger in this early text
strikingly links the project of destruction to the work of love in
human experience. More specifically: at stake in such destruction is a distinction Heidegger draws between philosophy as a
movement of love and the "logical tyranny"—often mistaken

for philosophy—that "frightens life" by staring at it (BP 198; 263). Rather than working to lock in upon objects (which will not get us closer to life), philosophy calls for a letting-go or a letting-be that enriches the self in the life one lives: "Philosophical activity itself requires a releasement [*ein Sich-Loslassen*] into the ultimate tendencies of life and a return into its ultimate motives" (BP 198; 263). It is from this perspective that the phenomenological method's "first step" is the "critical destruction" (BP 126; 164) of any objectification of life, of the self, and of its world:

> the having-me-myself does not involve staring at an object, it is not a fixed determination. It is rather the vital process of winning and losing familiarity with concrete lived life itself. As a process it is not a matter of dwelling upon an object. Rather, coming from out of life-experiences, it is a matter of leaning forward [*sich Vorneigen*] into new, vital horizons that are near. It is a coming from and a leaning-forward, wherein I, living, *am intelligible to myself*, even if what is experienced presents the most difficult puzzle of my existence. The intelligible context is life itself, and therein I have my self. (BP 126; 164)

If Heidegger is calling for a critical-phenomenological destruction already in the late teens and early twenties, *Being and Time* answers that call in a decisive way; and we can thus read these earlier claims—that understanding is in love, and that the critical-destructive work of philosophy is a work of love—as a version of the claim in *Being and Time* that understanding always has some "mood" [*Stimmung*] or that our affective disposition—neither simply "within" us nor simply "outside" us—is integral to the appearance of whatever appears to us in our world. As Heidegger notes, *Being and Time*'s insight into the disclosive power of mood has among its few precursors in the history of philosophy two notable instances: Aristotle's analysis of the affects (*pathe*) in book 2 of his *Rhetoric*, and then the tradition of Christian thinking in which Pascal, following Augustine, contends that certain forms of sight or understanding become possible thanks only to love. For both the Pascal and the Augustine whom Heidegger cites within his treatment of mood's role in disclosing the world and thus grounding the appearance of what appears, one enters the truth only through love or *caritas*. "One does not enter truth," Augustine writes in a passage that Heidegger cites, "except through charity."[22]

Among recent phenomenologists, Jean-Luc Marion richly argues that we find in this tradition of Augustine and Pascal not a correspondence theory of truth, where the mind seeks to form within itself a representation that would prove adequate to the thing, but instead an erotic truth. While in his development of that erotic mode of truth Marion attributes to Heidegger a failure or a forgetting with regard to love, arguing that a genuinely erotic truth departs from Heidegger's notion of truth as *aletheia* or un-concealment, Heidegger actually does understand love as inherent to this latter, alethic, notion of truth—and along lines that will prove important to our interest here in the question of imagination.

To say that understanding always has its mood is to signal the indissoluble link that Heidegger sees between the existential structure of projection and the existential structure of thrownness. This link implies in turn an inextricable tie between the temporal dimension (or "ecstasis" as Heidegger would put it) of futurity and the temporal dimension or ecstasis of pastness or the having-been. The fact that we are never without some mood, and the fact that we can shape but never escape or master our moodiness, discloses to us the facticity of our existence as such: the reality that we always already find ourselves existing in a given world and that we do not initiate or control such existence from the ground up. "The pure 'that it is' shows itself, but the 'whence' and the 'whither' remain in darkness" (BT 173; SZ 134). On this view, we find ourselves always already underway with existence as if "thrown" into it from God-knows-where. This seemingly passive aspect of our existence, however, according to which we receive existence without initiating or controlling it, remains inseparable from our active projection and pursuit, from out of such receptivity, of the possible ways of being that are opened up to us by our given world—which is to say, by the contexts of significance with which we are always already dealing pretheoretically and nonthematically but understandingly. To say that understanding always has its mood is to say that Dasein is *thrown* projection, or *factical* existence. "The understanding has in itself the existential structure that we call 'projection'" (BT 184–85; SZ 145), and thus the Being of Dasein in its primordial understanding is inherently anticipatory. The ongoing anticipation at the heart of Dasein's Being, however, its projection of possibility, must not be confused with any form of awaiting that can see (or calculate) ahead of time some planned or programmed actuality. The anticipatory movement of projection is irreducible, or ever open, and thus it does not (and cannot) amount to

comporting oneself towards a plan that has been thought out, and in accordance with which Dasein arranges its Being. On the contrary, any Dasein has, as Dasein, already projected itself, and as long as it is, it is projecting. As long as it is, Dasein always has understood itself and always will understand itself in terms of possibilities. Furthermore, the character of understanding as projection is such that it does not grasp thematically that upon which it projects—that is to say, possibilities. Grasping it in such a manner would take away from what is projected its very character as a possibility and would reduce it to the given contents that we have in mind; whereas projection, in throwing, throws before itself the possibility as a possibility, and lets it *be* as such." (BT 185; SZ 145)

Such a "letting-be" on the part of understanding—a phrase Heidegger often associates or even equates with love and its

essential anticipation—is understood here as nothing less than
sight, itself taken not as a function of the eyes but as the opening or clearing of the "there" where we always already find ourselves: "In its projective character," Heidegger writes in *Being
and Time*, "understanding goes to make up existentially what
we call Dasein's 'sight' [*Sicht*]" (BT 186; SZ 146), and he then explains, and cautions, that we go wrong in assuming an everyday
physiological understanding of sight. In order not to misunder-
stand the term "sight," we must see that "it corresponds to the
'clearedness' [*Gelichtetheit*] which we took as characterizing the
disclosedness of the 'there.' 'Seeing' does not mean just perceiv-
ing with bodily eyes, but neither does it mean pure non-sensory
awareness of something present-at-hand in its presence-at-
hand. In giving an existential signification to 'sight,' we have
merely drawn upon the peculiar feature of seeing, that it lets
entities that are accessible to it be encountered unconcealedly
in themselves" (BT 187; SZ 147). Along lines that resonate significantly with Heidegger's analysis of the imagination in Kant
as the common root of sensibility and understanding (an analysis to which we will turn momentarily), Heidegger notes that
"by showing how all sight is grounded primarily in understanding . . . we have deprived pure intuition [*Anschauen*] of its priority, which corresponds noetically to the priority of the present-
at-hand in traditional ontology. 'Intuition' and 'thinking' are
both derivatives of understanding, and already rather remote
ones" (BT 187; SZ 147).

PREDILECTION AND TRUTH

This understanding of sight as "clearedness," itself tied to the
notion that understanding is in love, goes hand in hand with
Heidegger's reinterpretation of truth as *aletheia*, in which he
likewise sees a role for love. Truth, he famously claims, does
not consist most fundamentally in the correspondence or ade-
quation between representations in the mind and things in the

world, however valid and important such a construal of truth may remain (and in our current political-cultural climate, it could not be more important); before we can even enter into a debate about the adequacy or inadequacy of our representations to a world of things "out there," however, these themselves—things and representations alike—must have come to light, and it is this coming-to-light that for Heidegger constitutes truth at its most fundamental level. Playing on the etymology of the Greek term commonly translated as "truth," *aletheia* (from the alpha-privative plus -*lethe*, meaning darkness or forgetfulness), Heidegger understands truth to be the "un-concealing" of things, the coming of things into light, visibility, and presence from out of a darkness or invisibility or absence that prove thus *inherent to* but also *concealed by* any and all appearance. As he lucidly puts it in a discussion of Greek understandings of *parousia* in *What Is Called Thinking?*, "this rise from unconcealment, as the entry into what is unconcealed, does not specifically come to the fore in the presence of what is present. It is part of presence to hold back these traits, and thus to let come out only that which is present. Even, and in particular, that unconcealment in which this rise and entry takes place, remains concealed, in contrast to the unconcealed present things."[23]

If the presence or appearance of things that appear as present conceals the concealment from out of which they appear, so likewise does it conceal the eventual disappearance that remains no less inherent to the appearance. *Parousia*, on this reading, is not a final and full or eternal presence but the durable interplay of presence and absence, or of presencing and absenting, that makes for any and all appearance. "Rest in duration," Heidegger notes, is not "the absence of movement. Rest, in the presence of what is present, is a gathering. It gathers the rising to the coming-to-the-fore, with the hidden suddenness of an ever-possible absenting into concealedness."[24] While the calculating rationality of modern logistics proves incapable of thinking this interplay of concealedness and unconcealedness because logistics reduces the real to objective presence, the thinking of heart to which Heidegger appeals may be so capable, and a movement of the heart is indeed inherent to truth as *aletheia*. In glossing Parmenides's fragment 5, "for it is the same to think and to be [*to gar auto noein estin te kai einai*]," Heidegger suggests that there is an essential belonging together of being as the presence of what is present (in the sense of *parousia* just signaled) and thinking as a taking to heart.

Such a linkage between *aletheia* and heart appears not only in a major later work like *What Is Called Thinking?* but already also in formative works from the 1920s and 1930s. In his notes for *Basic Problems of Phenomenology*, Heidegger glosses his suggestion that "understanding is in love" with the term *Besinnung*. In the page of notes just following that page on which Heidegger identifies love as motive ground of phenomenological understanding, he writes: "*Pre-theoretical* self-world experience—its character: understanding. (Therefore, *critical mindfulness* [*Besinnung*])" (BP 142; 185). This term signals a mindfulness or awareness whose character Heidegger develops at length in a large and dense work of the same title in 1938–39, wherein he again interprets the movement of philosophy as a movement of love.[25] In this case, the work of philosophy as work of love answers to the truth of Be-ing into which philosophy essentially inquires: "Philosophy means 'love of wisdom,'" Heidegger notes.

> Let us think this word out of a foundational mindfulness by relinquishing the representational domains of everyday life, erudition, cultural concerns and doctrines of happiness. Then the word says: "love" is the will that wills the beloved be; the will that wills that the beloved find its way unto its ownmost and sway therein. Such a will does not wish and demand anything. Through honoring, and not by trying to create the loved one, this will lets above all the loved one—what is worthy of loving—"become." The word "love" calls what is worthy to be loved "wisdom."[26]

Consistent with his perspective on the anticipatory character of understanding's existential sight, Heidegger is recurrently cautious to note that love's distinctive will—that the beloved be herself, himself, or itself—is not a grasping or controlling will that would impose its own form or idea on the beloved, so to "create" it (like an idol). Will here is more a letting or a releasing that seeks to enable and to enhance the free being—and thus becoming—of the beloved.[27]

The notion that love's will could never capture or contain the beloved in an idolatrous picture or program relates directly to Heidegger's contention that the love inherent to Being's truth has, like understanding, an essentially anticipatory character: "'*Wisdom*' is foundational knowing-awareness; is inabiding the truth of be-ing. Hence that 'love' loves be-ing in a unique 'fore-loving' [*Vorliebe*]. This: that be-ing 'be' is this love's beloved. What matters to this beloved, to its truth and grounding, is the will to foundational knowing awareness. Be-ing, however, is the ab-ground."[28] In the same year that he writes these lines in *Besinnung*, 1938, Heidegger also links, in an essay on the concept of *physis* in Aristotle, this enabling—and inherently anticipatory—movement of love explicitly to the construal of truth as *aletheia*. Contending that concealment is an essential condition of un-concealment, the essay concludes by seeing such concealment as inherent to the fore-structure of love:

Fragment 123 of Heraclitus (taken from Porphyry) says: *phusis kruptesthai philei*, "Being loves to hide itself." What does this mean? It has been suggested, and still is suggested, that this fragment means being is difficult to get at and requires great efforts to be brought out of its hiding place and, as it were, purged of its self-hiding. But what is needed is precisely the opposite. Self-hiding belongs to the pre-dilection [*Vor-liebe*] of being; i.e., it belongs to that wherein being has secured its essence. And the essence of being is to unconceal itself, to emerge, to come out into the unhidden—*phusis*. Only what in its very essence *uncon*-

ceals itself and must unconceal itself, can love to conceal itself. Only what is unconcealing can be concealing. And therefore the *kruptesthai* of *phusis* is not only not to be overcome, not to be stripped from *phusis*. Rather the task is the more difficult one of allowing *phusis*, in all the purity of its essence, the *kruptesthai* that belongs to it.[29]

If love's defining intention wills that the beloved be, or if love wills the "to be" of the beloved; and if such being cannot ever be brought fully to light and presence, exactly because being (infinitival) is insurmountably anticipatory, or always yet to be; then all love is inherently fore-love or predilection. The intimacy of love to the existential condition of all sight—the understanding—has everything to do with such a temporality of anticipation, and that same anticipation, we will see, proves fundamental likewise to the work of imagination. On our way toward a treatment of the anticipatory, and eventually loving, temporality of imagination, we should note that the disclosive power of love is perhaps most tested—and most crucial—where love seems most intense and visibility most lacking: in the death of a beloved.

LOVE'S DISCLOSURE AND THE INVISIBILITY OF DEATH

Love's disclosive power stands out especially in relation to death insofar as death remains finally invisible. The promise of death's presence is in fact the promise of an absence one could never fully see. As Jacques Derrida well puts it in "The Deaths of Roland Barthes," "the imminence of death presents itself; it is always at the point—in presenting itself—of presenting itself no longer."[30] Death "in itself" gives to us, as living, nothing to see or experience, but that invisibility itself appears distinctively— and perhaps in the end solely—to the look of love.

The role of love that I imagine here in rendering visible the invisibility of death should be all the more striking insofar as death's remaining invisible is tied intimately to death's touching us in our singularity and, thus, to its "nonrelational" character. Such invisibility and singularity stand out just where Heidegger's existential analysis takes up the question of death as experienced by others, wherein he is asking what the death of another can or cannot show me about my own death. If where death is I am not; or if death signifies my no-longer-being-able-to-be, then my death "in itself" gives to me nothing to see or experience, nothing that I myself could actually be as a Dasein, who always has its being to be. My "own" death, then, remains utterly invisible to me and beyond my own grasp even as it constitutes an inescapable, essential, or indeed intimate, possibility of my existence. If I can see nothing of death through my own death, it stands to reason that I might ask, what about the death of another? Can I not gain access to death, while remaining in life, through my experience of another's death?

Astute readers who are critical of Heidegger's emphasis on the nonrelational character of death—such as Robert Pogue Harrison—claim that Heidegger fails to appreciate the sociality from which alone I first glimpse my death and through which alone I finally accomplish my death. *Being and Time*'s analysis of human existence in its mortal character "fails by half," Harrison claims, because "it fails to interrogate the nature of Dasein's primitive access to the phenomenon of death." Noting that Heidegger never really explains how any given Dasein achieves its certainty about the possibility of its own death, Harrison argues that it must be the death of a beloved that first teaches such possibility to us. We gain access to our death, on this view, only through relations to the dead. "Only the shock of a loved one's death persuades us—against our deepest instinctual convictions—that we will or even *can* die," Harrison writes. "Only something as resistant as the insensate body of a loved one—the enigma of its expired life and remnant thinghood—could give the anthropomorphic mind its first access to what we abstractly call death, and with it to the ethos of finitude. In its perfect likeness of the person who has passed away, the corpse withholds a presence at the same time as it renders present an absence." If indeed it is the case that we first learn of our own death from the dead, Harrison richly conjectures, then the threefold temporality that Heidegger works out against the ultimate horizon of Dasein's own Being-toward-death would find its locus in the body of the dead: "In this void [left by the beloved dead] both past and future in their ecstatic reach come into 'being,' as it were. One could say that the corpse is the aboriginal locus of the temporal ecstasies (past, present, and future) in and through which our thinking, signifying, projecting, and recollecting derive their measure of finite transcendence." Emphasizing that the corpse is an "event of passage taking place before our eyes," Harrison argues with considerable force and insight that the temporalizing work a corpse can do for us is grounded in our affective relation to it: "The past (or no-longer-hereness of the person), the present (the corpse in its presence-at-hand), and the future (the fate awaiting those who follow in the footsteps of the deceased) all converge in the dead body, *as long, that is, as it remains an object of concern or solicitude for the living.*"[31]

While Harrison's analysis of the corpse and its potential temporalizing work involves a critical response to Heidegger, the center of that response—Harrison's claim that for Heidegger "the corpse is a mere 'thing'"[32]—is not only not supported but also, as I'll signal momentarily, clearly contradicted by Heidegger's text. That said, Harrison's analysis of the corpse and its temporalizing function does quite fruitfully push the question of death into proximity with the question of image and affection. It does this by highlighting the sense in which the corpse appears as enigmatic "likeness." The appearance of the dead to us is the appearance of a likeness or an image insofar as the dead person now appears as disappeared, presents herself as no longer present: her visible look has become the look of something invisible. In a discussion of the imagination in Kant and Heidegger, Dennis J. Schmidt also notes the proximity of death and the image by making much the same point as Harrison, but in the reverse direction: referencing Maurice Blanchot's claim in *The Gaze of Orpheus* that "man is made in his own image: this is what we learn from the strangeness of the resemblance of cadavers,"[33] Schmidt notes how it is that the image resembles a corpse: "Both the image and the corpse are and are not what they appear to be; likewise, both call attention to an absence. The corpse is, in one sense, *only* a likeness—in some sense it *is* its own image. A pure ambiguity, the corpse is the likeness of that which has withdrawn and can no longer appear as itself. One might also say that the corpse is as close to pure likeness, pure image, as can be found."[34]

The kinship between death and the image plays a central role not only, as just noted, in Harrison's analysis of the sociality that he believes would first teach us about our deaths but also in his analysis of sociality's indispensable role in accomplishing our death for us in our absence. In his chapter "The Afterlife of the Image," Harrison emphasizes both the image-like character of the corpse and the role of sociality in giving to the dead "their place in the afterlife of the imagination. For what is a corpse," he asks, "if not the connatural image, or afterimage, of the person who has vanished, leaving behind a lifeless likeness of him- or herself?"[35] Such an afterlife of the dead via the imagination is, as Harrison emphasizes, captured well in its social—especially familial and intergenerational—dimensions by ancient uses of the term *imago* (usually in the plural *imagines*) to mean the face of the dead ancestor. "Between the dead and undead," Harrison writes, "the essential difference lies in the release of the image":

> I speak of the image for several reasons. It is not by chance that the Romans called the ancestor's death mask the *imago*. The wax *imagines* that typically adorned aristocratic households were literally relinquished, or left behind, by the dead, such that the first image to emerge from the deliverance process was the likeness of a person taken directly from the corpse. Family members would

sometimes don these masks during burial ceremonies so that the dead ancestors would welcome a newcomer into their midst. This was personification in its primary dramatic mode, the word *persona* in Latin meaning precisely the actor's mask. It was as an image that the dead person lived on once the disembodiment process was realized.[36]

Similar meanings attach to the Greek *eidôlon* (from the verb *eidô*, "I see" or "I know"), which, giving the root of both "idol" and "idea" in English, can mean not only image, vision, or shape but also specter or phantom. Much as the Latin *imagines* conjure faces of the dead in their imaginal afterlives, so "in the ancient Greek imagination Hades (from *Aides*, 'the invisible') was the place where the shadow images of the dead lived on. Released from the body at death—either through the breath or through an open wound of the body—the *psyche* of the person became, precisely, an *eidôlon*, or image."[37] Both the image and the corpse, on this view, involve the presence of an absence or the proximity of a distance—which, as Schmidt suggests, with an inflexion diverging somewhat from Harrison, implies that our being with the dead entails a separation that is not to be overcome: "the *eidolon* was the strange presence in which one who must remain at a distance can still, in some sense, be present. Once we come to understand that this insurmountable distance proper to how we can 'see' the dead equally defines what it is that we 'see' in the image, we need to come to understand as well how it is that the image sets us in relation with that same distance."[38]

It is important to note that such separation between the living and the dead could, and I believe should, be understood in light of an often unacknowledged or disavowed separation already operative between the living. This is just the kind of separation that Harrison objects to within his critique of Heidegger's emphasis on the nonrelational character of our Being-toward-death. While I find quite compelling Harrison's emphasis on the social and intergenerational elements of care for the dead, and on the affective ground of the dead's appearance to us, he seems to me wrong concerning what Heidegger actually says of the corpse and, correlatively, concerning the implications of Heidegger's insistence on the nonrelational character of our Being-toward-death. Indeed, Heidegger's contention that death for each of us constitutes a limit to substitution or representation may actually reinforce Harrison's point about the role of love, and of intergenerational relation, in the appearance of death to us.

Within a brief but nuanced discussion of funeral rites, Heidegger in fact raises the notion that the corpse is a mere thing—but in order to reject that notion, not to assert or defend it as Harrison claims Heidegger does. Setting that exegetical disagreement aside, however, we should consider the senses in which Harrison's insight into the social dimensions of death may actually be reinforced by Heidegger's emphasis on death's nonrelational character. According to the logic of Heidegger's analysis, the distinctive character of the care, and grieving, involved in our being-with the dead—which is decidedly not a being-with some mere thing—depends on the insurmountable difference between my death and that of another Dasein. Heidegger is, to be sure, quite clear that in our Being-toward-death, we cannot stand in for one another. In facing death, we face rather, as individuals, a possibility that is distinctively our own, one that remains nontransferable and thus absolutely resistant to any substitution or representation. This limit to representation is linked for Heidegger to the role death plays in giving to me my existence "as a whole." My life comes to form *one* life, and my *own* life, only insofar as it is bounded by some limit and insofar as that limit differs from the limit of any other Dasein's life. While that limit of death is quite a strange one—insofar as I never myself actually reach it—it remains no less a limit that is certain, and that no one else can take from me or take over for me. Heidegger's insistence on the nonrelational character of my Being-toward-death can here be read to involve not a neglect or misunderstanding of the other's death but a respect for its character as something I cannot access or appropriate as my own. Respect for that uncrossable distance is central to his understanding of funeral rites, which he addresses in §47 of *Being and Time*, "The Possibility of Experiencing the Death of Others, and the Possibility of Getting a Whole Dasein in Our Grasp."

The section opens by noting the paradox that my existence as a whole—the appearance of my existence to me as one distinct life, and my own—is achieved thanks only to a limit—death—that I cannot myself access even while (and because) the death is mine: "when Dasein reaches its wholeness in death, it simultaneously loses the Being of its 'there.' By its transition to no-longer-Dasein [*Nichtmehr-dasein*], it gets lifted right out of the possibility of experiencing this transition and of understanding it as something experienced" (BT 281; SZ 237). This paradox that my death "itself" or "as such" remains inaccessible to me renders the death of others more conspicuous rather than less. The inaccessibility of my own death "makes the death of Others *more impressive*" (BT 281; SZ 238), Heidegger notes, insofar as the death of others might seem to offer me access to death "objectively." However, the objective character of such access is exactly what renders it inapplicable to my own death, which can never be an object for me. What the death of another can show me about my own death remains, therefore, limited—but it is just that limitation that leads Heidegger to consider more carefully the character of living Dasein's Being-with the dead.

Contrary to the criticism that Heidegger's emphasis on the *mineness* of death involves an impoverished sense of our Being-with others in relation to *their* deaths, Heidegger's discussion strives in fact to appreciate just what is distinctive about the death of others. In that direction, he emphasizes first that my Being-with the dead is, *contra* Harrison, not equivalent to Being-with a mere thing or object—the corpse—now simply present-at-hand. In fact, as he explicitly notes, "in this way of Interpreting the change-over from Dasein to Being-just-present-at-hand-and-no-more, the phenomenal content is missed, inasmuch as in the entity which still remains we are not presented with a mere corporeal Thing" (BT 282; SZ 238). And while not merely a thing present-at-hand, Heidegger continues, the dead one is also not something ready-to-hand like a tool or piece of equipment (such as the cadaver can be, for example, to the student of anatomy). Our Being-with the dead, Heidegger is clear, is not a mode of *concern* (*Besorgen*, which is the term Heidegger uses to name our dealings with things that have the character of tools or equipment), but a modified form of the *solicitude*, or care for other Dasein (*Fürsorge*)—which is always interwoven with concern but not equivalent to it. Heidegger's point along these lines (which the Levinasian perspective, among others, rejects or ignores) is twofold: we never deal with things in the world apart from our relations of care for other persons, and our care for other persons cannot bypass the world of things thanks to which alone we can sustain our relations of care for those persons.

As a form of solicitude, our Being-with the dead is a distinctive mode of Being in which we are deprived of one with whom we once shared a world: a person, that is, whose own being was defined as Being-in-the-world, and to whom we related in the mode of solicitude that was possible thanks only to our shared world. Being-with-the-dead constitutes an extension of that shared Being-in-the-world, but in the absence of the person with whom we once shared it. This latter point is crucial. By contrast to Derrida, who can suggest that death means, each time, the end of the world,[39] Heidegger's analysis implies that it is exactly the world's remaining—as what we once shared—and, in turn, our remaining in that world (whether we want to or not), that is essential to our being-with-the-dead as well as to the grief of our being left behind.

The "deceased" [*Der "Verstorbene"*] as distinct from the dead person [*dem Gestorbenen*] has been torn away from those who have "remained behind" [*den "Hinterbliebenen"*], and is an object of "concern" in the ways of funeral rites, interment, and the cult of graves. And that is so because the deceased, in his kind of Being, is "still more" than just an item of equipment, environmentally ready-to-hand, about which one can be concerned. In tarrying alongside him in their mourning and commemoration [*im trauernd-gedenkenden Verweilen bei ihm*], those who have remained behind *are with him*, in a mode of respectful solicitude [*ehrenden Fürsorge*]. Thus, the relationship-of-Being that one has toward the dead is not to be taken as *concernful* Being-alongside something ready-to-hand.

In such Being-with the dead [*Mitsein mit dem Toten*], the deceased *himself* is no longer factically "there." However, when we speak of "Being-with," we always have in view Being with one another in the same world. The deceased has abandoned our "*world*" and left it behind. But *in terms of that world* [*Aus ihr her*] those who remain behind can still *be with him*. (BT 282; SZ 238)

The indispensable role played here by the world in our Being-with the dead recalls insights (not fully accepted by their author) from book 4 of Saint Augustine's *Confessions*, where Augustine reflects on his Being-with a beloved friend, who has died, in light of the friend's absence—which appears through, and thanks to, the world they once shared.[40] Augustine's experience of the friend's absence is structured and sustained by the darkness and emptiness of all the worldly places in which he once enjoyed the friend's presence, and in which, during the friend's life, he could even in the friend's absence always anticipate his presence anew. Once the friend is irrevocably absent, that absence is made present in and through those once shared places. Much as in that Augustinian construal of place—as opened and sustained by the affection we have for the people with whom we share the places of our living and dying—so in Heidegger, I think, the experience of mourning is shaped decisively by the fact that, upon the death of a beloved, the world does not end but remains; the world remains, and even obtrudes, in a kind of suspension that illuminates the role previously played by love in sustaining those forms of recollection and anticipation that had rendered meaningful and enjoyable the shared places of that world. The distinctiveness of his world's places, Augustine realizes most fully only in the absence of his friend, was bound intimately to the unique love they shared. And we should add that the uniqueness of the one loved is bound intimately as well to the particular places of the beloved's living and dying in the world. By contrast, then, to a thinker like Levinas, for whom the singularity of the other is not at all constituted but indeed threatened or effaced by the other's placement in any context—whether world, culture, history, or the like—Heidegger, like Augustine, suggests to us an intimate tie between the uniqueness of the person and that person's place in the world. And this question of the other's uniqueness is very much at the heart of Heidegger's brief treatment of mourning and funeral rites.

Heidegger's contention that we do not gain access to our own death by witnessing or suffering the death of another stems, as we've noted, from his insight that death marks a limit to the logic of representation or substitution. Our everyday social life, Heidegger's analysis suggests, depends fundamentally on the various ways in which one person can indeed, and often must, "stand in" for another within a range of given concerns. An attorney, for example, can represent me in a court of law, dealing with a legal concern that is not really hers but mine; or I can hire a mechanic to replace leaking brake lines that are mine and not his. "Indisputably, the fact that one Dasein *can be represented* by another belongs to the possibilities of Being in Being-with-one-another in the world" (BT 283; SZ 239), Heidegger grants. But he then goes on to note the crucial limitation: "However, this possibility of representing breaks down completely if the issue is one of representing that possibility-of-Being which makes up Dasein's coming to an end, and which, as such, gives to it its wholeness. *No one can take the Other's dying away from him [Keiner kann dem*

Anderen sein Sterben abnehmen]" (BT 284; SZ 240). Or again: "In
'ending' and in Dasein's Being-a-whole, for which such ending
is constitutive, there is, by its very essence, no representing [*Im
'Enden' und dem dadurch konstituierten Ganzsein des Daseins gibt
es wesensmäßig keine Vertretung]"* (BT 284; SZ 240).

While the logic of representation or replacement is inherent
to any sociality, capitalist economies and related technological
cultures such as those we inhabit today push that logic to an
extreme that tends to forget or to efface the singularity of existence, and the absolute limit to representation, that are given
to us by death. One can read Heidegger's later work on modern
technology, calculating rationality, and the reign of the *Ersatz* as
expressing just such a worry that our technological being consists in little more than endless substitution or replacement, a
mindless and ever-accelerating movement wherein not only
other persons but indeed technology itself "leaps in" for us to
deal with everything and anything whatsoever, from driving to
thinking and perhaps even our dying. This would be the dysto-
pia that Taylor explores here with DeLillo, where we have given
existence over so thoroughly to our technological systems and
related fantasies that we grow incapable even of our own mortality. The possibility of my death, on the Heideggerian account,
and by extension the whole of an existence given to me within
the horizon of such a possibility, represents an absolute limit to
any such substitution, whether by other Dasein or by the machines and programs we currently invent to take over so many
of our life's concerns.

The experience of mourning and its "respectful solicitude"
would be a notable moment where we come to learn of that
limit (if we have failed to learn of it amidst the beloved's life):

> The greater the phenomenal appropriateness with which we take
> the no-longer-Dasein of the deceased, the more plainly it is shown
> that in such Being-with the dead, the authentic Being-come-to-
> an-end [*Zuendegekommensein*] of the deceased is precisely the sort

of thing which we do *not* experience. Death does indeed reveal itself as a loss, but a loss such as is experienced by those who remain. In suffering this loss, however, we have no way of access to the loss-of-Being as such which the dying man "suffers." The dying of Others is not something which we experience in a genuine sense; at most, we are always just "there alongside." (BT 282; SZ 238–39)

Contrary to charges of callousness, or of blindness to the essential roles played by interpersonal relation and affection in our lives, we should read here a respect for the other in the uniqueness—and nontransferable character—of her dying. Callous, indeed, would be to ignore that an individual's dying cannot, and ought not, be confused or exchanged with that of any other. The question then becomes the type of sociality involved.

The analysis of death and mourning in a Heideggerian register suggests that neither my own death nor the death of another ever becomes, "in itself," accessible to me in the presence of any experience. Because the transition to death lifts me out of my Dasein, I cannot, as Dasein, access that death in any actual experience; my death gives to me nothing that I myself could ever be, or see. But, likewise, the death of another remains inaccessible both in the sense that death as such never becomes present in any actual experience for that person, and then because the possibility of death remains, for each of us, uniquely our own and nontransferable. This double inaccessibility and the related limit to substitution should push us to reflect on the question of death's visibility—and on the relation of such visibility to mortal sociality, broadly, and then, more pointedly, to mortal love. This limit to representation, while a function of the nonrelational character of death, is not opposed to Dasein's sociality but an essential aspect of it, and one I believe crucial to the paradoxical appearance of a death that remains strictly invisible. In what follows I'd like to ask specifically about the role played by Dasein's love relations in grounding the paradoxical visibility of death's invisibility.

FACING THE INVISIBLE: BETWEEN ICON AND DEATH MASK

We can move toward an understanding of such paradox through a perhaps (at first glance) unexpected comparison between two figures or faces of the invisible. The first figure is the painted image of a face that seems to look everywhere, and at everything, all at the same time; this is an all-seeing portrait, built on a simple optical illusion, which serves in Nicholas of Cusa as an "icon of God" (*icona Dei*), an image in which, he tells us, the vision of God—which is itself absolute, infinite, and hence strictly invisible to our finite and relative perspective—nonetheless shows itself to us by a kind of similitude. The second figure is the photograph of a death mask; here we look at a face that itself does not look at all, a face whose look or gaze (*regard*) withdraws into an absolute nonseeing that, again paradoxically, shows itself to us. Just as I, finite and relative in my vision, can never put myself in the place of an all-seeing God, in order thus to exercise that God's absolute and infinite look; so I, inasmuch as living (or insofar as I am *Dasein* in Heidegger's sense), can never occupy the position or the perspective of the one who is dead. Both in the absolutely all-seeing look of a God and in the absolutely nonseeing look of a dead person, we glimpse something that remains strictly invisible. Such visibility of the invisible, I want to suggest, is grounded in a work of imagination whose power depends on our finitude and on the social, or indeed loving, relations we share as finite and mortal beings.

*
**

The panoptical dream for which our technological systems of facial recognition stand as an effective shorthand bear an interesting resemblance to theological visions of divine omniscience. One especially apt instance of such theological vision

FIGURE 3.2. Portrait of Rogier van der Weyden, from the Justice of Trajan and Herkinbald tapestry, ca. 1450. Historical Museum of Bern; https://en.wikipedia.org/wiki/The_Justice_of_Trajan_and_Herkinbald.

can be found in an extraordinary text from 1453 by the early modern theologian and philosopher Nicholas of Cusa: *De visione Dei (sive de icona), On the Vision of God, or On the Icon.*[41] In this text, which Cusa himself often referred to simply as "the image" or "the picture" *(icona)*, Cusa meditates on the relation between, on the one hand, an infinite, omniscient, and thus invisible God and, on the other hand, a community of finite believers who manage somehow to see such a God. Cusa figures this relation explicitly in terms of facial recognition. By contrast to our current systems of surveillance, however, which are driven by impersonal programs that capture all faces statistically and anonymously, the all-seeing face of God in Cusa reflects each and every human face, in its finitude and uniqueness, within a relation that is personal and mutually recognitive. It is also, we will see, a relation that lives thanks only to a sociality wherein the face-to-face between the couple of God and individual believer depends on countless other faces beyond these two.

While Cusa's text ostensibly concerns the vision *of God*, it can read like a treatise on the phenomenology of seeing more broadly, one according to which "to see" means always also to "be seen."[42] Such a co-implication of seeing and being seen has a rich trajectory in phenomenology from Heidegger to Maurice Merleau-Ponty, and it has been developed in more recent years, specifically with respect to questions of revelation, by Jean-Luc Marion. As in Marion's phenomenological and theological writings, "the icon" for Cusa is distinguished by a fundamental reversal of intentionality and by its (related) resistance to any objectification by the one who sees it. In looking at the iconic face, I do not first constitute an object that comes to be seen thanks to my intention or aim; I discover, rather, that the iconic face is already (and always) looking at me. Every time I myself turn toward the iconic God, he is already there, and I see that I am seen.[43] As Michel de Certeau emphasizes in his brilliant reading of Cusa in "The Look," the wondrous effect of the iconic look is that "there is no longer any *seen object* for the one who is *looked at* . . . . The observer believed himself to see. Transformed into one observed, he enters into an 'astonishment' that is not accompanied by any representation. The experience of the look is a surprise without object." Thus, by contrast—and in resistance—to the representational subject of a modernity marked for Heidegger by the "conquest of the world as picture," the iconic "look of the other excludes the possession of an image."[44]

The look of God in Cusa is, furthermore, equivalent to the word or the call of God that creates me, since within Cusa's thinking, "to be" means, for me as creature, "to be seen" by God. "Since your seeing is your being," Cusa writes in chapter 4, "I am because you look at me [*Et cum videre tuum sit esse, ideo sum quia tu me respicis*]" (chap. 4, 11). From this perspective, I am thanks only to the fact, and to the extent, that God's look sees me— in a seeing that does not follow after my being (in response to it) but rather that first engenders my being (in the mode of a divine *intuitus originarius*). To be is to be seen—but being seen for Cusa means equally, inherently, to return the look that first looks at me.

This is a crucial point in the Cusan analysis: the seeing of God that engenders my being—God's seeing me—is at the same time, equally, God's being seen by me, or my seeing God. In speaking about the vision *of* God here, we need for essential reasons to read the genitive in both its objective and subjective senses. "What does it mean to see, for you Lord, when you look at me . . . if not to be seen by me? In seeing me, you give yourself to me to be seen, you who are the hidden God. No one can see you except inasmuch as you give yourself to be seen. And you are seen only when you see the one who sees you [*Quid aliud, domine, est videre tuum, quando me . . . respicis, quam a me videri? Videndo me das te a me videri, quis es deus absconditus. Nemo te videre potest nisi inquantam tu das ut videaris. Nec est aliud te videre quam quod tu videas videntem te*]" (chap. 5, 15).[45]

Such coincidence between seeing and being seen is related

intimately for Cusa to the infinity of God's vision. Thanks to that infinity (and here, I think, we will begin to see Cusa diverging in notable ways from Marion[46]) the look of God fixes itself fully, and seemingly exclusively, on each one of us and on all of us at the same time—such that every finite face sees itself reflected entirely in the face of God, which thus appears as the living mirror of all our faces. "In this painted face [which serves as icon], I see a figure of infinity. For the look is not limited to an object or a place, and thus it is infinite. For it does not turn more toward one who looks at it than toward another. And, even though the look of this face is in itself infinite, it seems limited by whoever looks at it. For it looks so fixedly at whoever looks at it that it seems to look only at this latter and at nobody else. [*Video in hac picta facie figuram infinitatis. Nam visus est interminatusas obiectum vel locum, et ita infinitus. Non enim plus est conversus ad unum quam alium qui intuetur eam. Et quamvis visus eius sit in se infinitus, videtur tamen per quemlibet respicientem terminari, quia ita quemlibet respicit determonate, qui intuetur eam, quasi solum eum et nihil aliud*]" (chap. 5, 65). Because the look or face of God is infinite, it admits no more or less. Hence, when I look at this face, from the singular perspective of my finitude, I find there absolutely nothing other than myself. The infinite face of God, given wholly to each and every face, is thus the truth of my own—and of every—face. The face of God, as Cusa puts it, is the face of faces and "the most adequate measure" of all faces because it remains "absolute from any quantity" and hence "neither more nor less than any face whatsoever" (chap. 6, 19). By reason of his infinity, then, God can appear to me as my own image, or as the mirror that reflects me fully back to myself. This mirror, however, is not the invisible mirror of an idol as Marion understands it. For Marion the appearance of the idol is defined by the priority, limitation, and shape of my aim or intention, and it thus stands in sharp contrast or even antagonism with the icon, where I discover that prior to my aim or intention I am looked at by a gaze that radically precedes and exceeds me. In

Cusa's thinking, by contrast to that antagonistic contrast, when the face of God reflects my face fully, it is not I who project my limitations upon God. Rather, the fact that I see God within the finitude of my sight is itself a gift of God's infinity and not a shortcoming on my part. "For what you seem to receive from the one who looks at you," he states, "you yourself give [*Et ita id quod videris ab intuente recipere, hoc donas*]" (chap. 15, 67). To see, then, my own finite image in God is not other than to see the infinity of that God who is the truth of that image. Because his face admits neither more nor less, it is equal to all faces and to each face (*aequalibus omnibus et singulis*): "In this way, Lord, I discover that your face precedes every formable face and is the model and truth of all faces—and that all faces are the images of your irreducible and imparticipable face. Hence every face that can look into your face sees nothing that is other or different from itself, because it sees its own truth [*Ideo aequalis omnibus et singulis, quia nec maior nec minor . . . Sic igitur deprehendo vultum tuum, domine, antecedere omnem faciem formabilem et esse exemplar ac veritatem omnium facierum, et omnes facies esse imagines faciei tuae incontrahabilis et imparticibilis. Omnis igitur facies quae in tuam intueri faciem, nihil videt aliud aut diversum a se, quia veritatem suam*]" (chap. 6, 19).

We should note that the infinity of God, as coming to expression here in terms of God's face, applies also for Cusa to the world as a whole. In this direction, Cusa draws on the notion of the infinite sphere—whose center is everywhere and circumference nowhere—that derives from Alain de Lille and the *Book of the Twenty-four Philosophers*.[47] If the world has "its center everywhere and circumference nowhere, for its circumference and center is God, who is everywhere and nowhere,"[48] then God rests absolute, or distinct, from finite beings just insofar as he is totally present, or immanent, to them as their very being—and hence insofar as he is absolutely in-distinct. God is distinct, thus, in and through his absolute indistinction. "Lord my God," as Cusa puts it (chap. 13), "strength of the weak, I see that you are infinity itself. Thus, for you, nothing is other or different or opposed. Indeed, infinity suffers no alterity within itself: for since it is infinity, nothing exists outside it. For absolute infinity embraces and includes all things. [. . .] Infinity thus exists and enfolds all things, and nothing can be outside it. Consequently, in relation to it nothing is other or different. Infinity then is all things in such a way that it is no one of them. [*Domine deus meus, fortitudo fragilium, video te ipsam infinitatem esse. Ideo nihil est tibi alterum vel diversum vel adversum. Infinitas enim non compatitur secum alterittem, quia cum sit infinitas, nihil est extra eam. Omnium enim includit et omnia ambit infinitas absoluta. [. . .] Est igitur infinitas et complicat omnia, et nihil esse potest extra eam. Hinc nihil ei alterum vel diversum. Infinitas igitur sic omnia est quod nullum omnium]*" (chap. 13, 56).

Cusa's treatment of God's infinity recalls here the dialectic of distinction and in-distinction within God's relation to created beings as that dialectic is developed in Meister Eckhart, John Scotus Eriugena, or even already in Pseudo-Dionysius, where all created beings are distinct from one another but God is distinct by being indistinct from all created beings. And as in Eckhart, Eriugena, and Pseudo-Dionysius, Cusa's analysis highlights, and deploys, the essential co-implication within our relation to God of kataphasis or thesis (in order to *see* the invisible) and of apophasis or aphairesis (in order to see *the invisible*). According to this co-implication in Cusa, which is tied intimately to his famous text, and doctrine, on "learned ignorance," in order to see or to know God, I must see and know that I do not see and know God. Crucial to Cusa's staging of such nonknowing or nonseeing in *De visione Dei* is the role played by human sociality, which can be read as inherent, and indispensable, to the visibility of God's invisibility. For if I see only my image in the face of God without seeing that others see there also, equally, their own singular faces, which differ from mine but not from God's, then I do not see fully the invisibility of the face of God; that is, I do not see the infinite look that is, for Cusa, invisible in the (measureless) measure of its ubiquity. In order to see or glimpse the invisible ubiquity of God, Cusa suggests, I must capture it through the imagination (*imaginatio capere*), but that work of imagination takes place only through active and ongoing social relations, which alone will allow me to glimpse—thanks to a dynamic work of testimony and belief—that the face of God gives itself fully, and seemingly exclusively, not only to me, in my singularity, but also—simultaneously—to all others, and to each other, in each individual's singularity, which cannot be exchanged with mine. The ubiquity of God's all-seeing gaze becomes visible as invisible only through the play of testimony and belief among a multiplicity of unique finite beings.

The constructive work of these social relations comes to the fore in a cooperative exercise that Cusa recommends and explains in his prefatory letter to the Benedictine brothers at Tegernsee, to whom he sends his text on the vision of God as a practical and experimental introduction to mystical theology. As we will see momentarily, that exercise is governed by a logic that informs also Cusa's discussion, toward the text's conclusion, of a divine or infinitely powerful painter.

To enable the exercise he is recommending, Cusa sends along to his brothers the painting of a seemingly all-seeing face (said to be a self-portrait of Rogier Van der Weyden, itself now lost but preserved in a likeness within a Flemish tapestry). A practice yielding an experience that gives insight into mystical theology is thus to be made possible by entirely simple and common means (*simplicissimo atque communisimo modo*). Such gestures are characteristic of Cusa's thinking, where everyday material things—like spoons or bowling balls or paintings of faces—become mirrors of a kind. Rather than serving as idols reflecting a viewer's gaze back to the viewer within a closed circuit, however, the mirrors appearing in Cusa reflect, within the visible here and now, realities that both pervade and exceed the here and now. As Certeau points out, such use of the mirror function in Cusa's writing is akin to the practice of painters like Van der Weyden, Van Eyck, and the Master of Flémalle, who bring an otherness or outside—notably those of death and mourning—into the living frame of their paintings by means of the mirror painted within. In these rough contemporaries of Cusa, "the mirror is a place located *within* the painted framework and often decorated like the monstrance or the reliquary that circumscribes the manifestation of another world. On the inside, it presents to view a *beyond*—another time (death), another dimension (mourning, vice, etc.)—that is not visible in the scene represented by the painting, though it is *already* at work in it. It is the revealer (or the hallucination) of a history that is hidden, but present, the visibility of that which cannot be seen *there*."[49]

The everyday object—a painting whose seemingly all-seeing gaze is the function of a simple optical illusion—is to be attached to a wall, Cusa explains, and will thus form the point around which a semicircular space can be formed and become the place, and time, of a social practice. Around the almost-nothing of the point will open a vision of the infinite God who is immanent to everything. As Cusa explains, the individual can walk around the semicircle created by the point and feel as if the gaze follows him everywhere, resting wherever he rests, and moving wherever and whenever he moves. But this sense of a gaze that moves always and everywhere for the individual does not yet, and really never can, yield the appearance of a gaze that is truly ubiquitous—which is to say, everywhere and for everyone, all at the same time. This latter—the appearance of a ubiquitous gaze—requires a social cooperation among multiple, and finally innumerable, individuals who carry out the "same" experiment but always from each of their own, and clearly distinct, positions.

If one wants to have an experience of the all-seeing look through this practical and experimental engagement with the painting, one cannot remain alone. One should, Cusa recommends, arrange oneself so that "a brother moves from east to west, without leaving the eyes of the painting, while he himself goes from west to east; one will ask his partner in order to see if the image turns its sight continually toward him also, and one will learn by hearing that the look moves in the same way in the opposite direction; then he will believe. If he did not believe, he would not be able to grasp that this is possible [*et nisi crederet, non caperet hoc possibile*]. Thanks to the revelation of the witness [*et ita revelatione relatoris*], he comes to know that the face does not leave any of those who walk around it, even though their movements are opposed" (preface, 4).

That this sharing of finite visions by means of testimony and belief is indispensable to the appearance of God's strictly invisible infinity[50] is attested again toward the text's conclusion, where God is figured no longer as a painted face but as himself a painter endowed with infinite creative power. This painter, who fashions various figures in order to have an image of himself, shows himself (and thus hides himself) in the best way only through an infinite multiplication of figures; and he is glimpsed by us in the best way only in the measure that we share with one another our singular, even secret, perspectives, which are themselves without number. God, Cusa writes, is "like a painter [*quasi pictor*] who mixes different colors in order that he might finally paint himself [*qui diversos temperat colores, ut demum se ipsum depingere possit*]" (chap. 25, 111). And even though he is "one and cannot be multiplied," this painter "can nonetheless multiply himself, insofar as possible, in a very close similitude [*Cum ipse unus sit immultiplicabilis, saltem modo quo fieri potest, in propinquissima similutudine, multiplicetur*]" (chap. 25, 111). Such a similitude grows, Cusa suggests, evoking the essential interplay of apophasis and kataphasis commonly operative in mystical tradition, thanks only to such multiplication, "because the similitude of his infinite power can be unfolded in the best way possible only through a multiplicity of figures [*Multas autem figuras facit, quia virtutis suae infinitae similitudo non potest nisi in multis perfectiori modo explicari*]" (chap. 25, 111). In a manner recalling the exercise outlined in the text's preface, the visibility of the infinite power of this painter, which shows but also hides itself in and through each limited view it paints, requires a sharing among perspectives that are finite, singular, and innumerable: "And *all* intellectual spirits are useful to *each* spirit," Cusa explains. "And if they were not innumerable, you, infinite God, could not be known in the best way possible. For each intellectual spirit sees in you-my-God something without which the others—unless it were revealed to them—could not in the best manner possible attain to you-their-God. Filled with the spirit, they mutually reveal the secrets of their love, and thus the knowledge of God grows, and the desire to reach him, and the sweetness of their joy is enflamed [*Et sunt omnes intellectuales spiritus cuilibet spiritui opportuni. Nam nisi forent innumerabiles, non posses tu, deus infinitus, meliori modo cognosci. Quisque enim intellectualis spiritus videt in te deo meo aliquid, nisi aliis revelaretur, non atingeret te deum suum meliori quo fieri posset modo. Revelant sibi mutuo secreta sua amoris pleni spiritus, et augetur ex hoc cognitio amati et desiderium ad ipsum, et gaudii dulcedo inardescit*]" (chap. 25, 111).

If sociality among finite beings is indispensable to the visibility of the infinite look of God, at its core such sociality consists in a movement of loves that are shared but that remain, at the same time, and each time, singular and thus not susceptible to exchange or substitution. As suggested by the prefatory exercise, to see God means not only seeing that I am seen by God; it means seeing also—by hearing, and believing—that others are seen, all of them, and each of them, just as much as I am: fully and in a singular fashion. Here, though, we should recall that with respect to God in Cusa, seeing amounts not only to being but also to loving: "to see, for you, is to love [*videre tuum est amare*]" (chap. 5, 11), as he straightforwardly puts it. Thus, just as in order to see God, I must see not only that I am seen by God but also that others are seen just as much; so likewise, in order to love God I must love not only that I am loved but also that others are loved, just as much, and again in a manner that is each time singular. One has good reason, then, to claim that the phenomenology of seeing in Cusa—where seeing amounts to seeing that one is seen—is realized in and through the experience of love as a shared love, or a *condilectio*.[51]

*
**

The vision of God that is realized through the icon in Cusa, where seeing amounts to being seen, operates in a manner that comes strikingly close to phenomenological understandings of appearance—where to look at or to see anything means simultaneously to be looked at or to be seen by that thing. As Merleau-Ponty puts it in his seminal text on the chiasm, "the vision [the seer] exercises, he also undergoes from the things, such that, as many painters have said, I feel myself looked at by the things, my activity is equally passivity."[52]

An important source for Merleau-Ponty's thinking about the coincidence of (active) seeing and (passive) being seen is, of course, Martin Heidegger, and this coincidence figures prominently in Heidegger's treatment of the imagination within his important and much-debated reading of Kant just following *Being and Time*. Seeking to elucidate the image "in its original sense,"[53] Heidegger's 1929 book *Kant and the Problem of Metaphysics* explains that for anything to appear as the thing it is, it must take on and present to us the look or image of such a thing. Image here does not primarily mean copy or reproduction or imitation (as we may tend to assume both in everyday life and in the history of philosophy going back to Plato); it means rather the originary self-presentation of a thing in its recognizable shape or form. In this respect, the meaning of "image," or *Bild* in the German, comes quite close to the Greek notion of *eidos*, the form or the "idea" that makes a thing what it is. Within his discussion of the image's role in allowing things to come into visibility—a role it can play, we'll see, thanks to the schematizing work of the imagination—Heidegger notes that the image gives itself to be seen "as if it looked at us." A landscape, for example, "is called a look (image), species, as if it looks at us [*Sie wird ein*

Anblick (Bild), species gennant, gleich als blicke sie uns an]" (KPM 65; 93, trans. modified). In a passage of commentary on Heidegger's Kant book that Cusa himself could have written, Jean-Luc Nancy—in the well-titled essay "Masked Imagination"—sums up this Heideggerian analysis of the image: "The first image shows itself as a look turned toward us. The image constitutes an image by resembling a look. It is as if Heidegger was saying: the first image is always an image (resemblance) of an image (monstration). There is here, *at bottom*, a chiasm or a generative coiling: the image gives itself to be seen by resembling a seeing, the visible presents itself by seeing. The first image is always also *like a look*, it is thus image in being at the same time that which op-poses itself to the look and that opens itself as a look."[54]

From this chiasmic perspective, the image "as such" or "in its original sense" appears to us in a way that resembles the icon in Cusa: to look at the image is to look at a look that looks or seems to look at us—a look in which seeing and being seen coincide. Now, in Nancy's "Masked Imagination," as in the Heidegger passages on Kant that Nancy is interpreting (§20 of *Kant and the Problem of Metaphysics*, "Image and Schema"), one does not find the image that looks at us in an icon of God; rather, one finds such an image, and its face, in a death mask—or more precisely in the photograph of a death mask. Before exploring the significance of this specific and quite striking reference to the photograph of a death mask, we should sketch out the context in which it appears.

At the heart of *Kant and the Problem of Metaphysics* is Heidegger's interpretation of selfhood—via the imagination—in terms of primordial temporality. "Did Kant not show," Heidegger asks rhetorically, "in the Transcendental Deduction and in the chapter on Schematism that time takes part essentially in the innermost essential structure of transcendence? And does not transcendence determine the Being-as-self [*Selbstsein*] of the finite self?" (KPM 131; 188). Diverging from common understandings of Kant's *Critique of Pure Reason* as a work of epistemology aiming to advance a theory of knowledge, Heidegger argues that it entails more fundamentally "a laying of the ground for metaphysics." Such a ground-laying consists in an account of how we as finite thinking beings are able to turn toward and encounter beings other than ourselves. It is, in other words, an account of finite transcendence, of that movement through which we realize ourselves by standing out beyond ourselves within the enabling constraints of a world. As Heidegger puts it in relation to Kant, the "'from-out-of-itself-toward . . . and back to itself' first constitutes the mental character of the mind as a finite self. [. . .] As the ground for the possibility of selfhood, time already lies within pure apperception, and so it first makes the mind into a mind" (KPM 134; 191).

Essential to this finite capacity for encountering beings as they appear to us is the work of imagination. Within the Kantian context out of which Heidegger is thinking here, a being's appearance to us requires a synthesis of intuition and understanding; without the receptivity of sensible intuition there is nothing to see, but without the active ordering of the understanding, intuition gives us only the blurred flux of a sensible manifold. For Kant, it is the power of imagination that carries out this synthesis, by means of what he calls the "schematism," something he understands to constitute, as Taylor highlights in "Gathering Remains," "an art concealed in the depths of the human soul [*eine verborgene Kunst in den Tiefen der menschlichen Seele*]."[55]

On Heidegger's reading, the synthesizing work of the Kantian imagination has three modes that will relate fundamentally to the structure of primordial temporality: presentative or apprehensive, reproductive, and prefigurative or recognitive. He finds important ground for his interpretation in Kant's lectures on metaphysics:

In his lectures on Metaphysics, namely, in the Rational Psychology, Kant analyzes the "forming power" [*bildende Kraft*] in the following manner: this faculty "produces representations either of present time, or representations of past time, or even representations of future time. Hence, the formative faculty [*Bildungsvermögen*] consists of: 1. The faculty of taking a likeness [*Abbildung*], the representations of which are of the present time: *facultas formandi*. 2. The faculty of reproduction [*Nachbildung*], the representations of which are of a past time: *facultas imaginandi*. 3. The faculty of prefiguration [*Vorbildung*], the representations of which are of a future time: *facultas praevidendi*."[56]

While Heidegger acknowledges that Kant does not speak in this passage of the transcendental power of imagination, and while the passage seems to associate the imagining faculty solely with representations of past time, Heidegger takes from the passage a clue that the forming power of imagination is tied essentially to time in all three of its fundamental modes (or ecstases), much like the understanding in *Being and Time*. Presentation, reproduction, and prefiguration are grounded, indeed, in the primordial temporality whose threefold ecstatic structure *Being and Time* understands to ground the Being of Dasein as "care" (*Sorge*). A dense summary passage from *Kant and the Problem of Metaphysics* is worth citing here at length:

> Thus the way is opened to the original ground for the source of both basic sources [of the mind—namely, sensibility and understanding]. The interpretation of the transcendental power of imagination as root, i.e., the elucidation of how the pure synthesis allows both stems to grow forth from out of it and how it maintains them, leads back from itself to that in which it is rooted: to original time. As the original, threefold-unifying of future, past, and present in general, this is what first makes possible the "faculty" of pure synthesis, i.e., that which it is able to produce, namely, the unification of the three elements of ontological knowledge, in the unity of which transcendence is formed.
>
> The modes of pure synthesis—pure apprehension, pure repro-

duction, pure recognition—are not therefore three in number because they refer to the three elements of pure knowledge, but rather because, originally unified in themselves, as time-forming, they constitute the ripening of time itself. Only because these modes of pure synthesis are originally unified in the threefold unifying of time is there also to be found in them the possibility for the original unification of the three elements of pure knowledge. For that reason, however, the original unifying which is apparently only the mediating, intermediate faculty of the transcendental power of imagination, is in fact none other than original time. This rootedness in time alone enables the transcendental power of imagination in general to be the root of transcendence. (KPM 137; 196)

Crucial to this work done by the power of imagination is what Kant calls the schematism, which by making a concept sensible gives, in effect, the image of any eventual image, or the look of any eventual look. The need for this schematizing work arises from a notable tension in the appearance of any given thing: every given appearance is a particular "this-here" while depending also, at the same time, on the generality of a concept. The concept of house, for example, precisely as general, can never appear as a distinct "this-here," which is, exactly, not general; but no particular house could ever appear as house without the generalizing work of the concept for house. The imaginative work of the schematism thus entails an essentially anticipatory movement, for it gives the pre-view or the fore-look of (in this case) a house, without which no particular house could ever appear as a house. "Thus in the immediate perception of something at hand," Heidegger notes, "this house, for example, the schematizing premonition [*Vorblick*] of something like house in general is already to be found. It is from this pro-posing [*Vorstellung*] alone that what is encountered can reveal itself as a house, can offer the look of a 'house that is at hand'" (KPM 71; 101).

As operative within the irreducibly threefold temporality

of imagination, this anticipatory look of the schematism is included, and thus also recalled, within any given presentation in the "present." As is clear, however, from the analysis of temporality and care in *Being and Time*, that "present" is never fully and simply present; rather, it is differentially constituted through the interplay of the having-been and the yet-to-be of our Being-in-the-world as a being for whom any presence is given thanks only to a structuring absence. As natally mortal and mortally natal, Dasein encounters beings in their presence through the passively active and actively passive movement of Dasein's thrown projection—according to what we might call the middle voice of the imagination. "Original time," as Heidegger puts it in *Kant and the Problem of Metaphysics*, "makes possible the transcendental power of imagination, which in itself is essentially spontaneous receptivity and receptive spontaneity" (KPM 137; 196).

Insofar as Heidegger thus links imagination to the temporality that *Being and Time* develops in terms of *mortal* care, his pivotal—but conspicuously underdeveloped—reference in *Kant and the Problem of Metaphysics* to the photograph of a *death* mask can be all the more striking. Heidegger mentions such a photograph while discussing the originary self-showing of an image that is transmitted through a likeness and even a likeness of a likeness—as for example, the original self-showing of a dead person's look can be transmitted through a death mask, or even the photograph of a death mask. With each level of transmission, the originary self-showing is maintained, Heidegger suggests, even as a new showing (the look of a death mask, or then that of a photograph) enters the picture. Hence the photo of a death mask shows us not only the self-showing of a photo (in any particular photo, the photo is showing us how, in general, a photo looks), and not only the self-showing of a mask (in any given mask we must see simultaneously how a mask in general looks), but also, through these two, through the self-showing of the photo and through the self-showing of the mask, we see the self-showing of a dead person, or the look of a dead person's face. "Thus the copy," as Nancy glosses,

> does not lose the originary monstration: it maintains it and restages it in the ground of its own secondary monstration. Heidegger's aim here is clear: the primary sense of the image, the giving-itself-to-be-seen and the offering-its-look, the *Aussehen*, the looking-like-while-showing-itself of everything understood at the same time "as if it were looking at us" (*aussehen*, "to look," or "to seem (like)" breaks down literally into "seeing-outward"), forms the originary and proper value of the image, which is pre-served in the ground of every reproduction. (IM 86; 157)

Thus, in the case of the photo of the death mask, "this photo shows us itself and the mask itself, *and* that which the mask shows, namely 'the dead person such as he appears—*aussieht*—, shows himself or showed himself [*bzw. aussah*].' But this is also 'what a dead person himself can show,' namely '*wie das Gesicht eines Toten aussieht*,' 'how the face of a dead person seems/aims outward,' to transcribe literally according to the indication given above by Heidegger" (IM 87; 158, trans. modified).

As Nancy notes, Heidegger's reference to the photograph of a death mask has both empirical and transcendental reasons that Heidegger himself does not mention. Empirically, the photograph of a death mask very likely occurs to Heidegger thanks to the publication in 1926 of a work that drew significant attention among intellectuals and artists in Europe: Ernst Benkard's volume of photographs of death masks published under the title *Das Ewige Antlitz: Eine Sammlung von Totenmasken*, translated into English by Margaret M. Green and published in 1929 by Virginia and Leonard Woolf as *Undying Faces: A Collection of Death Masks*.[57] Among the death mask photographs contained in that volume is one of Blaise Pascal, whom Heidegger explicitly references in his 1925–26 course, closely related to *Kant and the Problem of Metaphysics*, published as *Logic: The*

〈11〉 BLAISE PASCAL
1623–1662

FIGURE 3.3. Death mask of Blaise Pascal, from Ernst Benkard's *Das Ewige Antlitz: Eine Sammlung von Totenmasken* (Berlin: Frankfurter Verlags-Anstalt, 1926), plate 11.

Question of Truth. There, while noting the tension between the appearance of a particular this-here (this particular face, this particular photograph) and the depiction of a concept (where, for example, the "photographic copy is used as an exemplary illustration of the sensible concept 'death-mask'"), Heidegger asserts—suggestively but without developing the matter— that "the *genuine* meaning of a photographic image is not 'illustrative example [of a concept]' and never can be." Rather, the meaning of the photograph here is tied to the unique person depicted: "What the photographic depiction depicts, is the face of a specific dead person—Pascal, for example—and not one particular case of 'Pascal' as an illustrative example of the concept 'Pascalness.'"[58]

The transcendental reason that Heidegger does not really note or develop concerns an intimate tie between the imagination and mortality. As Nancy is right to point out, it is remarkable that Heidegger—the great analyst of "Being-toward-death"—does not himself comment on the remarkable character of his "example" of the death-mask photograph. For such an image is, after all, decidedly not, as Heidegger seems to treat it, merely one example among others, comparable, say, to the landscape he mentions, or to a house, which we've just seen is another of his examples. The considerable contribution of Nancy's analysis in this regard is to underline that the example of the photo of the death mask is exemplary in the extreme; it is even "singular," as he puts it, "for the simple reason that the originary self-showing is here exemplified by the self-showing and the seeming of a dead person, which by definition does not show itself, but essentially withdraws from all monstration" (IM 91; 165, trans. modified).

To appreciate the paradox Nancy is pointing to here, we should recall Heidegger's insistence in *Being and Time* that the possibility of death offers to us nothing that we, as finite Being-in-the-world, might ever see or experience in any actual presence; it offers us, in his words, "no support for becoming intent

on something, 'picturing' to oneself the actuality which is possible [*das mögliche Wirkliche sich 'auzumalen'*], and so forgetting
its possibility" (BT 307; SZ 262). The thinker, then, for whom
death "as such" eludes all experience and hence any image or
representation, cites as an example of the self-showing of the
image as such—which means, recall, the self-showing of that
which gives itself as if it were looking at us—the image of a dead
person, whose look essentially withdraws or absents itself: a
face that simply does not look—or that no longer looks.

This latter qualification—the *no longer* looking implied in
the dead face's *not* looking—is crucial, because it calls to our
attention the temporality that lends to the self-showing of the
dead person's face an inherently double aspect: what shows itself in the present (the look of the dead face) can show itself as
such (that is, as dead, as a look now withdrawn, or not-looking)
only in light of the past or the having-been of the living look.
For there is not now any look or gaze in retreat or withdrawal if
there had not been previously a gaze or look that did present itself; to see *now* a look that *no longer* looks, I must simultaneously
see—or retain—the having-been of the living look. As Nancy
comments, "the dead man has a present aspect, insofar as he
does not see, and he has another aspect, insofar as he looked.
However, everything happens as if his image superimposed the
two aspects: one with respect to now, and one with respect to
before. As if the before (sight, *la vue*) remained in the now (non-
sight, *la non-vue*) or as if now (the non-sight) retroactively af-
fected the before (sight). There is prospection and retrospection
of the one into the other" (IM 93; 169, trans. modified).

In light of this superimposition or imbrication of prospection and retrospection, the image of the dead person exposes, in
a distilled or intensified manner, the temporal movement of any
and every image as a coming-into-presence haloed always also
by withdrawal into absence: a presence always already structured by absence just as a life is structured always already by
the death inherent to all life. The appearance or coming-forth

of any image presupposes a ground of withdrawal or disappearance; it depends, that is, on the finite and hence the mortal temporality of our Being-in-the-world—which, as we've seen, Heidegger equates with the power of imagination itself. It is "the transcendental power of imagination" that "allows time as a sequence of nows to spring forth, and as this letting-spring-forth it is therefore original time" (KPM 123; 175–76). Insofar as the power of imagination is thus equated with the primordial temporality of Dasein in its finitude, every given image lives thanks only to that temporality—presenting and absenting itself only in and through the always open interplay of prospection and retrospection, and hence of our natal Being-toward-death and our mortal Being-from-birth. Within that interplay, our access to the self-showing of the image implies—like the reception of our one life, as a whole—ever already its withdrawal. "Entering and exiting," as Nancy puts it, "is what the image does: appearing and disappearing" (IM 98; 178).

As a matter, then, for those who hold open the "between" of a having-been born and a being yet to-die, those for whom death is always immanent to life without ever presenting itself in the experience of any presence, every image is, in the end, not just a kind of mask but a kind of death mask—a formulation that itself may be redundant. For a mask as mask entails this double movement of a self-showing that hides itself and a self-hiding that shows itself. In this way, the mask realizes in a relative manner what the face of the dead person realizes in a more definitive manner.[59] From the face of the dead, through the death mask, to the photo of such a mask, the image shows (any given presence) only in hiding (the absence that structures it); to see the image, then, is to see—without seeing—that presentation of an absence and that absence of presentation. In this regard, the interplay within the image of presence and absence, or of showing and hiding, resembles quite closely the interplay of kataphasis and apophasis—or of immanence and transcendence, knowing and unknowing, visibility and invisibility—that we have pointed to in Cusa and his tradition. In light of this co-implication of arrival and withdrawal, coming and departing, Nancy can say of the photo, in the conclusion of his essay, what one must say of any image (and here we might note in passing a fairly deep resonance with Roland Barthes's emphasis on the mortal temporality that gives to photography its poignancy[60]): "And to finish finally: the photo *itself*, as a death mask, the instantaneous and always rebegun image as the casting of presence in contact with light, the casting of a presence fleeing into absence, which one neither captures nor represents but which one thus, paradoxically, *contemplates* (one comes into its *templum*, the time of its framing)" (IM 178–179; 99).

*
**

It is no small irony that today's techno-utopians would seek immortality within a culture of the digital image and its codes— if, after all, the image is grounded in the inescapably finite, mortal temporality of the imagination, and hence in the coincidence of appearing and disappearing: a presentation that withdraws and a withdrawal that presents itself. At this level, "death mask" is one possible name for a logic of the image that Cusa sees in the icon of God. Such a likeness or proximity between the death mask and the icon of God—which Christian tradition itself has brought to expression in the "true image" of the Shroud of Turin—can push us here to reflect on whether, and how, the sociality that proves essential to a visibility of the invisible God in Cusa might also prove operative in our relations with the faces of the dead. This is a question that Nancy in his treatment of the death mask does not himself pose explicitly, but he does—notably in his gesture toward the shared temporality of a con-templation—give us rich ground upon which we can pose it: if the sociality of a *con-dilectio* or a shared love among finite beings is for Cusa inherent to our vision of the infinite and invisible God, might we see a similar role played by sociality, and its love, in our vision of the nonvision of the dead face? The question of sociality seems especially important here insofar as

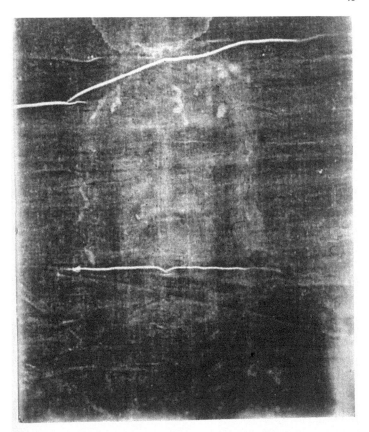

Torino - S.S. Sindone - ingrandimento Sacro Volto
dal negativo originale

FIGURE 3.4. Secondo Pia's 1868 negative of the Shroud of Turin; https://en
.wikipedia.org/wiki/Shroud_of_Turin.

it touches on that topic—Being-toward-death—where many
see Heidegger's failure to appreciate the social, and especially
the love, relations that constitute our existence. Adding to the
interest of the question: it could be Levinas who offers a first and
crucial bit of inspiration for it within his own understanding of
the relation between love and mortality.

SHARED LOVE AND THE VISIBILITY OF THE INVISIBLE

In what he intends as a sharply critical response to Heidegger's failure to appreciate the interpersonal ethical relation, or the face-to-face, Levinas asserts in *God, Death, and Time* that "what we call by the somewhat corrupted name of love is above all the fact that the death of the other affects me more than does my own. Love of the other is the emotion of the other's death. The reference to death is my welcome of the other, and not my anxiety before the death that awaits me. We meet death in the face of the other."[61] By insisting that death appears to me first in the face of the other, and that love means seeing the mortality of that face, Levinas believes himself at odds with the Heidegger for whom death is in each case "mine," a possibility of existence that, as nonrelational, remains resistant to any logic of substitution or representation. However, along lines more consistent with Heidegger than Levinas allows, we can well take up constructively Levinas's suggestion not only that my love of the other is conditioned by the other's mortality (a position at odds, we note in passing, with Augustinian theology) but indeed (and again rightly) that the death of the other shows itself, at bottom, primarily and perhaps exclusively to the look of love. In other words: if love means that the death of the other concerns me, or that it regards me, in a fundamental manner, one would also have to say, and see, that the look or gaze of the dead person—the withdrawn look of the dead face—regards me in the measure of my love. Recalling now what shows itself through the death mask: the dead face that looks at us in a manner that concerns us, the face that regards us, the most—and which does so just insofar as it no longer looks at all—is the face of a beloved.

Levinas thus signals an intimate, essential tie between love and the mortality that regards me in the face of the other: to love the other is inseparable from seeing death in the beloved's face. While taking inspiration here from Levinas, I am also imagining such an appearance of the other's mortality to the look of love in a way that diverges in two significant directions from Levinas's thinking. First, while Levinas's construal of the ethical relation focuses on the face-to-face between two, leaving the question of sociality both underdeveloped and in seemingly sharp (some would say insurmountable) tension with the ethical relation, the love for which mortality appears entails a sharing of that love, or a *condilectio*, that includes always more than just two. And second, while for Levinas the face of the other appears to me prior to and outside of any context, including culture, history, and world itself, the love for which I imagine the other's death to appear is a love that receives, and wills, the being of the beloved as her Being-in-the-world. To love the other, then, and to see death in her face, would demand that I love also the world that opens and sustains her being—and it would mean that through such love I see, along with her mortality, that world's fragility.

The ethical relation that preoccupies Levinas is a face-to-face relation between only two persons: between me and another who, always singular, calls or accuses me unconditionally in my own inescapable singularity. If we think about the appearance of death and its invisibility, however, on the model of Cusa's inherently social staging of the invisible God's appearance, then the enabling love involved must be shared beyond just two—and prove in the end to be innumerable. It would be, like existence for Rilke, "beyond number." The love in whose light the no-longer-looking look regards me is not only the singular, irreplaceable, non-exchangeable love that I hold for the dead person and that we shared during our lives; it is also, inextricably, the love that I must hold for the loves that others shared also with the dead person—loves, like mine, themselves singular, irreplaceable, and beyond exchange. (One can even say that within the love relation between two, there is always already a third, for in loving the other I love not just that person but also the love we share.)

For Cusa we see the invisibility of the absolute and infinite vision of God only through the active and constructive sociality of a *condilectio*, a love shared among, and a love for, countless perspectives that remain singular and irreducible to one another. So likewise with respect to the other's death: the withdrawal of the look appears to us, and precisely as a withdrawal that regards us, only through a sharing of the love relations that sustained the beloved in her lifetime, relations that remain themselves also singular and irreducible to each other while at the same time touching one another intimately. In fact, in loving the loves that others shared with the dead person, I am touched, at bottom, by the fact that those loves are not interchangeable or exchangeable with mine, even though they cannot be separated from mine.

This sharing of singular loves before the face of the beloved dead one is realized pointedly through the sorrow that stems from such love. Sorrow touches all of us even as each one of us suffers that sorrow in a singular way; we all suffer "together" or "with" one another, but in a way that the suffering of each, like the love that gives to sorrow its life, cannot be exchanged or transferred from one to the other. And just as I love not only the dead person herself but also the loves that others shared with her, such that these loves enrich and augment one another, so I sorrow not only over my own loss of the beloved but also over the sorrow that others suffer. Like the loving vision of God in Cusa, which gives itself to all and to each, sorrow touches, together, all who loved the dead one, but each in a singular way. If the contemplation of the all-seeing and thus strictly invisible face of God in Cusa transpires in and through this shared love, then our shared vision and time—our contemplation—of the nonlooking and thus invisible look of the dead beloved depends just as much on a *condilectio*. It would be such a *condilectio* alone that gives all of its force to what one calls, by a term perhaps itself also a bit corrupted, condolence.

Nancy's analysis of the death mask does not touch directly upon such a role for love in our vision of the dead one's look, but it does treat the mortal temporality that seems to me as indispensable to such love as it is to the imagination: the temporality of a con-templation in which *con-dilectio* and con-dolence coincide. By highlighting within the temporality of the dead face the superimposition of its prospective and retrospective aspects, one into the other—a superimposition without which one could not see the withdrawal of the look, or the look of one no-longer looking—Nancy can help us to see that this double aspect and its temporality inform already our relation with the face of the living. For just as in the face of the dead we look at a face that, previously, looked at us, so in the face of the living we look already at a look that, one day, will no longer look. (It is the coincidence of these two aspects that makes Barthes shudder while contemplating the photo of a condemned but—at the time of the photo—still living prisoner.) This look of death in the face of the other is exactly what Levinas calls, very rightly, love. But it is not Levinas alone who suggests to us that such a co-implication of prospection and retrospection is at bottom a work of love. Heidegger too states this quite directly.

He does so already in his early treatment of understanding, which, as "in love," is operative only in and through the temporal interplay of Dasein's thrownness and projection—and hence of its inheritance and bestowal of a world. And he makes this latter connection—between temporal love and intergenerational transmission—explicitly, and richly, also later in his writing on Rilke and the destitution of our age. In that context, Heidegger notes that love, or a thinking of the heart, attends at its core to our mortal—and natal—condition, for "it is only in the most intimate and invisible interior of the heart that man inclines toward what there is to love: the ancestors, the dead, the children, those who are to come [*Im unsichtbaren Innersten des Herzens ist der Mensch erst dem zugeneigt, was das zu Liebende ist: die Ahnen, die Toten, die Kindheit, die Kommenden*]."[62]

At stake in this intergenerational movement of love is nothing less than the inheritance and bestowal of worlds that we create—thanks to the imagination—without ever containing, controlling, or, still less, mastering them. As Taylor well argues in his essay here, "the activity of the imagination always *constructs* the world. However, this constructive activity always presupposes a more primordial passivity that *deconstructs* the notion of autonomous subjectivity."[63] While, as Taylor notes, such an insight has figured prominently in recent affect theory, it is already central to Heidegger's treatment of imagination in *Kant and the Problem of Metaphysics*, which (yet again contradicting the charge of some pretention to autarchy within his analysis of human existence) emphasizes that "all projection—and consequently, even all of man's 'creative' activity—is *thrown*, i.e., it is determined by the dependency of Dasein on the being already in its totality [*das schon Seiende im ganzen*], a dependency over which Dasein itself does not have control" (KPM 165; 235). The creativity of our thrown projection—which means also of our mooded understanding, or of our loving imagination—is exactly not the modern pretention to conquer the world as picture, for it depends on a totality that radically precedes and exceeds us, thus resisting those "one-world" illusions whose dangers Rubenstein here incisively calls out. If intergenerational love, in its essentially mortal and natal temporality, recalls those long dead while anticipating those to be born, it not only requires but itself already is a work of imagination. For it is not only the case that the work of imagination is inherently anticipatory; it is also the case that the time of anticipation calls essentially for imagination. We require imagination, and the affection of its temporality, to anticipate faces, and worlds, we cannot yet see, as likewise to recall those that have preceded us; and these two ecstatic movements remain inseparable, each being carried out only in and through the other. In recalling those who precede us, we recall their anticipation of us, even as in anticipating those still to come, we anticipate their recollection of us and of our anticipations. Within such anticipation we might do well to imagine, then, as lovingly as possible, what the children and those still to be born will see, or imagine, when they recall us. As

Taylor has argued here, the ground of such imaginative recollection, if it remains human, will remain inescapably material, earthly, and embodied—lived, as felt, in the flesh, and thus not reducible, without remainder, to the immaterial concept. To Taylor's critique of the latter-day "Gnostics eager to escape the confines of flesh and the 'corruption' of earthly existence,"[64] we might add this: the original Gnostics were condemned not only because they denied the goodness of creation and the reality of incarnation. They were condemned also—and this is essentially related—because, like their techno-utopian heirs today, they failed to understand, or to imagine, that we are saved, if at all, not by knowledge and its codes, but by love.

NOTES

1. Emmanuel Levinas, *Totalité et infini: Essai sur l'extériorité* (The Hague: Martinus Nijhoff, 1961); *Totality and Infinity: An Essay on Exteriority*, trans. Alphonso Lingis (Pittsburgh: Duquesne University Press, 1961).

2. "Nur noch ein Gott kann uns retten," SPIEGEL-Gespräch mit Martin Heidegger am 23. September 1666, published in *Der Spiegel*, May 31, 1976, 208; English translation (here modified), *Philosophy Today* 20 (Winter 1976), 277, cited and discussed by Rubenstein here, 147.

3. Martin Heidegger, "The Age of the World Picture," in *The Question Concerning Technology and Other Essays*, trans. William Lovitt (New York: Harper and Row, 1977), 134. On technological enframing, see esp. Heidegger's classic text "The Question Concerning Technology." Both essays are available in *The Question Concerning Technology and Other Essays*, trans. William Lovitt (New York: Harper and Row, 1977).

4. Emmanuel Levinas, "Heidegger, Gagarin, and Us," in *Difficult Freedom*, trans. Sean Hand (Baltimore: Johns Hopkins University Press, 1990), 233–34.

5. Levinas, *Difficult Freedom*, 234, 232, 232–33.

6. Likewise on the verge of becoming as easy and as common as word processing is gene editing, thanks to the technology of CRISPR (clustered regularly interspaced short palindromic repeats).

7. Tom Chivers, "What Do We Do about Deepfake Video?" *Guardian*, June 23, 2019; https://www.theguardian.com/technology/2019/jun/23/what-do-we-do-about-deepfake-video-ai-facebook.

8. https://www.youtube.com/watch?v=iHv6Q9ychnA.

9. In essays that have understandably enjoyed renewed attention in the Trump era, Hannah Arendt highlights well both the fragility of factual (by contrast to rational) truth, which is relatively easy to deny, ignore, or obfuscate precisely because it always could have been otherwise and thus lacks self-evidence, and, in turn, the potential political significance of a truth-telling that maintains such significance thanks to its refusal to enter the political fray. As she writes in "Truth and Politics," "Truthfulness has never been counted among the political virtues, because it has little indeed to contribute to that change of the world and of circumstances which is among the most legitimate political activities. Only where a community has embarked upon organized lying on principle, and not only with respect to particulars, can truthfulness as such, unsupported by the distorting forces of power and interest, become a political factor of the first order. Where everybody lies about everything of importance, the truthteller, whether he knows it or not, has begun to act; he, too, has engaged himself in political business, for, in the unlikely event that he survives, he has made a start toward changing the world"; in Arendt, *Between Past and Future: Eight Exercises in Political Thought* (New York: Penguin, reprint of the 1968 edition published by Viking Press), 251. This view on the political significance of truth-telling would be worth comparing with Max Weber's insistence in "Science as a Vocation" that university teaching best serves the "ethical forces" of clarity and responsibility by refraining from advocacy or leadership—a position that itself merits reconsideration in a time when many would-be progressive academics give far more ground than they should to charges from

the political and cultural right of ideology and tribalism in our colleges and universities.

10. Don DeLillo, *Zero K*, 259; cited and discussed here in Taylor, "Gathering Remains," 29.

11. While facial recognition systems have been shown to mis-identify people of color and women more frequently than they do white men, the effort to address this "problem" by simply making the systems more accurate may be itself problematic. As Timnit Gebru, computer scientist, technical colead of the Ethical Artificial Intelligence Team at Google until her controversial firing in December 2020, and cofounder of Black in AI notes, "A lot of times, people are talking about bias in the sense of equalizing performance across groups. They're not thinking about the under-lying foundation, whether a task should exist in the first place, who creates it, who will deploy it on which population, who owns the data, and how is it used." In Craig S. Smith, "Dealing with Bias in Artificial Intelligence: Three Women with Extensive Experience in A.I. Spoke on the Topic and How to Confront It," *New York Times*, November 19, 2019, updated January 2, 2020; https://www.nytimes.com/2019/11/19/technology/artificial-intelligence-bias.html.

12. Shoshana Zuboff, *The Age of Surveillance Capitalism: The Fight for a Human Future at the New Frontier of Power* (London: Profile Books, 2019).

13. John Naughton, "'The Goal Is to Automate Us': Welcome to the Age of Surveillance Capitalism," article and interview with Shoshana Zuboff, *Guardian*, January 20, 2019; https://www.theguardian.com/technology/2019/jan/20/shoshana-zuboff-age-of-surveillance-capitalism-google-facebook.

14. Taylor, "Gathering Remains," 73.

15. Naughton, "Goal."

16. Taylor, "Gathering Remains," 47–48.

17. Heidegger, "Age of the World Picture," 152–53. See also 128: "Certainly the modern age has, as a consequence of the liberation of man, introduced subjectivism and individualism. But it remains just as certain that no age before this one has produced a compa-

rable objectivism and that in no age before has this non-individual in the form of the collective come to acceptance as having worth."

18. Martin Heidegger, "What Are Poets For?" in *Poetry, Language, Thought*, trans. Albert Hofstadter (New York: Harper and Row, 1971), 114–15; "Wozu Dichter?" in *Holzwege* (Frankfurt am Main: Vittorio Klostermann, 1950), 292. Hereafter cited parenthetically as WPF with English pagination followed by German.

19. See sec. 125 of Nietzsche's *Gay Science*.

20. Martin Heidegger, *Being and Time*, trans. John Macquarrie and Edward Robinson (Oxford: Basil Blackwell, 1962), 187; *Sein und Zeit, Sechzehnte Auflage* (Tübingen: Max Niemeyer Verlag, 1986), 147. Hereafter cited parenthetically as BT and SZ.

21. Martin Heidegger, *Basic Problems of Phenomenology, Winter Semester 1919/20*, trans. Scott M. Campbell (London: Bloomsbury, 2013), 129; *Grundprobleme der Phänomenologie (1919/20)*, vol. 58 of the *Gesamtausgabe 2: Abteilung: Vorlesungen 1919–1944*, 168. Hereafter cited parenthetically as BP, with English pagination followed by German.

22. Cited in a note in *Being and Time* (BT 492; SZ 139), alongside corresponding passages from Pascal, whose understanding of our knowledge of divine things provides Heidegger's model: "but the saints, on the contrary [to knowledge of human things, which precedes a love of them], when they speak of divine things, say that we must love them before we know them, and that we enter into truth only by charity; they have made of this one of their most useful maxims."

23. Martin Heidegger, *What Is Called Thinking?*, trans. J. Glenn Gray (New York: Harper Collins, 1968), 236–37; *Was Heißt Denken?* (Tübingen: Max Niemeyer Verlag, 1997), 144.

24. Heidegger, *What Is Called Thinking?*, 237; *Was Heißt Denken?*, 144.

25. Martin Heidegger, *Besinnung* (Frankfurt am Main: Vittorio Klostermann, 1997), written in 1938–39; translated into English by Parvis Emad and Thomas Kalary as *Mindfulness* (London: Continuum, 2006).

26. Heidegger, *Mindfulness*, 52; *Besinnung*, 63.

27. It bears noting that the description that Heidegger provides here of love's relation to wisdom and Being repeats quite closely his descriptions of interpersonal love in letters to Hannah Arendt. For further discussion of these, see my *With the World at Heart: Studies in the Secular Today* (Chicago: University of Chicago Press, 2019), 128–39.

28. Heidegger, *Mindfulness*, 52; *Besinnung*, 63.

29. Martin Heidegger, "On the Essence and Concept of *Phusis* in Aristotle's *Physics* B, I," trans. Thomas Sheehan, in William McNeill, ed., *Pathmarks* (Cambridge: Cambridge University Press, 1998), 229–30.

30. Jacques Derrida, "The Deaths of Roland Barthes," in *The Work of Mourning*, ed. Pascale-Anne Brault and Michael Naas (Chicago: University of Chicago, 2001), 66.

31. Robert Pogue Harrison, *The Dominion of the Dead* (Chicago: University of Chicago Press, 2003), 91, 93, 92, 93, 93 (my emphasis).

32. Harrison, *Dominion of the Dead*, 92.

33. Maurice Blanchot, *The Gaze of Orpheus*, cited in Dennis J. Schmidt, *Between Word and Image: Heidegger, Klee, and Gadamer on Gesture and Genesis* (Bloomington: Indiana University Press, 2013), 155n57.

34. Schmidt, *Between Word and Image*, 33.

35. Harrison, *Dominion of the Dead*, 148.

36. Harrison, *Dominion of the Dead*, 148.

37. Harrison, *Dominion of the Dead*, 148.

38. Schmidt, *Between Word and Image*, 35.

39. *Chaque fois unique, la fin du monde* is the title given to the French edition of an essay collection that appeared first in English, Derrida's *The Work of Mourning*. The French volume appeared in 2003 with Editions Galilée. For a helpful study of this theme in Derrida's later thought and writing, see Michael Naas, *The End of the World and Other Teachable Moments: Jacques Derrida's Final Seminar* (New York: Fordham University Press, 2015).

40. For a fuller discussion of the phenomenological insights

gained (but also avoided) by Augustine through his experience of mourning, see chap. 2 of Carlson, *With the World at Heart*, "Mourning Places and Time in Augustine."

41. Citations to be given according to chapter and paragraph number, following the Latin text in Jasper Hopkins, *Nicholas of Cusa's Dialectical Mysticism, Text, Translation, and Interpretive Study of De visione Dei*, 3rd ed. In addition to Hopkins's Latin and English texts, I've consulted the English translation available in H. Lawrence Bond, trans., *Nicholas of Cusa: Selected Spiritual Writings* (New York: Paulist Press, 1997) and the French translation of Agnès Minazzoli, *Le tableau ou la vision de Dieu* (Paris: Belles Lettres, 2012).

42. In this direction, see esp. Jean-Luc Marion, "Seeing, or Seeing Oneself Seen: Nicholas of Cusa's Contribution in *De visione Dei*," trans. Stephen Lewis, *Journal of Religion* 96, no. 3 (2016): 305–31. For a reading of Marion and Cusa, see my own "Finitude and Sociality of the Self: Reading Cusa's *De visione Dei* with Jean-Luc Marion," *American Cusanus Society Newsletter* 32 (2015): 9–18.

43. Cusa, "To call you is to turn myself toward you. You cannot be missing to the one who turns toward you, and no one can turn toward you if you are not already present. You are present before I turn myself toward you [*Nam invocare te est me convertere ad te. Non potes illi deesse, qui se ad te convertit. Nec potes quis ad te converti, nisi adsis prius. Ades antequam ad te convertar*]" (chap. 5, 17).

44. Michel de Certeau, "Le regard: Nicolas de Cues," in *La fable mystique II* (Paris: Gallimard, 2013), 85.

45. This essential interplay, or coincidence, between seeing and being seen within Cusa's thought, recalling, we might note, the co-implication of theophany and anthropophany in John Scotus Eriugena, resembles also, and fairly deeply, the co-implication of givenness and the *adonné* in the phenomenology of Jean-Luc Marion; just as in Marion I receive myself only in giving myself, or in responding, to the call of that which always already first gives itself to me, in such a way that givenness appears only in the response that I, as *adonné*, make to it; and much as in Eriugena God shows himself and, in fact, creates himself, only in and through

the appearance of a humanity that responds, or cor-responds, to the appearance of God; so in Nicholas I am only inasmuch as I see God, which means only inasmuch as I see that God already sees me (which means also inasmuch as I respond to the call or the speech that Cusa equates with God's seeing). Through his vision of me God creates me, and thus gives me to myself, and precisely in order that I might see God in giving myself to him. For my reading of Eriugena in this direction, see "Theophany and the Chiaroscuro of Nature: Eriugena and the Question of Technology," in *Eriugena and Creation: Proceedings of the Eleventh International Conference on Eriugenian Studies*, ed. Willemien Otten and Michael Allen (Turnhout: Brepols, 2014).

46. See my "Finitude and Sociality of the Self."

47. On the history of thinking about the infinite sphere, see Georges Poulet, *Les métamorphoses du cercle* (Paris: Plon, 1961) and Dieter Mahnke, *Unendliche Sphäre und Allmittelpunkt* (Stuttgart-Bad Constatt: Friedrich Frommann Verlag, 1966). On the application to the universe of divine infinity, especially in Cusa, see the classic study of Alexandre Koyré, *From the Closed World to the Infinite Universe* (New York: Harper and Brothers, 1957) as well as more recent discussions in Mary-Jane Rubenstein, *Worlds without End: The Many Lives of the Multiverse*, esp. chap. 3, "Navigating the Infinite" (New York: Columbia University Press, 2014); and my own *The Indiscrete Image: Infinitude and Creation of the Human*, chap. 3, "The Living Image: Infinitude, Unknowing, and Creative Capacity in Mystical Anthropology" (Chicago: University of Chicago Press, 2008).

48. Nicholas of Cusa, *On Learned Ignorance*, bk. 2, chap. 12, para. 162, in H. Lawrence Bond, trans., *Nicholas of Cusa: Selected Spiritual Writings* (New York: Paulist Press, 1997), 161.

49. Michel de Certeau, "The Look: Nicholas of Cusa," in *The Mystic Fable*, vol. 2: *The Sixteenth and Seventeenth Centuries*, trans. Michael B. Smith (Chicago: University of Chicago Press, 2015), 32.

50. This is a central point of contention between Marion and Emmanuel Falque in their respective readings of Cusa, with Marion rejecting as "nontheological" and "hasty" the interpretation

according to which Falque, much in line with Certeau and my own reading, argues that "the filial yields to the fraternal in the vision of God" and that "faith . . . is not first that in God but in man or in the other" (Falque, cited in Marion, n. 11).

51. Emmanuel Falque reads Cusa in this direction, drawing on the analysis of *condilectio* in Richard of St. Victor—whose emphasis on the perfection of divine love within the trinity, and on the subjection of love to worth, differs markedly from the understanding of love I would advance here, which remains not only innumerable but also at odds with the logics of perfection and worth as Richard deploys them. See, e.g., bk. 3, chap. 19 in Richard's treatise on the Trinity: "Shared love is properly said to exist when a third person is loved by two persons harmoniously and in community, and the affection of the two persons is fused into one affection by the flame of love for the third. From these things it is evident that shared love would have no place in Divinity itself if a third person were lacking to the other two persons. Here we are not speaking of just any shared love but of supreme shared love—a shared love of a sort such that a creature would never merit from the Creator and for which it would never be found worthy"; in Grover A. Zinn, trans., *Richard of Saint Victor: The Twelve Patriarchs, the Mystical Ark, Book Three of the Trinity* (New York: Paulist Press, 1979). For Falque's reading, see "L'omnivoyant: Fraternité et vision de Dieu chez Nicolas de Cues," *Revue des sciences philosophiques et théologiques* 98, no. 1 (2014).

52. Maurice Merleau-Ponty, "The Intertwining—The Chiasm," in *The Visible and the Invisible, Followed by Working Notes*, trans. Alphonso Lingis (Evanston, IL: Northwestern University Press, 1968), 139; "L'entrelacs—Le chiasme," in *Le visible et l'invisible, suivi de notes de travail* (Paris: Gallimard, 1964), 181.

53. Martin Heidegger, *Kant and the Problem of Metaphysics*, trans. Richard Taft (Bloomington: Indiana University Press, 1991), 64; *Gesamtausgabe*, vol. 3: *Kant und das Problem der Metaphysik* (1951; Frankfurt am Main: Klostermann, 2010), 90–91. Hereafter cited parenthetically as KPM with English pagination followed by German.

54. Jean-Luc Nancy, "Masked Imagination," in *The Ground of the Image*, trans. Jeff Fort (New York: Fordham University Press, 2005), 87; "L'imagination masquée," in *Au fond des images* (Paris: Galilée, 2003), 158–59. Hereafter cited parenthetically as IM, with English page number followed by French.

55. Immanuel Kant, *Critique of Pure Reason*, A 141, B 180; cited in Heidegger, *Kant and the Problem of Metaphysics*, 71; *Kant und das Problem de Metaphysik*, 101.

56. Karl Heinrich Ludwig Pölitz, *Kants Vorlesungen über die Metaphysik*, 88, cited in Heidegger, *Kant and the Problem of Metaphysics*, 122; *Kant und das Problem der Metaphysik*, 174–75.

57. Ernst Benkard, *Das Ewige Antlitz: Eine Sammlung von Totenmasken* (Berlin: Frankfurter Verlags-Anstalt, 1926); *Undying Faces: A Collection of Death Masks*, with a note by Georg Kolbe, trans. Margaret M. Green (London: Hogarth Press, 1929).

58. Martin Heidegger, *Logic: The Question of Truth*, trans. Thomas Sheehan (Bloomington: Indiana University Press, 2010); *Gesamtausgabe*, vol. 21: *Logik: Die Frage nach der Wahrheit (WS 1925–26)* (1976; Frankfurt am Main: Vittorio Klostermann, 1995), 361–62.

59. For an astute treatment of the imagination as that which holds open this "between" of mortal existence, see the chapter in John Sallis's *Echoes: After Heidegger* (Bloomington: Indiana University, 1990) titled "Mortality and Imagination: The Proper Name of Man."

60. See Roland Barthes's *La chambre claire: Note sur la photographie* (Paris: Gallimard, 1980) as well as Derrida's text on Barthes in *The Work of Mourning*.

61. Emmanuel Levinas, *God, Death, and Time*, trans. Bettina Bergo (Stanford, CA: Stanford University Press, 2000), 105 (trans. modified); *Dieu, la mort et le temps* (Paris: Grasset, 1993), 122.

62. Heidegger, "Wozu Dichter?," 306.

63. Taylor, "Gathering Remains," 98.

64. Taylor, "Gathering Remains," 27–28.

INDEX

Page numbers followed by the letter *f* refer to figures.

promotional poster of, 168*f*.
See also space travel
nationalism, 10–11; American,
133–35, 158–59; humanitarian,
126; imperialism and, 119, 135;
and war, 146
National Space Council (NSC), 161
neoliberal globalized order, 10,
127–28. See also capitalism;
economy
Neuralink, 117
neuroscience, 92, 96–97
Newell, Catherine, 150–51, 154,
181n112
Newsweek, 146
New York Times, 144
Nicholas of Cusa, 14–15, 220–30,
231, 241–42, 254n45; *De visione
Dei* of, 14, 222–30, 231, 246
Nietzsche, Friedrich, 55, 70–72,
74, 132, 198; Works: *The Birth of
Tragedy*, 124; *Will to Power*, 63
nihilism, 11, 21, 72, 106; active,
169; black, 169
Nixon, President Richard, 148
Nokia, 68
Novalis, 95

Obama, President Barack, 161–62,
164
Oliver, Kelly, 142, 146, 149

Page, Larry, 30, 58, 68
Pan-Africanist Organization of
Afro American Unity (OAAU),
159
Parmenides, 206
Pascal, Blaise, 198–99, 202; death
mask of, 231*f*, 237
PayPal, 48, 117

Pence, Vice President Mike, 11,
158–62, 164
phenomenology, 190–91, 200–
202, 222; love as motive
ground of understanding in,
206; of seeing, 222, 231
philosophy: and art, 73–75, 94;
construal and practice of, 200;
critical, 81; history of, 60, 231;
idealistic, 32; modern, 74;
nineteenth-century specu-
lative, 40, 71; poetry and,
102; and religion, 75, 94; and
theology, 40–41; of transhumanism, 56; as a work of love,
201, 206. See also aesthetics;
epistemology; metaphysics;
phenomenology; theology
photography: of a death mask,
220, 232–43, 243*f*; of the earth
from space, 8, 117–72; mortal
temporality of, 242. See also
image
Picasso, Pablo, 121
Planetary Resources, 162
Plato: *Timaeus*, 129
pluralism, 133
poiesis, 95
posthumanism, 5–6, 51–73; as
antihumanism, 106; definition
of, 54–55; emergence of, 54;
era of, 85. See also technological singularity
postmodernism, 44, 76, 81. *See
also* postmodernity
postmodernity: and consumer
capitalism, 34. See also modernity; postmodernism
poststructural theory, 95
Prescod-Weinstein, Chanda, 165

conquest, 9; racist, 132, 169; of "unity," 132; untrammeled, 145
vision: of God, 223–30, 231, 242, 245–46; of the invisible, 14, 220–27; Kandel on, 97; technologies of, 13, 17n5; of the whole, 12. *See also* sight
von Braun, Wernher, 152–54, 160, 162, 170

Walkowicz, Lucianne, 161–64, 172, 186n156; "Becoming Interplanetary: What Living on Earth Can Teach Us about Living on Mars" (public forum, 2018) of, 164–67
Warhol, Andy, 36–38, 84, 90, 121
Warren, Calvin, 11; "Black Nihilism and the Politics of Hope" of, 169

Washington Post, 160
Weber, Max, 190
Weheliye, Alexander, 156
Wenig, David, 52
West, Cornel, 169
Whitson, Peggy, 163
Whole Earth Catalog, 111n50, 127–29, 130f, 149
Whole Earth Review, 63
Wired, 61
World Transhumanist Association, 57
Wynter, Sylvia, 149

Youngquist, Paul, 155

Zuboff, Shoshana, 12, 195
Zubrin, Robert, 165–66

Lightning Source UK Ltd.
Milton Keynes UK
UKHW022010080921
390193UK00001B/3